THE GREEK ECONOMY IN THE TWENTIETH CENTURY

THE GREEK ECONOMY

In the Twentieth Century

A.F. Freris

ST. MARTIN'S PRESS
New York

© 1986 A.F. Freris
All rights reserved. For information, write:
Scholarly & Reference Division,
St. Martin's Press, Inc., 175 Fifth Avenue, New York, NY 10010
First published in the United States of America in 1986
Printed in Great Britain

Library of Congress Cataloging-in-Publication Data

Freris, P.A.
   The Greek economy in the twentieth century.

   Bibliography: p.222
   Includes index.
   1. Greece—Economic conditions—1918–1974.
2. Greece—Economic conditions—1974–
I. Title.
HC295.F72   1986   330.9495'06   86-6669
ISBN 0-312-34724-3

CONTENTS

2298459

LIST OF TABLES

List of Tables

List of Tables

To my mother and memory of my father

PREFACE AND ACKNOWLEDGEMENTS

The writing of this book would not have been possible without the generosity of S.Gregoriou (1892-1976), deputy Governor of the Bank of Greece during 1945-1955, and of his widow, Eugenia. They kindly donated to me an invaluable collection of books, pamphlets, reports and journals covering developments in the Greek economy especially in the prewar years. Further research was undertaken in the National Library, Athens, the British Museum Library and at the London School of Economics.

The Editor of this series, Professor D.Aldcroft, offered constructive and useful advice and Mr. P. Sowden of Croom Helm showed exceptional patience and understanding.

The writing of this book was completed in Hong Kong during my tenure at the City Polytechnic of Hong Kong. The old Greek saying concerning something incomprehensible 'this is all Chinese to me' was proved wrong, but in reverse, by Elaine Yeung, Amy Mok and Candice Cheung who mastered quickly not only my handwriting but also the transliteration of Greek references into English. My thanks to them for their cheerfulness and speed in typing the manuscript.

To my friend and nth removed cousin, R.Koundouros, my thanks for his enthusiasm and support for this project.

Preface and Acknowledgements

Finally my wife, Anabella, bore yet again the brunt of my authoring activities with good cheer and humour including putting away the manuscript of this book to a safe and dry place during one of the periodic typhoons in Hong Kong.

A.F. Freris
Principal Lecturer in Economics
Department of Business and Management
City Polytechnic of Hong Kong
and Department of Economics
City of London Polytechnic

EDITOR'S INTRODUCTION

By comparison with the nineteenth century, the twentieth has been very much more turbulent, both economically and politically. Two world wars and a great depression are sufficient to substantiate this claim without invoking the problems of more recent times. Yet despite these setbacks Europe's economic performance in the present century has been very much better than anything recorded in the historical past, thanks largely to the super-boom conditions following the post-second world war reconstruction period. Thus in the period 1946-75, or 1950-73, the annual increase in total European GNP per capita was 4.8 and 4.5 per cent respectively, as against a compound rate of just under one per cent in the nineteenth century (1800-1913) and the same during the troubled years between 1913-50. As Bairoch points out, within a generation or so European per capita income rose slightly more than in the previous 150 years (1947-75 by 250 per cent, 1800-1948 by 225 per cent) and, on rough estimates for the half century before 1800, by about as much as in the preceding two centuries [1].

The dynamic growth and relative stability of the 1950s and 1960s may however belie the natural order of things as the events of the later 1970s and early 1980s demonstrate. Certainly it would seem unlikely that the European economy, or the world economy for that matter, will see a lasting return to the relatively stable conditions of the nineteenth century. No doubt the experience of the present century can easily lead to an exaggerated idea about the stability of the previous one. Nevertheless, one may justifiably claim that for much of the nineteenth century there was a degree of harmony in the economic development of the major powers and between the metropolitan economies and the periphery which has been noticeably absent since 1914. Indeed, one of the reasons for the apparent success of the gold standard post 1870, despite the aura of stability it allegedly shed, was the absence of serious external disturbances and imbalance in development among the major participating powers. As Triffin writes, 'the residual harmonization of national monetary and credit policies depended far less on ex post corrective action, requiring an extreme flexibility, downward as well as upward, of national price and wage levels, than on an ex ante avoidance of substantial disparities in cost competitiveness and the monetary policies that would allow them to develop' [2].

Whatever the reasons for the absence of serious economic and political conflict, the fact remains that through to 1914 international development and political relations, though subject to strains of a minor nature from time to time, were never exposed to internal and external shocks of the magnitude experienced in the twentieth century. Not surprisingly therefore, the first world war rudely shattered the liberal tranquillity of the later nineteenth and early twentieth centuries. At the time few people realised that it was going to be a lengthy war and, even more important, fewer still had any conception of the enormous impact it would have on economic and social relationships. Moreover, there was a general feeling, readily accepted in establishment circles, that following the period of hostilities it would be possible to resume where one had left off- in short, to recreate the conditions of the prewar era.

For obvious reasons this was clearly an impossible task, though for nearly a decade statesmen strove to get back to what they regarded as 'normalcy', or the natural order of things. In itself this was one of the profound mistakes of the first postwar decade since it should have been clear, even at that time, that the war and postwar clearing-up operations had undermined Europe's former equipoise and sapped her strength to a point where the economic system had become very sensitive to external shocks. The map of Europe had been rewritten under the political settlements following the war and this further weakened the economic viability of the continent and left a dangerous political vacuum in its wake. Moreover,

it was not only in the economic sphere that
Europe's strength had been reduced; in political
and social terms the European continent was
seriously weakened and many countries in the early
postwar years were in a state of social ferment
and upheaval [3].

Generally speaking, Europe's economic and
political fragility was ignored in the 1920s,
probably more out of ignorance than intent. In
their efforts to resurrect the prewar system
statesmen believed they were providing a viable
solution to the problems of the day, and the fact
that Europe shared in the prosperity of the later
1920s seemed to vindicate their judgement. But
the postwar problems - war debts, external
imbalances, currency issues, structural distortions and the like - defied solutions along
traditional lines. The most notable of these was
the attempt to restore a semblance of the gold
standard in the belief that it had been responsible for the former stability. The upshot was a
set of haphazard and inconsistent currency stabilisation policies which took no account of the
changes in relative costs and prices among
countries since 1914. Consequently, despite the
apparent prosperity of the latter half of the
decade, Europe remained in a state of unstable
equilibrium, and therefore vulnerable to any
external shocks. The collapse of US foreign
lending from the middle of 1928 and the subsequent
downturn of the American economy a year later
exposed the weaknesses of the European economy.
The stuctural supports were too weak to withstand
violent shocks and so the edifice disintegrated.

That the years 1929-1932/33 experienced one
of the worst depressions and financial crises in
history is not altogether surprising given the
convergence of many unfavourable forces at that
point in time. Moreover, the fact that a cyclical
downturn occurred against the backdrop of
structural disequilibrium only served to
exacerbate the problem, while the inherent
weakness of certain financial institutions in
Europe and the United States led to extreme
instability. The intensity of the crisis varied a
great deal but few countries, apart from the USSR,
were unaffected. The action of governments tended
to aggravate rather than ease the situation. Such
policies included expenditure cuts, monetary
contraction, the abandonment of the gold standard
and protective measures designed to insulate

3

domestic economies from external events. In
effect, these policies, while sometimes affording
temporary relief to hard-pressed countries, in the
end led to income destruction rather than income
creation. When recovery finally set in, in the
winter of 1932/33, it owed little to policy
contributions, though subsequently some western
governments did attempt more ambitious programmes
of stimulation, while many of the poorer eastern
European countries adopted autarchic policies in
an effort to push forward industrialisation.
Apart from some notable exceptions, Germany and
Sweden in particular, recovery from the slump,
especially in terms of employment generation, was
slow and patchy and even at the peak of the
upswing in 1937 many countries were still
operating below their resource capacity. A
combination of weak growth forces and structural
imbalances in development would no doubt have
ensured a continuation of resource
underutilisation had not rearmament and the
outbreak of war served to close the gap.

Thus, by the eve of the second world war
Europe as whole was in a much weaker state
economically than it had been in 1914, with her
shares of world income and trade notably reduced.
Worse still, she emerged from the second war in
1945 in a more prostrate condition than in 1918,
with output levels well down on those of prewar.
In terms of the loss of life, physical destruction
and decline in living standards Europe's position
was much worse than after the first world war. On
the other hand, recovery from wartime destruction
was stronger and more secure than in the previous
case. In part this can be attributed to the fact
that in the reconstruction phase of the later
1940s some of the mistakes and blunders of the
earlier experience were avoided. Inflation, for
example, was contained more readily between 1939
and 1945 and the violent inflations of the early
1920s were not for the most part perpetuated after
the second world war. With the exception of
Berlin, the map of Europe was divided much more
cleanly and neatly than after 1918. Though it
resulted in two ideological power blocks, the East
and the West, it did nevertheless dispose of the
power vacuum in Central/East Europe which had been
a source of friction and contention in the
interwar years. Moreover, the fact that each
block was dominated or backed by a wealthy and
rival super-power meant that support was forth-

coming for the satellite countries. The vanquished powers were not, with the exception of East Germany, burdened by unreasonable exactions which had been the cause of so much bitterness and squabbling during the 1920s. Finally, governments no longer hankered after the 'halcyon' prewar days, not surprisingly, given the rugged conditions of the 1930s. This time it was to be planning for the future which occupied their attention, and which found expression in the commitment to maintain full employment and all that entailed in terms of growth and stability, together with a conscious desire to build upon the earlier social welfare foundations. In wider perspective, the new initiatives found positive expression in terms of a readiness to co-operate internationally, particularly in trade and monetary matters. The liberal American aid programme for the West in the later 1940s was a concrete manifestation of this new approach.

Thus despite the enormity of the reconstruction task facing Europe at the end of the war, the recovery effort, after some initial difficulties, was both strong and sustained, and by the early 1950s Europe had reached a point where she could look to the future with some confidence. During the next two decades or so virtually every European country, in keeping with the buoyancy in the world economy as a whole, expanded much more rapidly than in the past. This was the super-growth phase during which Europe regained a large part of the relative losses incurred between 1914 and 1945. The eastern block countries forged ahead the most rapidly under their planned regimes, while the western democracies achieved their success under mixed enterprise systems with varying degrees of market freedom. In both cases the state played a far more important role than hitherto, and neither system could be said to be without its problems. The planning mechanism in eastern Europe never functioned as smoothly as originally anticipated by its proponents, and in due course most of the socialist countries were forced to make modifications to their systems of control. Similarly, the semi-market systems of the West did not always produce the right results so that governments were obliged to intervene to an increasing extent. One of the major problems encountered by the demand-managed economies of the West was that of trying to achieve a series of basically incompatible

5

objectives simultaneously - namely fully employment, price stability, growth and stability and external equilibrium. Given the limited policy weapons available to governments this proved an impossible task to accomplish in most cases, though West Germany managed to achieve the seemingly impossible for much of the period.

Although these incompatible objectives proved elusive in toto, there was, throughout most of the period to the early 1970s, little cause for serious alarm. It is true that there were minor lapses from full employment; fluctuations still occurred but they were very moderate and took the form of growth cycles; some countries experienced periodic balance of payments problems; while prices generally rose continuously though at fairly modest annual rates. But such lapses could readily be accommodated, even with the limited policy choices, within an economic system that was growing rapidly. And there was some consolation from the fact that the planned socialist economies were not immune from some of these problems, especially later on in the period. By the later 1960s, despite some warning signs that conditions might be deteriorating, it seemed that Europe had entered a phase of perpetual prosperity not dissimilar to the one the Americans had conceived in the 1920s. Unfortunately, as in the earlier case, this illusion was to be rudely shattered in the first half of the 1970s. The super-growth phase of the postwar period culminated in the somewhat feverish and speculative boom of 1972-73. By the following year the growth trend had been reversed, the old business cycle had reappeared and most countries were experiencing inflation at higher rates than at any time in the past half century. From that time onwards, according to Samuel Brittan, 'everything seems to have gone sour and we have had slower growth, rising unemployment, faster inflation, creeping trade restrictions and all the symptoms of stag-flation.'[4] In fact, compared with the relatively placid and successful decades of the 1950s and 1960s, the later 1970s and early 1980s have been extremely turbulent, reminiscent in some respects of the interwar years.

It should, of course, be stressed that by comparison with the interwar years or even with the nineteenth century, economic growth has been quite respectable since the sharp boom and con-traction in the first half of the 1970s. It only

6

appears poor in relation to the rapid growth between 1950 and 1973 and the question arises as to whether this period should be regarded as somewhat abnormal with the shift to a lower growth profile in the 1970s being the inevitable consequence of long-term forces involving some reversal of the special growth promoting factors of the previous decades. In effect this would imply some weakening of real growth forces in the 1970s which was aggravated by specific factors, for example, energy crises and policy variables.

The most disturbing feature of this later period was not simply that growth slowed down but that it became more erratic, with longer recessionary periods involving absolute contractions in output, and that it was accompanied by mounting unemployment and high inflation. Traditional Keynesian demand management policies were unable to cope with these problems and, in an effort to deal with them, particularly inflation, governnments resorted to ultradefensive policies and monetary control. These were not very successful either since the need for social and political compromise in policy-making meant that they were not applied rigorously enough to eradicate inflation, yet at the same time their influence was sufficiently strong to dampen the rate of growth thereby exacerbating unemployment. In other words, economic management is faced with an awkward policy dilemma in the prevailing situation of high unemployment and rapid inflation. Policy action to deal with either one tends to make the other worse, while the constraint of the political concensus produces an uneasy compromise in an effort to 'minimise macroeconomic misery'. [5] Rostow has neatly summarised the constraints involved in this context: 'Taxes, public expenditure, interest rates, and the supply of money are not determined antiseptically by men free to move economies along a Phillips curve to an optimum trade-off between the rate of unemployment and the rate of inflation. Fiscal and monetary policy are, inevitably, living parts of the democratic political process.' [6]

Whether the current problems of contemporary western capitalism or the difficulties associated with the planning mechanisms of the socialist countries of eastern Europe are amenable to solutions remains to be seen. It is not, for the most part, the purpose of the volumes in this series to speculate about the future. The series is designed to provide clear and balanced surveys of the economic development and problems of individual European countries from the end of the first world war through to the present, against the background of the general economic and political trends of the time. Though most European countries have shared a common experience for much of the period, it is nonetheless true that there has been considerable variation among countries in the rate of development and the manner in which they have sought to regulate and control their economies. The problems encountered have also varied widely, in part reflecting disparities in levels of development. While most European countries had, by the end of the first world war, achieved some industrialisation and made the initial breakthrough into modern economic growth, nevertheless there existed a wide gulf between the richer and poorer nations. At the beginning of the period the most advanced region was north-west Europe including Scandinavia, and as one moved east and south so the level of per capita income relative to the European average declined. In some cases, notably Bulgaria, Yugoslavia and Portugal, income levels were barely half the European average. The gap has narrowed over time but the general pattern remains basically the same. Between 1913 and 1973 most of the poorer countries in the east and south (apart from Spain) raised their real per capita income levels relative to the European average, with most of the improvement taking place after 1950. Even so, by 1973 most of them, with the exception of Czechoslovakia, still fell below the European average, ranging from 9-15 per cent in the case of the USSR, Hungary, Greece, Bulgaria and Poland, to as much as 35-45 per cent for Spain, Portugal, Romania and Yugoslavia. Italy and Ireland also recorded per capita income levels some way below the European average. [7]

Dr. Freris's account of the Greek economy in the twentieth century makes fascinating reading. Probably more than any other European country Greece experienced massive economic and social shocks and sustained ill-management and administration for long periods in its history that it is surprising how it managed to survive as an independent socio-economic unit. In the twentieth century alone it has had to face, among other things, two major wars, occupation by foreign troops, civil war, large scale migrations, a great depression, hyperinflation and a turbulent political and social background which for much of the time has been dominated by a repressive right-wing regime.

These events have undoubtedly had an adverse impact on Greece's economy in the twentieth century, the more so in that the country is not lavishly endowed with natural resources, while the scale of modern developments prior to the first world war was very limited. By any standards, Greece at that time was a backward country, with little in the way of modern industry, an antiquated agrarian system which depended on one or two cash crops such as currants and wheat, and a financially bankrupt state administration whose defence needs had put it heavily in debt to foreign powers. Such characteristics continued to dominate in the twentieth century, so that despite significant quantitative progress, the structure of the economy was slow to change. Even by the beginning of the second world war, after a decade of protective policies, Greek industry remained small, undiversified, ministering essentially to domestic needs, the structure of which had hardly altered in the past twenty years.

War, occupation, civil war and hyperinflation were soon to follow and had it not been for substantial US aid in the reconstruction period Greece would surely have lost its independent existence.

During the postwar period Greece made substantial economic progress but what is noticeable is that it has not radically altered the structural format of the economy. Agriculture still remains fragmented and inefficient even by West European standards, the industrial base is still too heavily geared to downstream low technology sectors - for example, food, drink and tobacco, textiles and clothing and shoes accounted for 46 per cent of industrial output in 1979 - while a large part of investment (some 65 per cent in the period 1961-80) was absorbed by the construction industry. Nor did the substantial inflow of foreign capital and direct investment do much to ameliorate the problems and structural weaknesses of the industrial sector; in fact, if anything, they probably tended to ossify the existing structure. To make matters worse the political regime allowed the economy to drift at a time when firm policy direction was required. As a consequence Greece has not been able to provide

gainful employment for all its population, a fact demonstrated by the large scale emigration from the country in the period 1951-80 , when it accounted for some 12.2 per cent of the population.
        Thus when Greece became a full member of the European Community in 1981, her level of income and the structure of her economy still compared very unfavourably with those of the constituent members. Whether membership of the Community will finally drag the Greek economy into the twentieth century remains to be seen. If it does succeed in so doing the process of transition will undoubtedly be a long and painful one.

NOTES

[1] P. Bairoch, 'Europe's Gross National Product: 1800-1975', The Journal of European Economic History, No. 5 Fall 1976, pp.298-99.
[2] R. Triffin, Our International Monetary System: Yesterday, Today and Tomorrow, Random House, New York 1968, p.14; see also D.H. Aldcroft, From Versailles to Wall Street, 1919-1929, Allen Lane, 1977, pp.162-64. Some of the costs of the gold standard system may however have been borne by the countries of the periphery, for example the Latin American.
[3] See P. N. Stearns, European Society in Upheaval, Macmillan, London 1967.
[4] Financial Times, 14 February 1980.
[5] J. O. N. Perkins, The Macroeconomic Mix to Stop Stagflation, Macmillan, London 1980.
[6] W. W. Rostow, Getting From Here to There , Macmillan, London 1979.
[7] Bairoch, 'Europe's Gross National Product', pp.297-307.

INTRODUCTION

    This book is about Greece's economic history
from the 1920s to the 1980s. It would be foolish
to pretend that Greece's turbulent and frequently
violent political history had no bearing on its
economic fortunes. Equally, it would be
short-sighted to draw a line in 1920 and not to
account, however briefly, for what had gone on
before. This introduction attempts to gather
together a number of threads so that what happened
after 1920 can be focused on more accurately and
linked to a number of significant developments in
Greece's past.
    Greece's overall economic experience,
although by no means unique, does contain special
lessons and examples of great interest to
historians and economists alike. The economic
development of the country and its considerable
achievements took place against an almost
unbelievably volatile political background,
continuously punctuated by bloody wars and
frequently dominated by short-lived and
incompetent administrations. Greeks like to pride
themselves on their native cunning referring back
to the 'wily Ulysses'. There are numerous
instances in Greece's economic history that it is
tempting to agree that the country somehow
survived as an intact social and economic unit
through sheer will-power rather than through
material resources.
    Greece's modern economic history is still
relatively unexplored. There are numerous
well-researched monographs on a number of issues
or short periods but no attempt has yet been made
to explore developments over a long time span.
Some of the best research has so far concentrated
primarily on the nineteenth century [1]. In

outlining the developments up to the 1920s
frequent and liberal use was made of these
sources. No excuses are offered for the brevity
of the treatment of some issues other than that
the space devoted to them is sufficient to set the
scene for what happened afterwards.

Greece's long occupation by the Ottoman
Empire reached the beginning of its end in 1821
when one more insurrection which lasted until 1829
took firm hold and led to a protracted and bloody
revolt against the Turks. Given the direct
interest of Britain, France and Russia in the fate
of the Ottoman Empire it was not surprising that
Greece's revolt was followed closely by these
three powers, who also effectively sealed its fate
by intervening openly on the side of Greece.
Turkey was forced to recognize Greece's autonomy
in 1829 and finally its independence in 1832.
Between 1827 and 1831 Greece was ruled by
J. Kapodistrias, an ex-minister of the Tzar, who
was given the title of Governor of Greece. His
obviously pro-Russian sympathies, and to some
extent his authoritarian rule, led to his
assassination by political rivals in 1831. The
three powers intervened again and offered the
crown to Prince Otto of Bavaria. He arrived in
Greece in 1833 still under age. He ruled without
a constitution for almost ten years until an army
revolt in September 1843 forced him to concede a
constitution and to dismiss most of his Bavarian
advisers in favour of a duly elected cabinet.

Otto's regime was marked by several crises.
In addition to his barren marriage which led to
speculation as to his succession, he never managed
to establish a firm hold over the political scene
or to inspire his subjects. Indeed, a humiliating
occupation of the port of Piraeus by an
Anglo-French fleet in 1854-57, in order to keep
Greece out of the Crimean War, disappointed the
growing nationalist feelings. The Ottoman Empire
still contained large tracts of land and included
a large number of subjects that Greece considered,
rightly, as Greek. In 1862 another revolt
expelled Otto and brought in his place a Danish
prince who became King George I and established
the Greek dynasty which sat, unstably, on the
throne until 1974.

At this point it is perhaps pertinent to note
that of the seven kings who ruled Greece in its
modern history two died in exile, one was
assassinated, and one still lives in exile. Of

the three who died on the throne, one was exiled
but reinstated, one died, after a brief reign, of
a septic bite from a pet monkey, and only one
ascended, stayed and died on the throne
uninterruptedly for a reasonable period of time.
If it was not for a number of tragic events
associated with their reigns, one could safely say
with Gilbert and Sullivan that the Greek Kings'
lot was not a happy one.

   King George I reigned until 1913. His long
tenure was marked by at least three important
events. Firstly, following the Russo-Turkish war
of 1877 and the Congress of Berlin, Greece was
awarded Arta and Thessaly with its rich
wheat-growing plain. Secondly, the still
unresolved issue of the large Greek communities in
Macedonia, Epirus, and Crete led to repeated
incidents with Turkey and finally to an
ill-advised invasion by Greece of the Turkish
occupied area north of Thessaly. Only the
intervention of the Great Powers stopped the
Turkish troops from marching almost unopposed all
the way to Athens. Greece was forced to pay large
reparations to Turkey. An earlier default in 1893
by Greece on its international loans was used as
an additional pretext to impose a tight
international financial control in order to secure
funds both for the reparation and the servicing of
the debt. By that stage Greece's fortunes had
reached an all-time low. Thirdly, in 1909 the
army revolted once again, but this time not
directly against the King but as a gesture of
protest against what it considered to be the
effective collapse and dissolution of Greece's
state and army following the 1897 defeat. The
political aspirations of the movement were
channelled and expressed by E. Venizelos, who had
distinguished himself in Crete following the
granting of autonomy by Turkey to the island in
1899.

   Venizelos' ascendancy to power marked
indelibly Greece's history. He continued to play
a leading role in politics until his death in
1936. The 1909 revolt presaged one more war
against Turkey, this time far more successful from
Greece's point of view. Greece, under the
inspired and confident leadership of Venizelos,
reorganized its army and navy and concluded
alliances with Serbia and Bulgaria. Given the
upsurge of nationalism in the Balkan areas still
under Turkish occupation, it was a matter of time

before war broke out. Turkey attacked Serbia and Bulgaria, and Greece in its turn declared war on Turkey. The first Balkan War (October 1912 - May 1913) ended victoriously with Greek forces occupying Salonica and Joannina and a number of islands in the Aegean. Crete was also finally ceded to Greece. Meanwhile King George I had been assassinated in Salonica and his son Constantine succeeded him to the throne. The peace between the warring neighbours did not last long. In June 1913 Bulgaria turned on its allies, first on Serbia and then on Greece. The attacks were unsuccessful and when Turkey and Rumania joined the fray, Bulgaria capitulated in July 1913 and lost most of the territorial gains of the first Balkan War.

The outbreak of World War I created a deep division in Greek politics that reverberated right down to the 1930s. The Venizelos Government was extremely keen to enter the war on the side of the Allies but the King, who was pro-German, preferred to keep Greece neutral. The division between the King and the elected government led to a virtual state of civil war with two rival governments, one in Athens with the backing of the King, the other in Salonica with Venizelos and the backing of the Allies. Finally the pressures on Athens grew too strong, Venizelos reoccupied the capital and the King was sent to exile. His son, Alexander, took over but was to die soon afterwards as a result of that infamous monkey bite.

The Versailles Peace Conference and specifically the Treaty of Serves in 1920, gave Greece some more of the Aegean islands, and ominously, a wide strip of Turkish territory around the important Asia Minor port of Smyrna. The Turkish nationalist movement of Kemal Ataturk soon clashed with the relentlessly expansionist Greeks who, crudely, were reliving their dreams of revenge upon the Turks for the four centuries of occupation and pursuing the re-creation of the Byzantine Empire. The latter was the materialisation of the so-called "Grand Idea", the expansion of Greece to some ill-defined Byzantine frontiers. The Greek army was initially successful in pushing the weak and disorganized Turks almost back to Ancara. Meanwhile at home Venizelos had lost the elections and King Constantine had returned. The Allies promptly withdrew their support for Greece and so it was only a matter of time before the Turks regrouped, attacked the hopelessly overstretched Greek communication lines and then pushed the remnants of the army back to Smyrna. There followed an orgy of destruction and widespread massacre of the Greek population throughout Asia Minor. More than 1.2 million refugees poured out of Turkey and into Greece shortly after 1922. This was perhaps the most traumatic event in Greece's modern history, not only because it redefined its political aspirations and geographical boundaries but because it changed significantly the social and economic structure of the country.

The reactions to these catastrophic events were understandable. King Constantine was exiled once again and was to die outside Greece. A military government took over and promptly shot most of the cabinet whom they considered responsible for the defeat. Greece was formally declared a Republic in 1924. (Confusingly, but perhaps significantly, the words republic and democracy are identical in modern Greek.) The first Greek Republic was to last until 1935 when a military coup brought back King George II, son of Constantine, following an outrageously rigged plebiscite. One year later in 1936, J. Metaxas established a dictatorship which stayed in power up to the outbreak of the World War II. These eleven years of the Republic were replete with political crises and repeated coups ranging from the dangerous to the truly farcical. Venizelos continued however to dominate the political scene. Soon after the Republic was established in 1924, General Pangalos led a coup and established a brief-lived dictatorship (1925-26). In addition to setting an unpleasant precedent for a succession of attempted coups, his dictatorship is best remembered for a police order that forbade the wearing of short skirts which apparently offended his prudish wife.

Venizelos was re-elected to power in 1928 and stayed there until 1932. These four years have been called the "golden four years" precisely because they constituted a landmark of relative political stability, with attempts at creative legislation and careful policy-making. Unfortunately he lost the 1932 elections to a coalition of anti-venizelist and pro-royalist supporters, the latter still pursuing a political vendetta against him as they considered him responsible for the split of the country during the First World War and the eventual demise of the

15

monarchy in Greece. Elections were held again in
1933. A Venizelist faction led by General
Plastiras made the fatal mistake of attempting to
overthrow the Government when it appeared that the
election results would go against Venizelos. The
coup failed, an attempt was made against
Venizelos' life and he was forced to retire to the
relative safety of his native Crete. There
followed another pro-venizelist coup in 1935 by
republican officers who feared that the Government
was planning to restore the monarchy. This coup
also failed but this time the pro-royalist
reaction was violent and thorough. The army was
purged of all republican sympathisers, Venizelos,
who had no part in nor approved of the coup, was
condemned to death in absentia and a rigged
plebiscite brought back King George II to Greece.
The King had been living in exile in London since
1923.

A further general election in 1936 produced a
hung Parliament with the Greek Communist Party
holding the balance. Increasing social unrest and
the deeply divided country over the
Venizelist-Royalist issue was the final pretext
that allowed General J. Metaxas, with the full
approval of the King, to dissolve Parliament and
establish a dictatorship in August 1936. Metaxas
used the threat of communism to the social and
economic fabric of Greece to justify a wide range
of repressive measures. It is perhaps a sobering
thought that after the attempted coup of 1935 the
Right ruled Greece continuously, except between
1963-65, until 1981. This is an important
consideration to keep in mind as it puts the civil
war that followed the German occupation into
perspective and also helps to explain the role of
UK and later of the United Sates in Greece's
political and economic affairs. The Greek Right
felt itself continuously threatened by both the
economic and political aspirations of a large
section of the population. The 1.2 million
refugees from Asia Minor proved themselves to be
not only active in the economic but also in the
political affairs of their new homeland. Their
initially miserable conditions of living and their
rightful wrath against the royalists, whom they
considered responsible for their plight, fuelled
political passions throughout this period. It is
not accidental that a substantial proportion of
the leadership of the Greek Communist Party (KKE
from its Greek initials) was of refugee origin.

Introduction

It is also indicative of the fear that social
unrest generated that the KKE was outlawed in 1936
and was not rehabilitated until 1974.
    Metaxa's regime was an unpleasant combination
of the vicious, petty and comical elements of the
Greek Right. The regime aped the Fascist models
of Italy and Germany by calling Metaxas the Leader
and Father of the Nation, by establishing a
fascist youth complete with smart uniforms and
fascist salutes and by imposing the usual
paraphernalia of police repression, torture, and
of exiling its political opponents to barren
islands. The Italian ultimatum to Greece in
October 1940 allowed Metaxas a brief moment of
popularity. By rejecting the ultimatum he united
the people behind him in repulsing the invader.
Although this was an interesting contradiction of
one purely fascist regime fighting a seemingly so,
it did nothing to atone either the King or the
government in the eyes of the people. After the
initial victories over the invading Italians the
Germans invaded in April 1941, and another four
years of far harsher and brutal sufferings were
visited upon an exhausted people. The resistance
movement that sprang up against the Germans
reflected the political divisions of the country.
Metaxas' fascist youth disappeared without a
single trace and a well organized and popular
resistance movement under the leadership of the
National Liberation Front (EAM from its Greek
initials) fought the Germans. The EAM from its
very inception was dominated by the KKE but its
followers encompassed practically the whole
spectrum of politics in Greece. Sounds of
discord, however, were soon heard which presaged
even more violent events. The EAM forces began
attacking royalist or noncommunist resistance
groups and its relationship with the Greek
government in exile grew more and more strained.
The British held the ring uneasily trying to make
the King, the government and the Resistance to
cooperate with each other, but becoming
increasingly weary over the political aspirations
of the EAM. The events after the liberation of
Athens in October 1944 were not surprising. The
resistance movement had virtual control over the
whole country whereas the returning exiled Greek
government could only rely on some loyal troops
and the British forces. Fighting broke out in
Athens in December 1944 and later the conflict
spread throughout the country. A protracted,

bloody civil war was fought until the Left was soundly beaten in the summer of 1949. The civil war was not about the division of Greeks between royalists and republicans for it initially assumed the form of almost a class struggle, additionally complicated by the cold war politics of the USA who backed the Athens Government as part and parcel of the policy of containing communist expansion. Although supporters of the Left do not wish to admit this, if the EAM had won, then Greece would have followed the fate of Eastern European countries. The KKE was blindly and unconditionally pro-Russian, even after it had become obvious that Stalin had bargained Greece off to the UK. King George II died in 1947 and was succeeded by his brother Paul, whose son, Constantine, was the last of the Greek monarchs. King Paul died in 1964.

From 1949 on, the Right ruled almost unchallenged until 1963 when a liberal government was elected in the teeth of bitter opposition. The King intervened once again and forced the resignation of the Liberal goverment in 1965. Elections were scheduled for 1967, but as the Liberals were bound to win, the military stepped in and established a dictatorship that lasted until 1974. Although avoiding some of the comical excesses of Metaxas, the regime was equally brutal and unpleasant in its liberal use of torturing, jailing and killing. The event which hastened its demise was a completely arbitrary interference with the internal politics of Cyprus including an assassination attempt on Makarios, the leader of the Greek Cypriot community. Turkey, under the pretext of protecting the Turkish Cypriot minority, invaded and occupied half of Cyprus. Thus a Greek totalitarian regime managed a tragic repetition of a parallel Asia Minor disaster but this time causing the loss of lives and loss of territory to an independent state. With the restoration of democratic rule in the summer of 1974 a plebiscite reestablished the Republic and King Constantine II became the last of his line to follow the well trodden path of Greek Kings to exile to England. The military junta had already forced the King to flee the country after he attempted his own coup against them. The elections of 1981 brought a socialist party into power, signifying both the acceptance of the inevitable by the Greek Right and the fact that it could not seek solutions any more by military or

18

Introduction

police interventions. The seal of political
maturity and of the change in the structure of
power sharing in Greece came by Greece's full
accession to the EEC in 1981 [2].

This brief outline of the political events,
although it does little justice to the complexity
of the issues involved, at least shows the
continuous turbulence of Greece's modern history.
A personal interjection here will perhaps
illustrate at the micro level the essence of these
events. A relative of the author, who died in the
mid 1970s, was called to the arms as a very young
medical undergraduate and in 1912 fought and was
badly wounded in the Balkan Wars, he was called up
in the First World War and was then again drafted
for the full campaign in Asia Minor during
1921-23. He had, literally, to swim for his life
at the evacuation of the remnants of the Greek
army at Smyrna. He was yet again called up as a
reservist in the medical corp during the Second
World War. All in all he spent some 12 years
under arms or in active duty. A whole generation
of Greeks right down to the end of the civil war
knew little else but continuous wars, political
instability and repressive regimes. It is a
salutory thought that the economic events to be
described and analysed took place against such a
shifting and shaky background.

Perhaps the most pressing problem facing the
young Greek state upon gaining its independence
was the issue concerning the large tracts of land
previously occupied by Turks but now belonging to
the State, the so-called 'National Lands'. The
Government had promised to distribute these to the
landless peasants, but progress was painfully
slow. In 1837, 65% of the peasants were landless,
and according to one estimate, about 70% to 75% of
all land, both cultivated and uncultivated,
belonged to the state. This was a unique
situation in Europe which was still dominated by
large private estates or small peasant ownership
[3]. A feeble attempt at a subsidised sale of
this land in 1835 failed because the peasants
could not afford the repayments. The existing big
landlords opposed the scheme because they feared
that they would lose the lucrative subcontracting
of the collection of land taxes once small scale
ownership became widespread.

In 1871 the State came to grips with the
problem [4]. Resisting calls to auction the land,
precisely because this form of sale would have

benefited large landowners, it offered some 350,000 individual plots for sale at low interest and long repayments. At that time, rough estimates placed about one third of all cultivated land in the hands of the state. In the intervening years since independence substantial tracts of lands had been illegally occupied or otherwise claimed by landless peasant and big landlords. About one third of all farmers were tenants of state-owned land. The land redistribution was accompanied by a change in agricultural taxes which encouraged greater production, especially that of cash crops [5]. This reform settled, at least partially, the issue of land ownership in Greece and established a pattern of small scale landownership which survived until today. However, more difficulties were in store when Greece acquired from Turkey Thessaly and a part of Epirus in 1877. The former contained the rich plain of Thessaly, traditionally the breadbasket and wheat growing area for Greece. The national territory expanded by 25% and the population by about 18% following these acquisitions.

Land tenure in the Ottoman Empire had developed its own peculiarities, customs and laws. Land in Thessaly was being held under the so-called 'tsiflik' system. This consisted of very large estates, sometimes encompassing several villages and even small towns. Although the peasants were tied to the land in a semi-feudal manner they enjoyed considerable protection under Ottoman law. Specifically, their form of share-cropping tenancy could be inherited and therefore they could not be ejected easily, if at all, from their land. In what now appears a perversion of the liberal, constitutional and democratic rule of Greece, compared to the absolute monarchy of the Ottoman Empire, these farmers actually became worse off once they came under Greek jurisdiction. For a start, the treaties under which Greece obtained these areas, protected the rights of the existing Turkish landlords. Significantly, they were given specific and absolute title to their lands. Fearful, however, of their future under Greek rule, these landlords sold off their properties to rich expatriate Greeks. The absolute title to the land now changed the position of the tenant farmers in the eyes of the law. In a sense they were not tied any more to the land, but neither

were the new landlords obliged to keep them there
and allow them to till it [6]. Through a series
of court decisions and amendments to legislation
the new Greek landlords established the right to
sign tenancy agreements or refuse to do so with
their farmers. The process of consolidation of
the 'tsiflik' meant that farmers previously tied
to their lands but at least with security of
tenure now found themselves at the mercy of their
new Greek masters who had different plans for
their land [7]. The areas so affected were very
large indeed. When Greece acquired, as a result
of the Balkan Wars, Macedonia and the rest of
Epirus, some 50% to 64% of all cultivated land in
Thessaly was under the 'tsiflik' system. The
equivalent figures for Macedonia were 41% to 52%
and 33% to 42% for Epirus. Indeed by 1922, when
the problems had become extremely pressing both
because of the influx of the landless refugees
from Asia Minor and because of the continuous
friction between landlord and tenants, some 33% of
all cultivated land in Greece was under the
tsiflik system involving about 13.5% of all the
farmers [8]. The land reform question was by no
means the only problem that faced Greek society at
that time. Three developments that took place
during the later half of the nineteenth century
affected to a great extent the later course of the
Greek economy.

Firstly, the tariff system of Greece
underwent a massive change in the 1880s [9].
Between 1857 and 1867 import duties on food and
wheat in particular were relatively light but with
manufactured goods bearing most of the duties.
Given that the land reform of 1871 had encouraged
the development of smallholdings, farmers shifted
production away from wheat, which required large
farms, to cash crops such as currants. The latter
involved labour intensive processes and was
ideally suited for family farms as well as having
a ready market in the UK. The tariff system at
the time protected industry without having any
particular effect on farmers. In 1884 this policy
was completely reversed. Import duties on wheat
increased fivefold and the industrial tariff was
extended to cover a wider range of goods. Indeed,
by 1905 wheat duties had increased by 2,400 times
their 1867 levels and they accounted for about 40%
of the value of the imported wheat. The tariff
also shifted the burden of duties on industrial
goods that could be produced in Greece. The way

Introduction

in which the import duties were calculated added
another escalator clause to the real value of
these tariffs. The duties were levied on a
notional drakma basis with a constant gold value.
Between 1885 and 1895 the foreign rate of exchange
of the drakma against the gold franc fell
continuously and so did the gold content of the
drakma. It therefore followed that as the import
duties were based on notional gold drakma they
yielded continuously higher revenues as the drakma
depreciated. Thus import duties increased
automatically in drakma terms as the foreign
exchange rate depreciated without the percentage
duty being affected.

The policy change on protectionism and
particularly the 'dear food' thrust of this
reversal have been the matter of extensive
discussion amongst Greek economic historians. One
approach has viewed the high duties on wheat,
imposed under the premierships of H. Trikoupis, as
a gesture towards the landed interests that arose
after 1881 and the entrance of the 'tsiflik'
landlords into the Greek political scene. What
made this change difficult to justify was the fact
that Trikoupis is considered as a liberal
moderniser who aimed to drag Greece into the
industrial age. But the fact is that tsiflik
landlords wielded considerable influence in
Parliament and were also themselves, or had the
backing of, rich expatriate Greeks.

The governments of the time were either
unwilling or unable to resist their pressures or
were afraid that funds which poured into Greece
for the purchase of these lands would dry up. The
high wheat import duties protected domestic
production which was primarily concentrated in
the newly acquired area of Thessaly [10].
Perversely, however, instead of encouraging the
expansion of domestic production and reducing
imports, the tariffs led to an increase in the
latter. Taking 1885 as the base year of 100, by
1911 the volume of wheat imports had grown to 176
and that of domestic output to 132 [11]. It
appears that the large landowners attempted to
maximize their revenues by changing land use
rather than by expanding output. Given the high
import duties, domestic wheat prices were driven
even higher by reducing the acreage devoted to
wheat and turning the land over to grazing,
especially to nomad shepherds who were willing to
pay high rents for it. The number of goats and

22

Introduction

sheep in Greece almost doubled between 1860 and 1879. The high wheat prices also enhanced rental income and drove land prices up. Furthermore, as a substantial proportion of the import trade in wheat was handled by the landlords themselves, this ensured their continued interest in high domestic prices.

Given Trikoupis' avowed aim to foster and encourage industry in Greece this protectionist policy appears contradictory as it led to higher food prices, and therefore higher industrial wages. But at the same time the high tariffs also protected domestic industry from competition. A pragmatic view, that these tariffs were yet another source of revenue for the Greek state, perhaps gets nearer to the truth. Industry in Greece at that time was effectively non-existent. The number of factories had risen from 95 in 1875 to 208 in 1873 and that of industrial workers from 7,000 in 1875 to 26,000 in 1911. But the country was still overwhelmingly agricultural [12].

The second important development concerned the dramatic change in the composition of agricultural output during this period. This was the outcome of the so-called 'Currants Crisis'.

Following the land redistribution and reforms of 1871 the growth of production of currants increased at an explosive rate. By 1900 one quarter of all cultivated land and one third of all the economically active population in farming was employed in producing currants [13]. There were three reasons for this expansion in output. Firstly, the cultivation of currants is ideally suited for small scale farms, exactly the kind that proliferated after 1871. Secondly, Greek currants had a ready market overseas and their export was linked to the imports of wheat. Indeed, during this period some 70% of foreign exchange earned from their export was spent on importing cereals. In addition to this, 50% to 75% of the value of exports was accounted for by currants. Farmers, exporters and the Government had every reason to encourage and foster their production. Finally, and most crucially, in 1878 the French vineyards were devasted by blight and by 1880 an increasing shortage of grapes drove the price of currants and of alcohol to high levels. The French vineyards did not recover until the late 1890s. In between, however, Greek farmers reacted by increasing the acreage under vine cultivation between 1881 and 1891 by more than one third, and expanding their output by about the same percentage. When the inevitable oversupply of currants did take place the smallholders and traders were hit very hard. The slow recovery of the French production was aided by high import duties on currants and alcohol and the rapid expansion of the Greek production finally drove down the prices of currants from 300 francs per 500 kilos in 1890 to 42 francs in 1894. (500 kilos being the approximate standard weight of trading currants) [14]. The Greek state had to intervene on an extensive scale to stave off the worst consequence of the crisis. An increasing percentage of currants normally destined for export was delivered directly to the Government who then sold it for spirits and alcohol production, forbidding any other uses. By 1903 almost a quarter of the currant crop was dealt with in that way. The proceeds from the sales of these currants were used to set up a special bank to provide subsidised loans to help growers during this difficult period. Finally, more desperate measures were introduced including land taxes payable in currants, thus raising the overall amount of the crop withdrawn from the open market to more than 35%. Throughout the crisis the government had to contend not only with the sufferings of the small farmers but also with considerable social unrest as farmers turned against the wholesalers blaming them for their plight. A direct consequence of the crisis was a massive emigration movement to the United States by the bankrupted or destitute farmers [15].

The third major development to be examined here concerns the continuous fiscal and monetary crises that plagued the Greek state since independence. These crises came to a head in 1893 when the government defaulted on its foreign debt payments. The default was compounded by the disasterous compaign against Turkey in 1897. The ensuing defeat brought not only humiliation for Greece but also the imposition of international financial control which lasted until the outbreak of the Second World War. As the events leading up to the default and the imposition of control are rather complex, they will be examined here in roughly chronological order.

On the establishment of the Greek independent state and after initially unsuccessful experiments with banks, the government licensed the National Bank of Greece, which had been established in

1841, to issue bank notes which were convertible to gold. The convertibility of the currency never lasted for long and even during the periods when it was effective it resembled a gold exchange rather than pure gold standard. In 1848, 1868-70, 1877-1884 and 1885-1928 convertibility was suspended [16]. The reasons for this monetary instability were primarily the permanent deficit in the balance of trade, the continuous political crises and the inability of the Greek state to raise sufficient funds either via taxation or borrowing at home or overseas. This meant that the State had to resort to the printing press for its needs.

The previous short outline of the political history indicated that until Greece's frontiers were firmly established and the majority of the Greeks living under Ottoman rule were grouped together, the country was for long periods at a state of war. The percentage of the state budget devoted to defence rose continuously from 27.7% in 1866-70 to 48.6% in 1883-95 [17]. During the premierships of Trikoupis (1883-95), Greece embarked on an extensive developmental and modernization effort. Trikoupis' vision of a strong Greece was a combination of the expression of rising middle class values and the appreciation of the realities of power politics that hemmed in and frequently humiliated Greece. Trikoupis' protectionist policies towards the landed interests should not detract from his extensive public works programmes which included the building of railways and the excavation of the Corinth canal [18]. To finance these projects and the growing defence expenditures, the Greek state reverted to massive external borrowing, especially after 1879. This was an important date for later fiscal developments in Greece. Repeated problems with the servicing of the external debt incurred during the period of the revolt against the Turks meant that between 1844 and 1879 there were virtually no external loans. The international banking community refused to enter into any new commitments before the outstanding arrears had been settled. The situation during this period was not particularly difficult for the Greek state, because during the regime of King Otto the Government relied extensively on taxation to meet its expenditures and the external situation limited spending on defence. After 1879, however, and following an agreement with the main creditors, primarily the UK, France and Germany, the Greek state began to borrow extensively overseas. Perversely enough, despite the previous record of defaults, the international financial community lent freely to the Greek Government [19].

Trikoupis' problems with the finance of the extensive public works programme were compounded by three factors. Firstly, the state had to rely increasingly on indirect taxation, particularly levies on tobacco, spirits and kerosene. In 1871 the ratio of direct to indirect taxes in terms of revenue stood at 1.61, in 1880 at 0.86 and finally in 1895 at 0.85 [20]. Although indirect taxes are meant to minimize the disincentive effects on savings and investment they are, of course, regressive. Trikoupis' popularity therefore sank to a very low level as his public works programme expanded. Secondly, the relative decline in the level of international trade during this period meant that revenues from import duties also declined. For example, the value of imports into Greece declined continuously between 1882-85 and fluctuated between 1886 and 1893 reaching a low level of 91.4 million drakmas in 1893 and a high level of 140.3 million drakmas in 1891 [21]. Finally, the onset of the currants crisis in the 1890s, hit the public purse in two different ways. It reduced the foreign exchange receipts from exports and it increased government expenditures on subsidies and on the various schemes for controlling the production and exports of currants. There was a vicious circle of these threefold effects pressing on the state finance : budget deficits financed by external loans, the continuing deficit in the trade balance necessitating further inflows of foreign capital and the fluctuating fortunes of the import trade which provided duty revenues for the state budget. It is at this particular juncture of Greece's economic history that even the most charitable approach cannot fail to generate amazement at the foolhardiness of Greece's creditors and the inability or unwillingness of the Greek state to put some semblance of order in its finances. Greece's foreign debt problems have their origins in this time and they continued to plague its monetary and financial affairs right down to the outbreak of World War II.

By 1893 Greece had borrowed 585.4 million of gold francs. This sum on its own is not particularly meaningful unless it can be related to some other stock or flow figure. Thus for example in 1893 some 30% of all public expenditure in Greece was directed towards servicing the internal and external debt [22]. In an extensive and detailed study of Greece's foreign debt during this period, Levantis aptly summarised the situation that finally led to the official default in 1893. He starts by outlining the balance of trade situation and then links this with the fiscal policies pursued [23].

"It is safe to state however that the international outgo surpassed the international income by a figure ranging between 40 and 50 million/drakmas annually. This figure corresponds to the amount of annual borrowing from abroad for the twelve year period of 1879-1890. It was through this continuous capital importation that Greek international accounts kept their equilibrium. The moment the flow stopped the difficulty was apparent in the inability to meet debt charges. Default could not be avoided; it could only be postponed." (Levantis, p.75)

He then goes on to discuss the uses of the capital funds borrowed and the conditions of the loans that the Greek state had to accept:

"If we exclude the insignificant sums appropriated for the construction of railway lines and public works, the biggest portion of borrowed funds was consumed by the pyramiding charges of the growing indebtedness, the huge outlays in armaments and the covering of recurring budgetary deficits ·······. From 1879, a year that marks the beginning of importation of capital from abroad, to the year 1897 which signalises the advent of the international financial control 470.4 million drakmas were paid for the servicing of debt, an amount that corresponds approximately to the total actually borrowed. In other words over a period of scarcely twenty years the borrower had paid in service charges the amount actually received, while the

27

largest portion of the contracted
indebtedness still remained
unliquidated." (Levantis p.72-73)

Angelopoulos [24] covering much the same ground
adds further aggravating factors such as the
issuing of loans at deep discounts, high real
interest rates, excessive provisions for sinking
and amortization funds and so on. He points out
that for the loans issued between 1821-1893, 34%
of the proceeds never reached Greece, being
absorbed by commissions, fees, discounts etc.
Foreign borrowers were willing to take on the risk
of lending to Greece, precisely because the
expected returns were made so attractive. There
was also the additional factor that some 15% to
30% of all the foreign bonds were held by
expatriate Greeks who were quick to bring pressure
to bear on the Greek Government if their interests
were affected [25].
In December 1893 Trikoupis announced from the
speaker's stand in Parliament the default on
foreign loans using an expression that has passed
down in the annals of Greece's history,
'Unfortunately, gentlemen, we are bankrupt'. This
was by no means the first official default on
Greece's international obligations. In 1827, and
again in 1847 Greece had stopped payments on its
external debts. What made this occasion special
was the adamant refusal of Greece's creditors to
negotiate and their continuous pressure for some
sort of international control over Greece's
finances. Their chance came with Greece's defeat
in the 1897 war against Turkey. As a part of the
peace settlement an International Commission of
Economic Control (ICEC) was set up. The basic
aims of ICEC was to ensure that war reparations
due to Turkey were promptly paid but without any
prejudice to the interests of the existing lenders
and bondholders. The original instrument setting
up the ICEC specified that:

"For this purpose an International
Financial Commision shall be instituted
in Athens composed of the
representatives of the mediating powers,
one member being appointed by each
Power. The Hellenic Govenment shall
pass a law which shall previously be
accepted by the Powers, regulating the
working of the Commission and according

> to which the collection and employment
> of revenues sufficent for the service of
> the war idemnity loan and the other
> national debt shall be placed under the
> absolute control of the Commission."
> (Lenantis, p.98)

The Greek government was obliged to assign for these purposes the revenues from the state monopolies of salt, cigarette paper, matches, playing cards, abrasives and kerosene and the revenues from tobacco, stamp and import duties collected in the custom offices of Piraeus, supplemented if necessary by the revenues from a number of other customs posts. The revenues so collected by the ICEC were to be used to create a sinking fund for the repayment of the debts. Any excess revenue not used for this purpose was to be shared equally by the ICEC and the Greek Government. The provisions of the agreement forbade the Greek state to impose any duties or taxes on the interest receivable by the foreign bondholders and it was further severely restricted in enacting tax changes without the prior approval of the ICEC.

The overall effect of the imposition of financial control on Greece was an abrogation of the sovereignty of the state and a vindictive and humiliating set of conditions and restrictions. It is indicative of both the strictness by which the commission enforced the settlement and the willingness of the Greek governments to comply, that all payment to the ICEC were made in physical gold even during periods of extreme foreign exchange instability or rapid devaluation of the drakma. This resulted in an increasing real burden being imposed on a weak and underdeveloped country. Furthermore, all the calculations of repayments assumed that bonds were to be redeemed at par despite the fact that the majority of them were issued at heavy discounts. The final picture of the ICEC in action is given by Levantis who quotes evidence to the fact that right down to March 1941 and one month before the Germans occupied Greece, and whilst the country was fighting for its life the ICEC commissioners in the Bank of Greece continued to remit gold payments abroad [26].

Greece entered into the twentieth century with the burden of a large number of problems and with unsettled political and territorial questions. The industrial framework of the economy was virtually non-existent. In percentage terms the progress made by 1892 was impressive precisely because it started from a zero base. Greece was predominantly an agricultural country with well over 65% of the population employed on the land [27]. The outbreak of the Balkan Wars and later of the World War I gave a considerable boost to the small scale industry that supplied the army, particulary in victualling, blankets and boots. Also the Greek shipping sector, which stood at 900,000 gross tons in 1915, was started on its path of growth, recovering quickly the large losses suffered due to enemy action during the Great War and regaining to its prewar level by 1925 [28].

The agricultural sector was still burdened however by the unsolved problems of the 'tsiflik', the large estates. At the outbreak of the First World War the 'tsiflik' occupied about 33-35% of all the cultivated land in Greece. The currants crisis had put an end to over-specialization in one crop but had not helped to diversify or expand the range of cultivation. Wheat prices were kept artificially high by import duties but this did not encourage the 'tsiflik' owners to expand their production or to invest in their farms. It encouraged them instead to extract higher rents which in turn meant that the tenants had neither the income nor the incentive to invest in their holdings.

There is an extreme paucity of data concerning estimates of the level and composition of GNP during this period. The picture becomes even more confused as the geographical area and the population of Greece increased in 1881 and again in 1913 and 1920. Irrespective however of the exact size and growth of the different sectors or of overall economic activity, proximate reasons can be put forward to explain why Greece remained an agricultural country for nearly the first 80 years of independence. For a start, the protracted war of independence led to severe privation and physical destruction of the meagre capital and infrastructure that was available at the time. The country was saddled at an early stage by large external debts and the situation was aggravated by repeated wars of territorial expansion right down to 1922. The role of the state in the developmental process was limited to acting as an intermediary between landlord and

Introduction

peasant, embarking during one period only on a
programme of public works and in general pursuing
laisse-faire policies with the exception of the
increases in tariffs on wheat imports in the
1880s. Greece's lack of raw materials and fuel
made the economy dependent on imports. This
worsened the chronic domestic shortage of funds
either for investment or as sources of taxable
income flows by adding a balance of trade
financing requirement [29]. Indeed recent
research has come to question the wisdom of
Trikoupis' extensive public works programme by
pointing out that although a railway system was an
essential aspect of the infrastructure of a
country, in the case of Greece it did not really
help the development of industry. In fact it
burdened the balance of trade even more since all
the capital equipment had to be imported.
Furthermore, the railways competed with coastal
shipping and as a result stunted its growth. This
was unfortunate as this was an area where Greek
tradition and inclination might have given it a
comparative advantage as the coastal shipping
developed overseas links [30]. Funding
development by foreign capital was not an option
open to Greece because the majority of foreign
funds was absorbed by state loans. Most of the
foreign investment that took place during the
second half of the nineteenth century and in the
first ten years of the twentieth was directed
primarily to mining, gas, telegraph, public
transport and in some instances, banking. Foreign
investors also participated in the building of
railways. Here again the investment was
concentrated in infrastructure facilities and did
little or nothing for the industrial or export
sectors [31]. Nor should one fail to mention the
role of expatriate Greeks from Turkey, Egypt,
Levant or Europe and especially that of A. Syngros
the 'eminence grise' of this extraordinary group
of people. Motivated by a combination of
patriotism and greed they proceeded to contribute
directly to Greece's finances by buying large
amounts of its overseas issues of bonds, but there
was little to show in terms of direct industrial
investment. None of these expatriate Greeks seem
to have suffered losses in their involvement with
the mother country. A number of them left all
their fortunes to the Greek state upon their
death. Some of the most imposing buildings and
avenues in Athens still bear their names or the

evidence of their, possibly, belated generosity to their country of origin [32].

Greece entered the First World War with an economy that had changed very little if at all over a period of more than sixty years. The events that followed the Great War created economic and political upheavals unprecedented in the history of a country which already had its share of wars and instability. Greece was never the same after the defeat by the Turks in 1922, but the economy once again changed very little. What change there was, was too little and too late to steer the economy and society towards a different path of development.

NOTES

[1] Specific and separate reference will be made to these monographs later on. The following is a fairly comprehensive sample of a number of sources that deal primarily with the nineteenth century, or at least attempt a more global approach to Greece's recent economic history.

  a. L. Th. Houmanidis, Oikonomiki Istoria tis Ellados, Ethnikon Kentron Koinonikon Ereunon, Athens 1973 (Covers the economic history of classical Greece to the fall of Constantinople in 1453).

  b. A. Papadimas, Protes Rizes tis Neas Ellinikis Oikonomias, Piraeus, 1967.

  c. V. I. Filias, Koinonia kai Exousia stin Ellada, Syhrona Keimena, Athens 1974 (covers the 1800-1864 period).

  d. I. Kordatos, Eisagoyi is tin Istorian tis Ellinikis Kefalaiokratias, Epikairotis, Athens 1972.

  e. M. Nikolinakos, Meletes pano ston Elliniko Kapitalismo, Nea Synora, Athens 1976 esp. pp.17-142.

  f. P. Rodakis, Taxeis kai Stromata sti Neoelliniki Koikonia, Mykinai, Athens 1975.

  g. P.K. Raptarhis, Istoria tis Oikonomikis Zois tis Ellados, Athens 1934.

  h. E.J. Tsouderos, Le Relevement Economique de la Grece, Berger-Levrauet, Paris 1920.

Introduction

i. K. Moskoff, I Ethniki kai Koinoniki Syneidisi stin Ellada 1830-1909, Salonica, 1972.
j. N.P. Mouzelis, Modern Greece: Facets of Underdevelopment, Macmillan, London 1978.

[2] For a good, short, factual outline of Greece's modern history see E.S. Forster, A Short History of Modern Greece 1821-1956, Methuen, London, 1958. The standard short Greek reference is N.G. Svoronos, Episkopisi tis Neoellinikis Istorias, Themelio, Athens 1976, esp. pp.9-156. For a more detailed exposition
see D. Dakin. The Unification of Greece 1770-1923, St. Martin's Press, London 1972.

[3] Istoria tou Ellinikou Ethnous (various editors and contributors), Ekdotiki Athinon, Athens 1977-78, Volume 14, pp.94-105.

[4] K. Vergopoulos, To Agrotiko Zitima stin Ellada, Exantas, Athens 1975, p.85. For a more general introduction see I. Kordatos, Istoria tou Agrotikou Kinimatos stin Ellada, Boukoumanis, Athens 1975.

[5] T. Lignadis, I Xeniki Exartisis kata tin Diadromin tou Neoellinikou Kratous, Athens 1975, pp.57-83.

[6] Istoria, Volume 15, pp.69-72.

[7] Vergopoulos, To Agrotiko, pp.85-114.

[8] Ibid., pp.151-53.

[9] For a comprehensive history of Greece's external trade policy see A. I. Andreas, I Exoteriki Emporiki Politiki tis Ellados 1830-1933, Athens 1933, esp. pp.83-106. See also X. Zolotas, I Ellas is to Stadion tis Ekviomihaniseos, Bank of Greece, Athens 1964, pp.30-31, and pp.126-133.

[10] Vergopoulos, To Agrotiko, pp.115-137.

[11] Ibid, p.127.

[12] a. G. Dertilis, Koinonikos Metashimatismos kai Stratiotiki Epemvasi 1880-1909, Exantas, Athens 1977, pp.85-98.
b. P. Agianoglou, To Perasma apo tin Fedouarchia ston Kapitalismo stin Ellada, Athens 1982, pp.254-264.

[13] Istoria, Volume 15, pp.10-14.

[14] Istoria, Volume 15, pp.65-68 and 170-171.

[15] K.Vergopoulos,Kratos kai Oikonomia ston 19 on Aiona, Exantas, Athens 1978, pp.103-108.

[16] a. K. Varvaresos, Istoria kai Provlimta tou Ellinikou Nomismatikou Systimatos, Pyrsos, Athens 1939, pp.1-17.

33

Introduction

b. X. Zolotas, Nomismatika kai
    Synallagmatika Fainomena en Elladi
    1919-22, Greka, Athens 1928, pp.6-10.
c. For a general discussion see
    C. J. Damiris, Le Systeme Monetaire Grec
    et la Change, Volumes I-II, M. Giard,
    Paris 1920, passim.
[17] a. Istoria, Volume 15, p.14.
b. K. Tsoukalas in Koinoniki Anaptyxi kai
    Kratos, Themelio, Athens 1981,p.63, gives
    the following data concerning the
    structure of Governemnt budgets (in %):

	Defence	Servicing of Debt	Other
1866-70	27.7	11.6	60.7
1871-75	25.1	21.3	53.6
1876-80	41.9	19.3	38.4
1881-85	48.6	26.8	24.6

[18] L. Papagiannis, Oi Ellinikoi Sidirodromoi
     1882-1913, Morfotiko Idryma Ethnikis
     Trapezis, Athens 1982, passim.
[19] A. Th. Angelopoulos, Ai Dimosionomikai
     Synepiai tou Daneismou tis Ellados, in
     Epitheorisis Koinonikis kai Dimosias
     Oikonomias, May-August 1936.
[20] Istoria, Volume 15, p.72.
[21] Zolotas, Nomismatika, pp.213-214.
[22] Angelopoulos, Ai Dimosionomikai, pp.11-12.
[23] J.A. Levantis, The Greek Foreign Debt and the
     Great Powers 1821-1898, Columbia University
     Press, New York 1944.
[24] Angelopoulos, Ai Dimosionomikai, passim.
[25] For extensive, but primarily quantitative,
     surveys of Greece's foreign indebtedness in
     the pre-war period see:
a. G. Haritakis, (Ed.), Oikonomiki Epaitiris
    tis Ellados 1932, Athens 1933, article
    entitled Analysis tou Dimosiou Hreous tis
    Ellados, pp.493-590.
b. A. Agiopetritis, Ta Exoterika Dimosia
    Daneia apo tis Epanastaseos tou 1821
    mehri Simeron, in Statistikai Meletai
    1821-1971 published by Ethnikon Kentron
    Koinonikon Ereunon, Athens 1972,
    pp.292-332.
[26] a. Levantis, The Greek, pp.98-106.

b. For an informative discussion of the ICEC see S.P. Kouvelis, Diethnis Oikonomikos Eleghos en Elladi, in Archeion Oikonomikon kai Koinonikon Epistimon, Oct-Dec 1938.

c. For background material to the 1893 bankruptcy see T. Vournas, Ta Lavreotika Kai i Hreopia tou 1893, Fitrakis, Athens 1976.

[27] For example, the horsepower employed in the 22 factories existing in 1867 was 300. The situation in 1889 was 143 factories using 8568 HP. See Istoria, Volume 15, pp.10-14 and 33-56.

[28] a. Istoria, Volume 16, pp.79-80.

b. For a more general introduction to the earlier history of Greek shipping see K. Papathanasopoulos, Elliniki Emporiki Nautilia 1833-1865, Morfotiko Idryma Ethnikis Trapezis, Athens 1893.

[29] a. N. Vernikos, I Ellada Brosta stin Decaetia tou' 80, Exantas, Athens 1973, pp.28-30.

b. Zolotas, I Ellada, pp.28-30.

c. Tsoukalas, Koinoniki, pp.28-30.

[30] a. Dertilis, Koinonikos, pp.76-84.

b. Agianoglou, To Perasma, pp.257-264.

[31] A. Freris, To Xeno Kefalaio stin Ellada, 1840-1940, Oikonomikos Tahydromos, 29/1/76, pp.12-13.

[32] N. Psiroukis, To Neoelliniko Paroikiako Fainomeno, Epikairotis, Athens 1974, esp. pp.166-202.

Chapter One

THE TURBULENT 1920s : THE ASIA MINOR DISASTER AND
AFTER

1.1   INTRODUCTION

Greece's involvement in the Balkan Wars (1912-13)
and the First World War yielded at least one
important gain, namely that of increasing its
territory and population by about half. In
addition to this, the disruption of external trade
forced the government to rely extensively on
domestic supplies for the war. Industries such as
textiles and food processing benefited
considerably from the war effort [1]. Greece
however still remained a predominantly
agricultural economy. The distribution of the
population amongst the major sectors of economic
activity had hardly changed for more than half a
century as the data in Table 1.1 testify.

TABLE 1.1   Composition of economically active
population 1861 and 1920 (%)

Sectors	1861	1920
Agriculture	74.0	70.0
Industry and Handicraft	10.0	13.1
Commerce and Transport	6.1	9.2
Public Administration	4.4	2.0
Professional and Other	5.5	4.8

Source: K.Tsoukalas, Exartisi kai Anaparagogi,
Themelio, Athens 1977, p.183

Industry, however, did make impressive advances
precisely because it started from an almost zero
36

TABLE 1.2   Results of 1917 Industrial Census

A total of 2,213 establishments were surveyed
which employed 36,124 workers and utilised 7,000
HP.

(a) Analysis of establishments:

No. of Workers employed per Establishment	No. of Establishments	Total No. of Workers
1 - 5	1,188	3,579
6 - 25	743	8,845
25 and over	282	23,700

(b) In specific (partial coverage):

Industry	No. of Establishments	Total of Workers	Employment as % of total
Food Processing	1,244	10,136	34.4
Spinning and textiles	173	10,680	36.25
Timber processing	135	1,235	4.19
Chemicals	132	2,967	10.11
Engineering	132	2,820	9.57
Paper and printing	117	1,617	5.48
	1,933	29,455	100.00

Sources:

(a) G.A. Anastasopoulos, Istoria tis Ellinikis
     Viomihanias 1840-1940, Vol.II (1885-1922),
     Elliniki Ekdotiki Etairia, Athens 1947,
     pp.950-951.
(b) G. Haritakis, Oikonomiki Epaitiris tis
     Ellados for 1933, Athens 1934, p.600.
(c) M. Gevetis, I Statistiki tis Viomihanias kai
     Viotehnias is tin Neoteran Elladan, in
     Statistikai Meletai 1821-1971, pp.245-291.

base.   Considerable   controversy   surrounds   this
particular   issue.   One   approach   considers   the
1920s   as   the   time   when the Greek economy took an
important turning   towards   industrialisation   which
was   cut   short   by   the depression of the 1930s and
the outbreak   of   the   Second   World   War.   Another
approach   views   the   relative   rise   in the role of
industry   as   a   natural   aspect   of   the   overall
underdevelopment   of   the   Greek   economy.   In other
words,   the   spurt   of   industrialisation   indicated
both the strengths and   the   limits   of   an   economy
with   few   raw   materials   or   energy   resources,   a
limited   domestic   market and a permanent balance of
trade constraint.   Industrial   censuses   undertaken
in   1917,   1920   and 1930 provide useful information
in helping   to   appraise   both   the   state   and   the
dynamics of Greece's industry during this period.
        Table   1.2   summarises   the   results   from   the
1917   census.   This   census   was   incomplete because
there   was   considerable   difficulty   in   obtaining
answers   to   the   questionnaires.   Furthermore, the
survey   covered   only   the   purely   manufacturing
sector   leaving   aside   handicrafts   or   very   small
establishments.   The   data   indicate   clearly   the
importance of food   processing   and   textiles.   For
the   purpose   of   all   the   censuses   the   word
'establishment' was taken   to   mean   a   place   where
one   or   more   persons   were   permanently   occupied
under   managerial   supervision   in   the   production,
repair   or   assembly   of   goods   or   occupied   in
services ancillary to that production.
        The   1920   and   1930   censuses   were   far   more
comprehensive   and   also   more accurate.   Tables 1.3
and 1.4   summarise   their   findings.   They   covered
both   manufacturing   and   handicrafts   using   the
criterion   as   to   whether   an   establishment   was
'manufacturing'   the   use   of   some   sort   of machine
powered   by   electricity,   steam   etc.   This
particular   classification   and   the   fact   that the
1920   and   1930   censuses   included   handicrafts
explain   the   large   discrepancies   in   the   data
between 1917 and   1920.   It   also   exaggerates   the
importance   of   'industry'   in   these   two   later
censuses.   For example, if one was to   include   only
purely   manufacturing   establishments   on   the basis
of their use of   some   sort   of   mechanical   power,
then   the   number   of   establishments   for 1917 would
be reduced from   2,213   to   2,050,   those   for   1920
from   33,811   to   2,900   and   those   for   1930   from
76,591 to 3,900 [2].
        The   data   available   for   1920   did   not   give

The Turbulent 1920s

TABLE 1.3   Results of the 1920 Industrial Census

A total of 33,811 establishments were surveyed employing 154,633 workers and utilising 110,674 HP, i.e. 3.27 HP per establishment or 0.71 HP per worker.

Analysis of establishments:

No. of Workers Employed per Establishment	No. of Establishments	Total No. of Workers	Employment as % of Total	HP Used	HP pused as % of total
1 - 5	30,958	84,434	54.6	38,322	34.6
6 - 25	2,365	28,050	18.1	19,726	17.8
25 and over	488	42,149	27.2	52,626	47.5

Sources:

(a) Haritakis, Oikonomiki Epaitiris for 1933, p.600.
(b) Gevetis, Statistikai Meletai, pp.258-261.

TABLE 1.4 Results of the 1930 Industrial Census

A total of 76,591 establishments were surveyed employing 280,331 workers and using 357,338 HP, i.e. 4.66 HP per establishment or 1.27 HP per worker.

(a) Analysis of establishments

No. of Workers employed per Establishment	No. of Establishments	Total No. of Workers	Employment as % of Total	HP Used	HP used as % of Total
1 - 5	70,644	121,198	43.2	90,102	25.2
6 -25	4,900	49,665	17.7	58,677	16.4
25 and over	1,047	109,468	39.0	208,559	58.3

(b) Percentage of total industrial personnel per sector (partial coverage of sectors).

Food processing	16.5
Hides; skins and animal products	11.4
Building materials	10.4
Clothing	9.0
Textiles	8.0
Transport and communications	9.7
Wood and timber	6.0
Engineering	7.9
Paper and printing	2.5
Tobacco processing	1.9
Chemicals	1.8

Sources:
(a) Anastasopoulos, Istoria, Vol.III (1923-1940), pp.1259-1267.
(b) Haritakis, Oikonomiki Epaitiris for 1933, p.600.

any details for individual sectors but comparisons of the 1930 with 1917 data (allowing for the incompleteness of the latter) make it unlikely that significant changes took place between 1917 and 1920 and then again between 1920 and 1930. Some further industrial data to be reviewed later on confirm this supposition.

The data from the last two censuses give a more accurate perspective of the growth of the industrial sector in Greece during this period. By 1930 the overwhelming number of manufacturing establishments was very small. The degree of mechanisation increased by an impressive percentage between 1920-1930, 78% on HP used per worker and 42.5% on HP per establishment. But in view of the fact that both surveys included handicraft establishments which may well have used very few or no powered machines or tools at all, these percentages may be misleading. Indeed it is far more likely that as a large number of small establishments entered the manufacturing sector, a growing percentage of the employment and HP used was concentrated in the larger firms. This is confirmed by the percentage data in both Tables 1.3 and 1.4.

The contribution of industry to GNP and to the balance of trade requires national income and trade statistics. The former are scanty, and where available, inaccurate for the early 1920s and not much better for the 1930s. Trade statistics were collected and recorded far more accurately after 1930. The available evidence will be presented and discussed in Chapter Two. For the time period under scrutiny here, the contribution of industry can be analysed in terms of the proportion of active population engaged in it. Table 1.5 summarises the relevant data from the population censuses of 1907, 1920 and 1928.

The data in Table 1.5 do indicate a four percentage point increase in industrial employment between 1920-28. The majority of the active population however remained in agriculture. Comparisons between 1907 and 1920-28 are not appropriate because of the drastic changes in the geographical and demographic structure of Greece following the Balkan and First World Wars and the Asia Minor campaign. So, for example, in 1907 Greece covered 63,000 square kilometres, in 1920, 150,000 sq.kl. and in 1928, 129,000 sq.kl. Indeed, the 1920 census results, which were published in 1928, had to make special allowances for the fact

TABLE 1.5 Percentage Distribution of Economically Active Population 1907-1928

Sectors	1907	1920	1928
Agriculture	35	48.9	53.5
Animal Husbandry, Hunting and fishing	10.42	8.15	7.5
Industry	25.74	13.23	17.79
(1) General industry	-	8.7	-
(2) Textiles	-	4.1	-
(3) Chemicals	-	0.36	-
Mining and construction	-	4.8	0.26
Rest of Sectors (Services, Trade, Professional Administration,Transport)	28.8	24.92	20.95

Source: E. Makis, O Oikonomikos Energos Plythysmos tis Ellados kai i Apasholisis Autou, in Statistikai Meletai, pp.147-181, various tables. The data for the 1907 census, and in particular for agriculture, are not reliable.

that,at the time of the census Greece covered
150,000 sq.kl., but by the time of publication it
had lost 21,000 sq.kl., following the 1923
conference of Lauzanne. Irrespective of the
variations in the size of the territory, the major
change was undoubtedly in the size and composition
of the population following the influx of refugees
from Asia Minor.

1.2 THE ASIA MINOR DISASTER AND THE REFUGEES

Greek history up to 1922 is replete with examples
of waves of refugees pouring through its
frontiers. The existence of large Greek
communities in areas still occupied by Turkey
ensured that each local insurrection or border
clash displaced large groups of people who still
considered Greece as their mother country. After
the 1842 and 1866-68 revolts in Crete some 50,000
refugees came to Greece. In 1906 Bulgaria
expelled another 50,000 Greeks and later they were
joined by more than 60,000 following the Balkan
Wars and Russian Revolution.
    The Asia Minor campaign started in March 1921
and ended with the evacuation of the Greek army
and the destruction of the port of Smyrna in
September 1922. Greece signed an agreement with
Turkey in January 1923 involving an exchange of
populations. But before that, more than 900,000
Greeks had already left Turkey. By December 1924
when the exchange of populations had been
completed , 1,221,849 Greeks and 45,000 Armenians
had come to Greece and 610,146 Turks and
Bulgarians had been sent back to their respective
countries [3]. This massive and rapid movement in
population created an enormous economic upheaval.
The cost in terms of pure human suffering is,of
course, incalculable. The population of Greece
increased almost overnight by 13 per cent. This
would have been equivalent to allowing some 7
million new settlers into the UK in a single year
in the mid 1980s!
    Desperate times required desperate measures.
The first obvious problem was housing. Thousands
of refugees congregated in urban centres, creating
wretched camps and squatter villages not only in
the outskirts of cities but literally in their
centres. The Government opened up schools,
theatres and seaside hotels and billeted the
refugees in every available building. One of the

biggest and most fashionable theatre in the centre of Athens was partitioned with makeshift curtains and housed scores of families. But the most urgent policy was the resettlement of refugees in lands evacuated by the exchanged Turkish populations. One of the first actions of the Greek Government was to approach the League of Nations in February 1923 and to ask for financial and administrative assistance for the resettlement effort. The League set up a body, the Autonomous Committee for the Resettlement of Refugees.

It had four members, two Greek, one British and one American and its primary task was to supervise the distribution of land to, and the building of houses for the refugees. The Greek State contracted a special 12.3 million loan and obtained further funds and loans in 1928. By 1930, when the Committee was dissolved and handed back to the Greek state its functions and assets, it had resettled more than half a million people. Another 650,000 were resettled either by the Government or by their own efforts, especially in urban centres. The refugees who were settled in farms were not given their smallholdings outright. For those who had left properties behind, the estimated value of that property was subtracted from their land grant and the difference, if any, was repaid by a loan. There was considerable controversy over this procedure as it was generally believed that the Greek government had overvalued the property left behind by the Turks and thus indirectly cheated the refugees of the true net value of the properties they received in exchange [4]. Furthermore, there was the problem of refugees who either did not have an exchangeable property or were not farmers to start with. These people, in addition to being uprooted, were burdened with loans and could only settle in urban areas where housing and working conditions were, in general, poorer than in the countryside. The original agreement for the exchange of populations included arrangements whereby the two governments would present estimates of the exchanged properties and settle the financial differences as appropriate. Needless to say, this part of the agreement proved completely unworkable and the two countries agreed not to pursue any counterclaims but to settle the matter internally with their own refugees. The Committee for the Resettlement of the Refugees put the value of the Turkish properties in Greece at

9.9 billion drakmas. Other estimates are considerably smaller at 5 billion drakmas. There are also conflicting estimates of the value of the Greek properties abandoned in Turkey ranging from 40 to 100 billion drakmas, thus leaving a substantial net loss on the Greek side. All these estimates were in current prices for the late 1920s [5].

The consequences for the Greek economy of this influx were on first sight momentous. Recent research however has cast doubt as to the catalytic effect of refugees on Greece's economic development. At the risk of oversimplifying a complex issue, what is claimed is that refugees did create quite an impact which accentuated already existing trends in the Greek economy. Without the refugees, the direction of the Greek economy would have been much the same, except, absolute levels of activity might have been smaller. Earlier authors and commentators had overstated their claims by implying that the course of the Greek economy had somehow changed after the Asia Minor disaster. The discussion that follows touches on the key issues involved, although we shall be returning to some of the points raised in the last section of Chapter Two.

For a start, the influx of refugees changed the demographic structure of Greece. In 1920, 80.75% of the population were of Greek origin and 14% were Turks. In 1928 these proportions had changed to 93.8% and 1.6% respectively. For the first time in its modern history, the Greek nation was almost completely Greek in its ethnical composition. Athough that in itself had no specific economic effect, it did change the outlook and perhaps the psychology of the public. The dream of the Grand Idea laid in ruins, but at least now all the major Greek communities in Turkey and in the Balkans were gathered together.

The refugees also gave an impetus to the rapid development of urban centres. The 1920 census showed that 63.7% of the population lived in rural settlements, 9.7% in semi urban and 26.6% in urban centres. The 1928 census showed that these percentages had changed to 54.4%, 14.5% and 31.1% respectively [6].

Despite the tendency of the refugees to settle in urban centres, they did provide the reason to finalise the remaining land redistribution issues still lingering in Greece. As the Introduction to this book indicated, a very substantial proportion of all cultivated land, more than 30%, still remained under the 'tsiflik' system at the outbreak of World War I. Between 1900 and 1917 the Government had taken a number of steps that presaged the final demise of large land ownership in Greece. In 1907 the government passed a law that enabled it to purchase, compulsorily if necessary, large estates and then, resell the land to refugees from Rumania and Bulgaria. Surprisingly enough, the large land owners did not raise too many objections because they preferred selling their estates to the government rather than to their tenants. Also from a legalistic point of view, landless peasants could now demand the expropriation of estates, not as a political favour but as an exercise of the government's legal rights. Between 1907 and 1914 one-sixth of all the remaining 'tsiflik' estates were purchased and resold to tenant farmers [7].

Furthermore, when Macedonia was annexed by Greece in 1913, the Government forbade any changes in land tenancy and ownership rights, thus forestalling any attempt on the part of the landlords to acquire absolute land rights which they could not enjoy under Ottoman law. When Venizelos, after coming into conflict with King Constantine over Greece's participation in the First World War, had fled Athens to establish a rival government in Salonica, he grasped the opportunity to deliver one more blow against the landed interests. A special act passed in 1917 allowed the complete and systematic expropriation of all large 'tsiflik' estates. This law was little used until refugees started to arrive in waves after 1922.

The final push to expropriate the estates was not just a political move but also made a lot of economic sense at the time. The 'tsiflik' system had simply increased Greece's dependence on wheat imports despite the high tariff duties. The owners preferred to restrict their own wheat production in order to keep domestic prices high and concentrated instead on raising rents and letting the land out for grazing and pastures. By the early 1920s more than 40% of the value of all imports was accounted for by wheat and flour [8]. Following the 1917 Law the pace of expropriation speeded up. Between 1917 and 1920, 64 estates were bought out. In 1921-22 the figure was 12 but it shot up to 1,203 in 1923-25. Towards the end of 1920, Greece had become a country of small owner farmers and was to remain so until the present day. Table 1.6 shows that the size distribution of farms between 1929 and 1950 changed very little if at all.

TABLE 1.6   Distribution of farms on the basis of acreage (% of total number of farms) 1929 and 1950

Size in Acres	1929	1950
0-2.4	37.5	28.5
2.4-24	58.6	68.4
24-123	3.6	3.1
123 and over	0.3	0.1

Source: Vergopoulos, To Agrotiko,   p.188.

The usual problems of small scale agricultural production were aggravated in Greece by the fact that the existing smallholdings were also fragmented into strips. So in Thessaly, for example, during this period 15.5% of all farms were held in 10 strips, 17.5% in 7 strips and 14.3% in 6. In Macedonia the picture was similar with 42% of all the farms held in 5 strips and 24.6% in 6 strips. Despite the detrimental effects that this fragmentation and the encouragement of smallholdings had on efficiency and productivity, one must not underestimate the magnitude of the land redistribution undertaken in Greece during that time. More than 85% of all the cultivated land in Macedonia, 68% in Thessaly, or an overall national average of 40% was subject in one way or another to redistribution or expropriation [9].

The effect of the resettlement of refugees on agricultural output is rather difficult to gauge precisely because some of the land they took over had been previously cultivated by the departed Turkish owners. Some regional data available for Macedonia indicate that the increases in the area cultivated between 1922 and 1932 were well above the national average in areas populated by refugees. The Committee for the Resettlement of Refugees and various state schemes helped to irrigate or drain considerable areas which were then handed over to the refugees, thus confusing the picture a little further [10].

But the refugees did help to change the composition and structure of agricultural production in Greece. For a start , they accelerated the process away from the cultivation of currants which had for so long dominated both agriculture and the export trade of Greece. Refugees introduced the cultivation of traditional crops from Turkey such as tobacco, cotton, and extended the production of sultanas and wine grapes. Between 1911-1920 the average output of tobacco stood at 23,335 tons per annum and for cotton 6,700 tons p.a. The averages for 1921-30 increased to 53,600 and 9,419 tons respectively. Refugees also specialised in the production of wheat, of mulberry bushes used for raising silkworms, hemp for rope making and garden vegetables. The refugees' contribution to the tobacco industry was a lasting one despite the fact that in the late 1930s overspecialisation in the production and exporting of tobacco replicated to some extent the currants crisis of the late nineteenth century.

The refugees' contribution to industrial development is considerably more controversial. The net addition of 0.6 million consumers to the domestic market undoubtedly benefited the output of food processing, textile and clothing industries. The efforts to rehouse them also gave a boost to the building and construction industry. Refugees established industries that were familiar to them, such as silk and carpet weaving, but new for Greece. The immense economic problems and pressures that faced refugees on their arrival in Greece also brought out the best in their entrepreneurial skills. Industrialists such as Bodosakis Athanasiadis, whose name was synonymous with the chemicals and munitions industry in Greece and of , course , Aristotle Onasis, the shipping magnate, were both of refugee origin.

A quantitative approach to the effects of the refugee influx on industry can be attempted by comparing the situation in 1930 (Table 1.4.) with that of 1920 (Table 1.3). Industrial employment between 1920 and 1930 increased by more than 80% and the number of industrial establishments by 126.5%. Although the number of establishments with more than 25 workers increased, the number of employees per establishment in total decreased from 4.5 in 1920 to 3.6 in 1930. The changes in the composition of industrial output are more difficult to gauge as

48

TABLE 1.7 Number and type of new enterprises 1921 - 1937

Year	Number	Horse Power	Sector (Number of enterprises, sample only)
1921	56	1,821	27 Food
1922	46	371	25 Food
1923	41	1,277	19 Food
1924	107	2,518	60 Food, 12 Timber
1925	132	4,624	50 Food, 15 Engineering
1926	124	3,145	80 Food, 11 Engineering, 11 Tobacco
1927	214	6,105	155 Food, 24 Spinning, Textiles
1928	192	6,340	147 Food, 13 Timber
1929	63	3,715	35 Food
1930	45	1,636	20 Food
1931	93	2,751	70 Food
1932	50	1,003	24 Food, 11 Spinning, Textiles
1933	37	1,613	20 Food
1934	67	1,969	38 Food, 11 Chemicals
1935	113	3,254	81 Food, 11 Chemicals
1936	124	2,925	77 Food, 16 Chemicals, 14 Engineering
1937	160	4,538	93 Food, 18 Chemicals, 10 Engineering

Source: G. Haritakis (Ed.), Oikonomiki Epaitiris tis Ellados for 1937 pp.230-31, Athens 1938. Food stands for Food Processing.

there are no detailed data in the 1920 census. An insight, however, into the dynamics of industry can be obtained by examining the number and type of enterprises entering the various sectors. This is done in Table 1.7. The rapid increases of new entrants from 1924 to 1929 was undoubtedly influenced by the influx of refugees. It is also interesting to note that the majority of the new firms were concentrated in the food processing sector.

Finally, Table 1.8 shows the changes in the composition of industrial output between 1921 and 1938. The data here show that textiles grew slowly during the 1930s to become the key industry despite the large number of entrants into food processing. Tanning declined overall, whilst chemicals, after showing little change, increased at the end of the period. It is interesting, however, that over the eighteen years the same four industries accounted for more than 60% of the

TABLE 1.8   Percentage contribution of individual sectors to total value of industrial output (current prices), 1921-1938

Year	Spinning, Textiles	Food Processing	Chemicals	Tanning
1921	9.2	22.7	15.0	15.3
1922	23.5	21.1	14.8	19.0
1925	20.3	21.8	15.0	17.5
1926	22.6	23.2	14.7	15.0
1927	23.3	20.1	15.0	17.3
1928	25.0	20.0	14.0	14.0
1929	26.0	20.7	14.7	10.0
1930	27.6	18.7	13.5	9.0
1931	27.0	20.0	11.1	9.0
1932	27.4	20.2	12.2	8.0
1933	30.8	16.6	14.7	10.0
1934	33.5	16.2	14.0	9.0
1935	32.0	15.4	16.2	8.5
1936	31.3	16.1	17.7	9.0
1937	29.0	17.5	20.4	8.2
1938	27.0	17.3	21.7	7.5

Source: G. Haritakis (Ed.), Oikonomiki Epaitiris tis Ellados for 1938, Athens 1939, p.283.

total manufactured output. Electricity generation by the end of the period was accounting for about 10% of industrial output.

If the refugees did have an impact on industry this was to reinforce tendencies that were already present. Greek industry by the outbreak of the Second World War was small scale, undiversified, ministering to domestic needs and its structure had hardly changed over almost 20 years [11].

One frequent suggestion that has been made about the effects of the refugees on the economy is that they provided a cheap source of labour and helped to keep real wages low. In the absence of any reliable wage and price data this proposition cannot be put to the test [12]. But what is undisputed is that the Greek labour movement took real roots and developed rapidly during this period. Although the history of the socialist and labour movement in Greece goes well back into the nineteenth century, the movement had no real substance until the late 1920s. A form of a socialist association, 'The Federation' including members from a number of trades, was formed in 1909 in Salonica. In 1918 the first TUC-type body was set up, the General Confederation of Greek Workers (GCGW) which was followed shortly by the foundation of the Socialist Labour Party of Greece [13]. In 1926, after the Socialist Party had turned itself into the Communist Party of Greece (KKE after its Greek initials), the GCGW and the KKE severed their links. Indeed, by 1928, the leadership of the GCGW was in non-communist hands. This led the KKE to create a splinter GCGW. The Greek labour movement remained weak and continuously persecuted both by the political authorities and the employers. Labour legislation passed by Venizelos in 1911-14 concerning minimum working age, Sunday working, hours of work etc. was never actively enforced [14]. As already mentioned, refugees played an active and leading role in the organization of trade unions and in the foundation of the KKE. They also provided constant support to Venizelos' Liberal Party and were deeply anti-royalist. Given their justifiably radical political views and their reduced circumstances, the refugees provided a large and identifiable group of disaffection within an already impoverished and divided land.

But perhaps the most important and direct impact on the economy by the refugees was the

51

The Turbulent 1920s

fiscal costs or benefits that their presence involved. Greek economists and politicians of the day attempted what would be now called a crude cost benefit analysis of the net contributions or costs of the refugees. One study, for example, added up the loans contracted by the Greek government for resettlement purposes, the sums spent on ancillary services for the refugees including compensation payments plus 15% of all the expenditures of the Ministries of Justice, Internal Affairs, Education and Domestic Economy. This 15% represented an estimate of the percentage of refugees to the total population directly affected by these expenditures. These sums aggregated over 1923-29 came to some 7.2 billion drakmas. The refugees however also contributed to taxes. Using again the 15% rule on all relevant taxation revenues this yielded the sum of 8.6 billion drakmas for the 1923-29 period, thus leaving a net 1.4 billion fiscal contribution by the refugees. Even these extremely crude figures are an underestimate of the net contribution of refugees since the loans contracted on their behalf by the Greek state were of course being repaid by them, either partially or in full, over a number of years [15]. Another estimate covering the 1922-32 period yielded the following figures. Interest rate and capital repayments on loans came to 5.3 billion drakmas, housing and resettlement 3.3 billion drakmas, and an apportionment of general public expenditures on refugees to 2.5 billion drakmas, a total of about 11 billion drakmas. The refugees however contributed over the same period some 10.5 billion drakmas in taxes plus 0.5 billion drakmas on loan repayments. Their net contributions or costs by 1932 was therefore almost zero [16]. Although initially the presence of the refugees generated a great deal of sympathy and united the nation in its effort to cope with their problems, during later years the indigenous population came to resent their presence and their continuous demands for special treatment and help. Matters were made worse by the political divisions which also branded the refugees as "Venizelocommunists", a rare political animal indeed! But there is little doubt that their contribution to the Greek economy was greater than the costs they imposed.

Overall, the refugee problem in Greece was solved relatively quickly. Despite the weaknesses of the economy the refugees did not create an

52

uncontrollable sociopolitical problem. What undoubtedly helped was the fact that they were of Greek origin, most of them spoke Greek and considered Greece, ultimately, as their homeland. The existence of a large stock of land, either in the form of abandoned Turkish farms or expropriated estates made resettlement faster and with no attendant social or economic counter effects. The refugees boosted the already existing local industry, helped to change the composition of agricultural output, provided a source of relatively cheap labour and generated entrepreneurial skills. But although their overall contribution to costs and benefits yielded a surplus, had the Asia Minor disaster never happened, it is unlikely that the course of the Greek economy would have followed a fundamentally different path. All the available evidence indicates that the refugees accelerated already existing developments or generated changes that did not create conditions for radical shifts in the direction in which the economy was already moving.

1.3 THE MONETARY MAELSTROM 1921-28

The events associated with Greece's monetary and fiscal system during this period were truly monumental and left their mark right down to the postwar period. In order to avoid any artificial chronological divisions, the events described and analysed here extend into the decade of the 1930s as well. In order to facilitate the presentation of a large number of interrelated data Table 1.9 brings together the salient quantitative features of Greece's monetary and fiscal history from 1914 till the outbreak of the Second World War. Frequent reference will be made to this table but great caution will be exercised in interpreting the data as the statistical sources for this period can be extremely inaccurate and misleading. Table 1.9 carries a long footnote qualifying or explaining some of the time series presented [17].

The Balkan Wars of 1912-13 were financed without undue recourse to emergency taxation or extensive loans. In fact the figures in Table 1.9 show a surplus in the government budget right down to the outbreak of the First World War. All the available evidence points to a careful fiscal

TABLE 1.9 Inflation and Inflationary Factors 1914-1940

YEAR	Bank Notes in Circulation M1 Drks	Sight Deposit Accounts M1 Drks	% Change in Bank Note Circulation Over Previous Year	Cost of Living Index 1914 = .100	% Change in Cost of Living Index Over Previous Year	Deficit (-) or Surplus (+) of State Budget M1 Drks	Index of the Price of £ in Drks 1914 = 100	Index of the Price of $ in Drks 1914 = 100	Index of French Franc in Drks 1914 = 100
1914	236			100		+76.9	100.0	100.0	100.0
1915	291		23.3	117	17.0	+57.7	99.4	101.9	94.5
1916	464		59.4	159	35.8	+94.8	97.8	100.3	88.0
1917	670		44.3	256	61.0	+126.0	97.7	100.0	89.9
1918	1084		61.7	366	42.0	-195.5	98.6	100.0	92.5
1919	1333	1357	22.9	323	-11.7	-224.8	97.1	106.9	77.7
1920	1425	2105	6.9	351	8.6	-28.4	136.0	184.7	65.3
1921	1832	2989	28.5	398	13.3	-194.6	281.7	353.7	138.3
1922	2094	3390	14.3	636	59.7	+1119.0	661.7	718.5	290.5
1923	4152	4600	98.2	1181	85.6	-1015.0	1117.8	1237.9	393.0
1924	4646	6147	11.8	1235	4.5	+224.6	982.9	1084.7	291.0
1925	5266	6117	13.3	1414	14.4	+1081.0	1243.0	1252.6	305.0
1926	4519	6898	-14.1	1633	15.4	+820.9	1536.1	1538.8	255.0
1927	4952	7219	9.5	1790	9.6	+1226.0	1464.6	1466.5	297.0
1928	5445	*10242	9.9	1868	4.3	+1105.0	1482.1	1481.8	300.0
1929	5388	*11343	-1.0	1923	2.9	+374.7	1490.0	1490.7	301.0
1930	4895	*6735	-9.1	1682	-12.5	+217.1	1490.0	1490.9	302.0
1931	4268	11068	-12.8	1671	0.6	-21.6	1402.2	1496.7	304.0
1932	4256	*7753	-0.2	1773	6.1	+27.3	1879.5	2585.6	535.0
1933	4912	10099	15.4	1904	7.3	+770.3	2368.0	2804.0	705.0
1934	5373	11671	9.3	1937	1.7	+419.0	2161.7	2094.7	706.0
1935	5623	11109	4.6	1957	1.0	+597.7	2102.9	2096.7	709.0
1936	5758	11773	2.4	2028	3.6	+560.5	2143.0	2102.5	659.0
1937	6457	13106	12.1	2185	7.7	+718.8	2186.0	2154.5	451.0
1938	6789	14513	5.1	2173	-0.5	-85.0*	2170.0	2158.0	318.0
1939	8481	15511	24.9	2167	-0.2	-250.0*	2170.0	2392.0	308.0
1940				2399	10.0	-	2129.0	2882.0	308.4

Sources: See Note [17]

policy under the circumstances [18]. What created
a truly dangerous situation which then snowballed
into uncontrolled inflation and finally financial
chaos were the monetary arrangements made in
conjunction with the inability of the government
to borrow at home. It is important at this stage
to present a brief outline of the history of the
banking system in Greece to that date in order to
put the events in proper perspective.

Soon after gaining independence, the Greek
state made a number of attempts to establish a
bank which culminated with the setting up in 1841
of the National Bank of Greece. This bank
dominated the monetary and banking scene in Greece
until the foundation in 1928 of a genuinely
independent central bank. From its inception the
National Bank had the privilege, although not the
monopoly, of issuing banknotes. Three other
banks, and in particular the Ioanian Bank in
Corfu, had also note issuing rights. By 1920
however the National Bank had established a de
facto monopoly by taking over two of these banks
and by the Ioanian Bank rescinding its note
issuing rights. As the National Bank expanded its
activities it came to dominate completely the
credit market and was acting as the unofficial
central bank until 1928. The National Bank
remained a private bank although the state had a
majority shareholding. From its foundation in
1841 until 1897, in addition to the note issuing
franchise which was renewed on several occassions,
the bank was gradually allowed to enter a number
of fields and activities, such as issuing bonds,
extending agricultural loans and mortgages,
dealing in foreign exchange, participating in the
organizations set up to control the production and
export trade in currants and, in general, to act
as the Government's agent on all important
financial occasions. But, far more importantly,
the bank became the major domestic creditor to the
Government [19]. Table 1.10 sets out a
comparative picture of the deposit and lending
activities of the National Bank over the 1841-1938
period. The original franchise of the bank
allowed it to issue bank notes which were
convertible to gold. During four periods in its
history however the Bank was relieved of this
obligation. Firstly for a brief period in 1848
following the widespread political unrest in
Europe, then again in 1868-1870, and 1877-1884
when the government borrowed heavily from the Bank

TABLE 1.10 Structure of Greek Banking and the National Bank of Greece 1847-1938 (percentages of totals).

Year	Total Deposit										1930			1935			1938		
---	---	---	---	---	---	---	---	---	---	---	Total Deposits (Sight plus savings) etc (A)	Short Term Loans (Less than 3 months) (B)	Long Term Loans (More than 3 months) (C)	(A)	(B)	(C)	(A)	(B)	(C)
	1847	1850	1860	1870	1880	1895	1900	1908	1919	1921									
National Bank of Greece	100	100	99.0	89.0	79.0	72.0	58.0	50.0	52.0		49.0	37.7	45.0	58.6	56.7	48.0	51.0	52.0	23.7
Next Five Biggest Banks	-	-	-	-	-	-	-	-	-	-	30.4	35.6	*6.1	23.6	21.0	*5.0	22.5	22.0	*4.0

Source: G. Haritakis Oikonomiki Epetiris for 1938, pp.195-201, and for 1931, pp. 380-381.

The data for 1847-1921 are incomplete. For 1847-1895 the sample contains eight banks, for 1900-1921 eighteen, and for 1930-38 forty-six. Lack of data and the dominance of the National Bank of Greece during 1847-1921 made the share of the next biggest five banks impossible or irrelevant to calculate.

NB Total deposits are in million drakmas and they include sight, savings, and time deposits, and for 1930-38 only, bonds issued by banks.

* The National Land Bank provided 37.1% of these loans in 1930, 30.5% in 1935 and 42% in 1938. Also the newly founded Agricultural Bank was providing 12% and 26% of the total long term loans in 1935 and 1938 respectively.

and finally from 1885 till 1928. So for most of
the periods of its operations as a quasi central
bank, the National's note issue was not convertible
into gold [20]. Although at the time
convertibility appeared to be a very significant
issue, what in fact mattered more were the
constraints imposed by the continuous deficit in
the balance of trade and the fact that the note
issue was being used progressively as a major
source of government finance. As the data in
Table 1.11 indicate, an increasing percentage of
the loans of the National Bank after 1910 were to
the state with these loans representing a growing
proportion of the the bank's total assets. The
relative fall in the National Bank's exposure to
the state between 1895 and 1910 was in no small
measure due to the provisions of the international
financial control imposed on Greece. Under these
provisions the Greek state was forced to withdraw
and burn every year 2 million drakmas worth of
banknotes. This novel process of reducing the
money stock was soon to be surpassed by the
ingenuity of the fiscal and monetary policies
implemented during 1922-26 [21].

TABLE 1.11   Loans by the National Bank to the
             Greek State 1885-1927

Year	Direct loans and state bond holdings as % of total loans	Direct loan and state bond holdings as % of total assets
1885	35.7	31.5
1895	59.8	52.4
1900	53.3	45.3
1910	42.3	31.9
1915	49.5	27.4
1920	73.7	51.7
1925	69.9	56.7
1927	75.0	63.9

Source :   Based on data from Haritakis, Oikonomiki
           Epaitiris for 1937, p.285.

     In 1910 the Government managed to ease the
monetary constraints imposed by the international
financial control on Greece by passing a law that
enabled the National Bank to issue more bank notes
than its original franchise allowed as long as

these notes were used to purchase gold and foreign exchange in the open market. Furthermore, the bank was obliged to resell the gold and foreign exchange so obtained at the purchase price. The basic idea behind this measure was to increase monetary circulation without compromising the convertibility of the drakma. In practice , the drakma continued to be nonconvertible after 1910 because the law covered only additional issues and not the existing bank notes. As the foreign exchange rate data in Table 1.9 indicate the drakma stayed fairly constant against sterling and the dollar and it even appreciated against the franc in the period up to 1919.

This was roughly the picture of the monetary system in Greece at the outbreak of the First World War. During the War, the Allies as part of their wartime aid to Greece, guaranteed credits of £12 million, FF300 million and $50 million. These loans were not actually released but were meant to be drawn on and settled at the end of the war. Indeed the Greek government was encouraged to use these standing credits to issue more banknotes to finance its war effort. There was a clear understanding that this was not a fiduciary issue as it was backed by an equivalent amount of foreign exchange credits. In 1920 , when the pro-Allies Venizelos lost the elections and the exiled pro-German King Constantine returned to the throne, the Allies refused to honour their promises and the National Bank ended up with a large proportion of its note issue backed by nothing [22]. As the data in Table 1.9 indicate the budget swung into a deficit in 1918 and stayed so until 1921. By March 1922, with the war raging in Asia Minor, the Greek state found itself unable to raise revenues either by taxation or overseas borrowing. There followed a remarkable feat of monetary and fiscal ingenuity that has gone down in Greece's financial history as the 'dichotomization of the drakma'. A historian relying on an eye witness account , described the events as follows [23] ,

"The Finance Minister, P.Protopapadakis, at the end of a private meeting with the Prime Minister, suddenly stood up and said 'I have got the money'. He took out a 100 drakma note and tore it in half. The Prime Minister thought he had gone mad".

On 25 March 1922 the Greek Government swiftly and
under a cloak of secrecy announced that
henceforth all notes were to be literally cut in
half. One half was to be retained by the owners
and used normally as currency worth only half its
nominal value, and the other half was to be
surrendered within a particular time period in
exchange for a 20 year 6 1/2% loan. At the date
of the announcement the total note issue stood at
3,100 million drakmas. The state should have
therefore received 1,550 million drakmas by this
compulsory loan. In fact the proceeds came to
1288 million because of a number of banknotes in
the hands of the state itself and because foreign
subjects were exempted from this measure. As the
cut notes were liabilities of the National Bank,
the Bank could then proceed to print an equivalent
amount which it handed over to the state. This was
in a sense the counterpart of the 20 year loan.
The subsequent impact on inflation and on the
stock of money was minimal. Indeed monthly data
available for the average circulation of notes of
the National Bank show that in February 1922 the
note issue stood at 2,217 million drakmas, in
March 1922 it had fallen to 1,197 million but by
August 1922 it was back to 2,039 million [24].
This amazingly bold experiment in fiscal
policy was repeated on 23 January 1926 when , once
again , the inability of the state to raise revenues
via taxation led to another forced loan. This
time the proceeds of the loan were used to pay
back some 1,200 million drakmas of short term
state debts to the National Bank. The terms and
conditions of this loan involved the cutting in
half of all banknote over 50 drakmas, except the
half this time represented three quarters of its
value, the other one quarter being exchanged for a
20 year 6% loan. As on the previous occasion
foreign subjects and bank deposits were exempted.
This new loan raised 1,250 million drakmas. The
circulation of the note issue in December 1925
stood at 5,266 million drakmas and in January 1926
at 4,194 million. Unlike the 1922 experiment
however, the note circulation did not rise back to
over 5,200 million drakmas before October 1927
precisely because the government did not demand
more notes to be printed.
These two sudden reductions in the stock of
money, and the element of compulsory loans which
accompanied them, did not have a clear-cut effect
on inflation. As Table 1.9 shows, the rate of

inflation measured by the cost of living index
increased between 1921-22 reflecting the effects
of the war expenditures. But inflation speeded up
in 1923. For 1926-27 the story is different as
the rate of inflation fell and kept falling till
1931. The rate of the exchange of the drakma
against sterling also tells the same story with
the 1926 events having a more direct impact. The
1922 measures were not meant to be counter-
inflationary but simply a source of finance.
The fall in banknote circulation was immediately
made up and thus there was no lasting effect on
prices. Indeed an argument has been put forward
to the effect that the velocity of circulation
increased during 1923 and that the forced loan
actually increased spending. Savings previously
held in banknotes had now to be brought out and
circulated as half of them were turned into a
forced loan and the other half remained in cash
form. The implication here being that people
would avoid holding banknotes and would switch
into other assets or goods. As it turned out that
would not have been a bad idea as in 1926 the
notes were cut again!
     The 1926 events did have a more discernible
effect on inflation not only because the amount of
banknotes did not increase immediately but also
because the National Bank raised interest rates
and followed a restrictive credit policy.
Irrespective however of the exact circumstances
surrounding these two events, the bisection of the
notes must have had an overall deflationary effect
despite the fact that in 1923 the note issue rose
again almost immediately. For a start , the poorer
sections of the population traditionally kept
their savings in cash. Suddenly one half, and
later on one quarter, of these savings were frozen
in the form of the compulsory loans whereas owners
of other financial assets were not affected. As
it is likely that the marginal propensity to
consume of the poorer sections of the population
would have been higher than the average mpc, then
the reduction in the liquidity of their wealth
holdings may well have affected their spending.
On both occasions there was a transference of
wealth from the poorer section of the population
to the Greek state. In 1926 the proceeds of the
loan cleared short-term government debt to the
National Bank. In 1923 the reduction in the
liabilities of the National Bank was followed by
an equivalent rise in the loans made to the

Government and then by a proportional rise in its liabilities as the Bank printed more notes. In 1926, however, there was nothing to oblige the Bank to make up by more lending the fall in both its note issue and loans outstanding to the goverment. The effect here was purely deflationary and this was reflected clearly in the rate of exchange of the drakma against the sterling and the dollar between 1926-27. The deflationary effect was compounded by interest rates rising from 7 1/2% - 8 1/2% to 11% in 1926 [25].

The events between 1922 and 1926 were a clear indication that the monetary and fiscal system in Greece was long overdue for a radical overhaul. Although the fiscal situation could only change as the structure of the economy changed, thus allowing for different venues and sources to raise taxes, the monetary system suffered from institutional shortcomings. The situation where the government had to rely on a private bank for the majority of its loans was not acceptable anymore. The foreign exchange parity of the drakma also needed readjusting, and in the process of doing so, the confidence of the population in a currency that had undergone two radical interventions within a very short period of time had to be re-established.

1.4 THE FOUNDATION OF THE BANK OF GREECE : MONETARY STABILITY AND CAPITAL FLOWS

In April 1927 after long and protracted negotiations Greece settled the question of debts and loans outstanding since World War I with France and the UK. These were the same loans that had led to the 1922 monetary crisis by leaving uncovered the note issue. The settlement of these loans was essential because at the same time Greece was applying to the League of Nations for a £9 million loan to be used for the stabilisation of currency, to cover government deficits and continue the resettlement of refugees. The League of Nations sent to Greece a team of experts to report on the financial situation. It then imposed as a condition for sponsoring the loan the foundation of a real central bank rather than the ambiguous situation that existed at the time with the National Bank acting as an unofficial monetary authority [26].

The Bank of Greece was formally established

in May 1927 and commenced its operations a year
later. Its foundation and first year of life was
replete with controversies [27]. The National
Bank put forward strong arguments in favour of
separating its note issuing function from its
commercial activities in order to maintain its
privileged position and to avoid having a central
bank set up. When these arguments did not win the
day and the time came to surrender its note issue
plus the gold reserves backing it, there developed
an extremely acrimonious dispute over the exact
evaluation of these reserves. The National Bank
had habitually undervalued the gold acquired by
accounting for it at historic cost rather than at
market prices and also the successive increases of
fiduciary issue had devalued the gold content of
drakma. The Bank of Greece, therefore, found a
shortfall of 938 million drakmas in the gold
surrendered. The dispute soon developed into a
political debate with threats of litigation or
even legislation to settle the issue. Finally the
Bank of Greece was awarded 60% of the disputed
sums. As events showed later on, the National
Bank appeared to harbour a grudge against the new
and rival institution and for a time refused to
admit that its supremacy over Greece's monetary
affairs was over [28]. The new central bank took
its role extremely seriously and from the outset
its governor made it very clear that its foremost
aim was to restablish monetary stability in order
to heal the wounds of the chaotic 1922-26 period.
    For a start, the exchange rate of the drakma
against the sterling was stabilised at 1 = 375
drakmas (or 1.952 grams of gold = 100 drakmas).
The drakma was made fully convertible against
foreign exchange and hence indirectly against
gold. The Bank of Greece had to observe a legal
minimum of 40% gold and foreign exchange reserves
against the note issue, but it started its
operations with reserves in excess of 80%. So for
the first time since 1885, the gold exchange
standard was in operation with the drakma fully
convertible. The Bank's first report is well
worth quoting as it encapsulated both the spirit
of the time and the great caution, and perhaps
trepidation, with which the Bank approached the
tasks in view of the circumstances surrounding its
foundation [29].

    'For the first year of management the
    guiding principle was to establish the

62

> stability of the drakma, that is an equivalent parity of our monetary unit and a specific weight in gold ·····. The policy which started in 1921 to finance the state budget deficit by the issuing of paper notes or short term debt had as a fateful and inevitable result the complete shattering of public finances, the devaluation of the currency and therefore the consequent dislocation of the economy ·····. The ways used to finance these deficits were the ones usually observed in the more destructive periods of economic history, that is increases in the paper note issue, use of short term loans, advances from the National Bank, various unpaid accounts dragged on from year to year and finally compulsory loans, all of which damaged the economy, casting severe doubts on the credit-worthiness of the country and creating a sense of fear and uncertainty, of an uncontrolled slide ·····. The state's demands generated an intolerable shortage of capital and continuous increases in interest rates.'

Up to 1932 when the reverberations of the depression finally reached Greece, the country experienced a brief period of stability and fairly coherent economy policy. It is not surprising that these years, which coincided with Venizelos' rule, were dubbed the "four golden years'. The settlement in 1927 of the outstanding issues concerning Greece's foreign debts opened up another period of extensive direct foreign investment in Greece.

As the Introduction to this volume has indicated, Greece had borrowed extensively until its default in 1893. But in addition to outright loans to the state, there was also direct foreign investment in Greece in a number of areas and sectors. An extensive survey of direct investment separated these activities into five distinct periods [30]. The first period covers 1830-1878 and it involved primarily French companies investing in mining, production of gas and railroads. The activites of one particular French company in a silver mine near Athens at Lavrion caused the first and only South Sea type-bubble on

the then primitive unofficial stock market in
Athens. The company quite illegally utilised not
only the silver lodes in the mines which dated
back to the classical antiquity, but also the
ancient slag heaps which reputedly contained a
fortune in unprocessed ore. The shares of the
company traded feverishly in Athens, until the
government stepped in to claim its legal rights,
only to embroil itself in a protracted legal
battle with the company. The second period covers
1879-1893 and coincides with Trikoupis' extensive
public works schemes. Here the inflows were
primarily state loans. In the third period
1894-1914, despite Greece's default, but perhaps
because of the imposition of the international
finance control, there was renewed interest in
investment in banks, commercial and trading
undertakings, insurance companies, railways, and
so on. The fourth period, 1915-1919 covering the
years of the First World War, involved only state
loans.
    The final period, spanning 1920-32, witnessed
considerable investing activities particularly in
infrastructure and communications. For example, in
1925 the British company Power and Traction signed
an agreement with the Greek government which gave
it the monopoly in the generation and distribution
of electricity in Athens and Piraeus, and a
monopoly in the operation of electric trains and
buses in Athens and some suburbs. In 1925 an
American company, Ulen Co., undertook to build a
dam near the ancient battlefield of Marathon to
solve Athens' water supply problems. Further
investment and construction undertakings in the
period involved either direct participation in
production or simply the execution of a project.
The monopoly production of matches was given to a
Swedish firm and a German firm extended the
telephone network. The resurgence of private
foreign investment in Greece was undoubtedly the
outcome of growing confidence in Greece following
the restructuring of the banking system and the
settlement of international debts. Rates of
return, however, were also comparatively higher in
Greece than in other countries. So for example,
discount rates in Greece stood at between 6-12% in
the 1920-40 period whereas for the same period in
UK they varied between 2-6.6% [31].
    There are a number of problems in assessing
the overall effects of these capital inflows on
Greece's economic development. For a start, there

The Turbulent 1920s

is a lack of systematic estimates on a consistent
monetary base. In addition, these inflows were
primarily associated with state loans and aspects
of currency stabilisation. Data, however, for the
balance of payments are almost nonexistent up to
the mid 1920s. Finally, the contribution of these
inflows to capital accumulation cannot be guessed
at because there are no reliable national income
data for almost the whole of the period up to
World War II. Table 1.12 summarises one of the
best aggregate estimates of these inflows divided
into different categories and time periods [32].

TABLE 1.12   Total inflow of loans and investment
              funds 1830-1932. In million gold
              francs.

Year	State Loans	Loans to public bodies or corporations	Direct private investment
1830-1878	60	-	100
1879-1893	640	90	130
1894-1914	535	100	160-180
1915-1919	562.5	-	-
1920-1932	1,152.8	125	130
Total	2,950.3	315	520-540

Source : Giannitsis, Oi Xenes, p.236

Another estimate excluded all state loans and
concentrated instead on direct foreign
investment. The inflows were then valued in term
of current drakmas using the appropriate rates of
exchange for the gold franc - drakma for each
period. The total estimates were then revalued at
1975 drakma levels (allowing for the
hyperinflation during the Second World War). The
sum total varied from 5.7 billion drakmas in 1930
to 51.9 billion in 1939, the extreme differences
being indicative of the uncertainty in the
calculation [33]. A separate estimate of the
total official external debt of Greece in 1932 put
it at 2.3 billion gold franc of issued debt at
nominal prices. The UK was the chief creditor
with 28.5% of the total followed by France with
22%, the US with 11%, Germany with 4.5% and
Belgium with 3.5% [34].

All these diverse estimates must be related to some other stock or flow variable in order to determine their overall significance and influence on the economy. One approach examined the servicing burden imposed on the economy by the total domestic and foreign, state debt. This worked out at 25.4% of the total current state revenues in 1893, 25.7% in 1910, 26.2% in 1922 and finally almost 33% in 1932. Since the ratio of external debt to total debt during these periods stood at 84.8%, 82.6%, 73.9% and 77.2% respectively, it would then follow that the servicing of the external debt absorbed easily 20% or more of all the state revenues [35].

Another estimate used the extremely conservative assumption that the rate of return on foreign investment in Greece during the 1910-1940 period was 10% and therefore absorbed about 2% of GNP. The estimate is somewhat heroic in view of the paucity of data on national income accounts for the period. But it did lead to the conclusion, especially when taken in conjunction with the other estimates, that foreign investment simply perpetuated the balance of payment deficit [36]. For example, one source quotes that between 1921-32 Greece received in overseas loans 19.4 billion drakmas but had to pay back in capital and interest payments 25 billion. The same source also estimates that the servicing of these loans absorbed about 9.25% of the GNP at the time [37]. The continuing discrepancies between these inflows and outflows could only lead to repeated defaults. Direct foreign investment made little difference to Greece's economic development except where it involved infrastructure such as telecommunications and transport. We have already reviewed the evidence on the structure of industry and agriculture over several decades when very little changes or progress took place. State loans raised abroad were crucial for the short term fiscal balancing act of the Greek government but provided neither the time nor the incentive for longer term adjustments. To the deficit in the balance of trade there was now added the outflows necessary to service the loans and capital invested. This generated yet another cycle of borrowing and the story was repeated. But perhaps more perniciously, this financial and economic dependence on overseas sources produced a political dependence as well, as witnessed by the imposition of the international financial control

in 1897 and the events surrounding the establishment of the Bank of Greece.

1.5 THE GREEK ECONOMY JUST BEFORE THE DEPRESSION

The state of the Greek economy just before and
after the influx of the refugees has already been
reviewed in Section 1.1 of this chapter. To all
intents and purposes Greece entered the 1930s as a
primarily agricultural country with a small
industrial base. The refugees helped to change
marginally the composition of industrial output
and more so that of agriculture, but their
presence and activities accelerated existing
trends rather than changed the course of the
economy. Two further aspects of the relative
underdevelopment of the economy need some
exploration. Firstly, the balance of trade as
shown in the figures in Table 1.13 was permanently
in deficit.
    Data for the overall balance of payments
during this period are very incomplete or
nonexistent until the Bank of Greece started to
collect more systematic information after 1928.
The structure of import and exports is better
documented and is shown in Table 1.14. As can be
seen the imports of industrial goods continued

TABLE 1.13 Balance of Trade 1920-1930 (million
            drakmas, current prices)

Year	Imports	Exports	Deficit
1920	2,177.5	686.3	1,491.2
1921	1,725.6	947.7	777.8
1922	3,085.4	2,458.0	626.4
1923	6,035.3	2,545.1	3,490.2
1924	8,053.7	3,276.9	4,876.8
1925	10,209.5	4,541.3	5,668.1
1926	10,004.9	5,429.7	4,575.1
1927	12,590.6	6,040.0	6,550.6
1928	12,416.9	6,331.0	6,085.9
1929	13,276.1	6,960.0	6,316.1
1930	10,525.2	5,985.7	4,539.5

Source: (a) Andreas, I Exoteriki, various tables.
         (b) Zolotas, Nomismatika, p.214.

TABLE 1.14 Composition of imports and exports 1918-1931 (percentage of total)

Years	IMPORTS				EXPORTS			
	Live animals	Food & Drink	Raw material & Semi-processed goods	Industrial goods	Live animals	Food & Drink	Raw material & Semi-processed goods	Industrial goods
1918	–	50.1	7.2	42.5	–	43.0	55.6	1.2
1919	–	31.0	9.0	59.9	–	37.5	40.1	22.3
1920	–	34.3	11.0	54.5	–	37.9	40.4	21.6
1921	–	40.8	12.9	46.2	–	53.9	32.2	13.8
1922	–	49.7	12.0	38.1	–	35.1	58.3	6.4
1923	–	53.0	11.9	34.9	–	46.9	55.9	7.0
1924	–	45.4	9.8	44.7	–	35.9	58.3	5.7
1925	–	42.3	12.0	45.5	–	38.5	56.1	5.3
1926	4.3	43.5	20.4	31.6	3.0	30.5	65.9	3.3
1927	6.3	38.6	20.0	34.8	0.02	32.9	64.8	2.1
1928	4.0	36.3	21.6	37.9	0.01	33.8	60.3	1.7
1929	3.9	36.3	22.2	37.4	0.04	33.9	63.9	2.0
1930	3.6	32.6	22.9	40.9	0.02	29.3	65.1	1.7
1931	4.6	29.4	23.0	42.8	–	35.3	61.4	2.2

Source: Anotaton Oikonomikon Symvoulion, To Exoterikon Emporion tis Ellados kai ai Symvaseis Antallagis Emporeumaton, Athens 1933, pp.26 & 29.

to dominate the picture, although food and drink declined relatively as agricultural output recovered after 1922. The exceptionally high industrial exports between 1919-21 may well reflect the effects of the war effort in Asia Minor or could simply be due to classification adjustments. The structure of exports remains unchanged except for a rise in the exports of raw materials and semi-processed goods (primarily ores, minerals etc.).

A study of the financial inflows and outflows relating to the balance of payments in Greece between 1929-31 highlights the second important aspect of the underdevelopment of the economy. During these three years receipts from exports accounted for more than 36% of the total inflows of foreign exchange. Remittances from immigrants came a clear second with 19% of the total receipts [38]. Emigration overseas, in the late 1920s, had became a permanent feature of the Greek economy. The first recorded increase in overseas emigration and particularly to the United States came as a result of the currants crisis in the 1890s. There were further increases in the early years of the twentieth century and although the flow to the US was interrupted by the First World War, it continued unabated until the quota restriction imposed in the late 1920s and the depression checked it considerably. In order to illustrate the magnitude of this population movement it is perhaps indicative to point out that in the first decade of the twentieth century some 2.3% of the total population of Greece emigrated. This rose to about 6% by the 1920s and fell back to less than 2% by 1928. These are perhaps somewhat misleading comparisons however, not only because they involve stocks and flows but because the population of Greece changed considerably during these years as a result of the war and influx of refugees. Indeed there is reason to believe that the refugee problem would have been that much more difficult to cope with had it not been for the continuing exodus of both the indigenous population and of the newcomers from Asia Minor to the United States. The issue of emigration did not end here because it became again an extremely serious and damaging phenomenon for the Greek economy after the Second World War. Although economists and commentators of the time did not seem to have concerned themselves with the seriousness of the problem, there is some

The Turbulent 1920s

scattered evidence that the government encouraged
emigration as a solution to rural underemployment
and as a source of foreign exchange. Indeed,
there were even accusations that in the chaotic
years before and soon after the Asia Minor
disaster, when brigandry and lawlesness were on
the increase in the countryside, the local
authorities closed their eyes when some of the
less desirable local residents applied for
passports. But perhaps an important element that
helped to increase the numbers leaving the country
was the continuous threat of military service and
the disruption of farming activities by seemingly
nonstop wars after 1912. Indeed the number of
people in the countryside who had become potential
lawbreakers by consciously or unknowingly evading
military service or even deserting was so great,
and the issues so complicated, that Drafting Laws
and Induction Ordinances in the early 1970s were
still amnestying classes of draftees or deserters
of the 1920s, almost half a century earlier!
Table 1.15 summarises the data on emigration
between 1896 and 1940.

As the turbulent decade of the 1920s came to
an end Greece entered the period of the depression
with a much better organized government and
financial sector, with a number of outstanding
political problems solved and with its territory
almost equal to the present one except for the
Dodecanese which were returned to Greece after the
Second World War. The refugees had been absorbed
speedily although their economic plight was still
great. The structure of the economy had changed
relatively little with agriculture still the
leading sector. The dependence of the state on
foreign finance both for normal fiscal needs and

TABLE 1.15   Permanent Overseas Emigration 1896-1940

YEARS		YEARS	
1896-1900	11,189	1921-1925	50,531
1901-1905	51,479	1926-1930	40,838
1906-1910	122,634	1931-1935	14,797
1911-1915	128,521	1936-1940	15,703
1916-1920	67,598		

Source: Statistical Year Book of Greece, National
Statistical Service, Athens 1981.

also for balancing the current account remained undiminished. It is perhaps indicative that, when the shock waves of the 1929 crash reached Greece, the effect was primarity on the foreign exchange rate and on the balance of payments rather than on the production side of the economy. The inward-looking industry dedicated to serving domestic markets and the more robust agriculture, strengthened by the influx of refugees, created the circumstances under which Greece's response to the Depression was predictable. The economy retrenched its position, the role of foreign trade diminished and drastic but at least orderly state intervention was used to cope with the external financial situation.

NOTES

[1] Istoria, Vol.16 pp.327-342. For a general introduction to Greece's economy in the early 1920s see D.E. Protecdicos, Greece Economic and Financial, Eyre and Spottiswood, London 1924, passim.

[2] Haritakis, Oikonomiki Epaitiris for 1933 p.601

[3] S.V. Markezinis, Politiki Istoria tis Neoteras Ellados, Vol.II (1922-24), Papyros, Athens 1973 p.370

[4] (a) M.I. Notaras, I Agrotiki Apokatastasi ton Prosfygon, Athens 1934 pp.1-16 & 172-84
   (b) Markezinis, Politiki, pp.376-378

[5] (a) The Oikonomikos Tahydromos dedicated a special issue, 26/4/1973, on the impact of refugees on modern Greece: Oi Prosfyges stin Ellada. The issue contains contributions from a number of authors. References will be made on an author basis.
   (b) I. Angelis, in Oi Prosfyges, p.30

[6] G. Dafnis, in Oi Prosfyges p.12

[7] Istoria, Vol.16, p.196

[8] (a) Vergopoulos, To Agrotiko, pp.139-175
   (b) Istoria, Vol.16, pp.296-303

[9] Agianoglou, To Perasma pp.293-301

[10] D. Damaskinidis, in Oi Prosfyges, p.20 and M.Negreponti-Delivani in Oi prosfyges, p.76

[11] (a) A. Damaskinidis and S. Drosos in Oi Prosfyges, pp.19-22 and 57-58 respectively

71

(b) Agianoglou, <u>To Perasma</u>,pp.304-7.
[12] E. Mears, <u>Greece Today : The Aftermath of Refugee Impact</u>, London 1930, pp.115-117.
[13] A.G.B. Leon, <u>The Greek Socialist Movement and the First World War</u>, Columbia University Press, New York 1976, esp. pp.100-121.
[14] (a) A.Benarogias , <u>I Proti Stadiodromia tou Ellinikou Proletariatou</u>, Olkos, Athens 1975, pp.48-86 & 264-275.
(b) D. Livieratos, <u>To Elliniko Ergatiko Kinima</u> 1918-1923, Karanasis, Athens 1976, pp.22-30.
(c) I. Kordatos, <u>Istoria tou Ellinikou Ergatikou Kinimatos</u>, Athens 1956,passim.
[15] S. Nikolaidis, in <u>Oi Prosfyges</u>,p.42.
[16] G. Damaskinidis in <u>Oi Prosfyges</u>, p.19.
[17] Table 1.9 is based on a large number of sources cross-checked where possible for consistency. Primary use was made of
(a) G. Haritakis (Ed.), <u>Oikonomiki Epaitiris tis Ellados</u> for 1929,Athens 1930, p.287, for 1931, Athens 1932, p.385, for 1938, Athens 1939, pp.189-201.
(b) Anotaton Oikonomikon Symvoulion, <u>I Oikonomia tis Ellados kata to 1937</u>, Athens 1938,p.39.
(c) Zolotas, <u>Nomismatika</u>, Statistical Appendices.
(d) A. F. Freris, <u>O Plithorismos stin Propolemiki Ellada</u> 1914-1940 in <u>Oikonomikos Tahydromos</u>,7/8/77, pp.14-15.
The following notes and caveats should be read in conjunction with the data in the Table.
i) Bank notes in circulation are yearly averages. Up to 1928 when the Bank of Greece was established, the right to print notes rested with the National Bank of Greece. Until 1919 two other banks also issued notes,but the overall amount was very small in proportion to those of the National Bank of Greece. After 1928,the issuing right rested with the Bank of Greece.
ii) The sight deposit etc. figures are for year ending. The figures for deposits cover the largest commercial banks including those of the Agricultural Bank. The starred items are approximations only. Confusingly some sources add sight and deposit accounts

held with the Bank of Greece. These
have been eliminated from the figures in
order to give a more accurate picture as
the accounts with the Bank of Greece
were primarily held by other banks and
the government. The large jump in
deposits after 1928 presumably occurred
because of the stabilisation measures of
1928 when confidence in the drakma was
quite strong. Overall these estimates
are not reliable because different
sources give different figures or do not
include the same institutions on a
consistent basis. The annual reports of
the Bank of Greece do not give any
consistent or continuous data either.
iii) The cost of living index has been
calculated and published since 1914. No
reference has been discovered to any
change in base or recalculation since
1914. The changes in the structure of
population of Greece following the
influx of the refugees from Asia Minor
must have distorted considerably
spending patterns. Hence the index
values for the 1930s can only be
considered as broadly indicative.
iv) The calculation of the deficit in
central government spending in Greece
approaches that of a black art rather
than statistics. Official sources (Bank
of Greece, Anotaton Oikonomikon
Symvoulion) are either silent on actual
estimates or give conflicting figures.
Some of the more consistent estimates
(Haritakis) are clearly marked
'accounting deficits not real ones'.
The nearest explanation for the
discrepancies and lack of data is that
the Greek Treasury apparently carried
over from year to year surpluses and
deficits and then reallocated them.
There is also considerable confusion
over the distinction between capital and
current expenditures. Also the actual
outcome of fiscal activity of any single
year was not published until two to
three years later. So the figures in
the table are purely indicative. From
1918 onwards the fiscal year straddled
two years instead of one calendar year

so the figures for 1918 refer to 1918-19 and so on.

[18] (a) H.Papadas, I Axiothaumasti Dimosionomiki Politiki tis Horas mas kata tin Periodon 1917-1922 in Oikonomikos Tahydromos, 10/2/83, pp.51-52.

(b) A.D. Stragos, Les Finances de Guere de la Grece 1912-23, Union, Strasbourg 1928, passim.

[19] There is a large number of histories of the National Bank of Greece. For a concise treatment see G.Haritakis (Ed.), Oikonomiki Epaitiris tis Ellados for 1937, Athens 1938, Part II, pp.271-297. See also S. Spiliotopoulos, Istoria tis Ethnikis Trapezis tis Ellados, Ikaros, Athens 1949. For a general introduction to the history of the Greek banking system see K.I. Siamsiaris, I Elliniki Trapeziki Organosis, Bank of Greece, Athens 1965, passim. Two interesting monographs cover certain aspects of the operations of banks in Greece between 1871 and 1900: G. Dertilis, To Zitima ton Trapezon 1871-73, Morfotiko Idryma Ethnikis Trapezis, Athens 1982 and S. Thomakis, Pisti kai Ekhrimatismos tis Oikonomias, Morfotiko Idryma Ethnikis Trapezis, Athens 1981.

[20] (a) Varvaresos, Istoria, pp.1-13.
(b) Zolotas, Nomismatika, pp.6-7.

[21] Varvaresos, Istoria, p.14.

[22] Papadas, I Axiothaumasti, p.52.

[23] Markezinis, Politiki Istoria, Vol.I, p.272.

[24] The discrepancy in the March bank note figures relating to circulation and to the sum of cut notes reflects the fact that the state calculated the proceeds of the loan on the basis of the maximum notes that the National Bank could print under its existing franchise and not the actual notes in circulation.

[25] (a) For an extensive discussion of the background before and after the 1922 and 1926 events see T.M. Veremis, Oikonomia kai Dictatoria, I Syghyria 1925-26, Morfotiko Idryma Ethnikis Trapezis, Athens 1982, passim, but in particular pp.58-63.

(b) Zolotas, Nomismatika, pp.68-76, 107-108, and 223-224.

[26] (a) Markezinis, Politiki Istoria, Vol.III, pp.105-159.

    (b)   Veremis, Oikonomia, pp.115-117.
[27] (a)   G.A. Pyrsos, Symvoli is tin Istorian tis Trapezis tis Ellados, Vol.A, Kyklos, Athens 1936, passim.
    (b)   G. Vouros, Ta Deka Eti tis Trapezis tis Ellados, 1928-38, Athens 1938, passim.
    (c)   S. Gregoriou, Sheseis Trapezis Ellados kai Kratous, Pyrsos, Athens 1939, passim.
[28] (a)   K. Vergopoulos, Ethnikismos kai Oikonomiki Anaptyxi, Exantas, Athens 1978, pp.55-59.
    (b)   Istoria, Vol.16, pp.337-338.
[29] Ekthesis epi tou Isologysmou for 1928, Bank of Greece, Athens 1929, pp. IV, XIII & XXI.
[30] A.K. Giannitsis, Oi Xenes Ameses Ependyseis kai i Diamorfosis tis Neoellinikis Oikonomias, 1830-1939, in Epitheorisis Koinonikon Ereunon, No.30-31, 1977, pp.234-253.
[31] (a)   D.S. Stefanidis, I Eisroi ton Xenon Kefalaion kai ai Oikonomikai kai Politikai Synepiai, Salonica 1930, passim.
    (b)   Istoria, Vol.16, pp.335-338.
    (c)   Vergopoulos, Ethnikismos, pp.63-68.
[32] (a)   A.F. Freris, To Xeno Kefalaio stin Ellada 1840-1940, Oikonomikos Tahydromos, 29/1/1976, pp.13-14.
    (b)   T.Kapsalis, La Balance des Comptes de la Grece, Librarie Payot, Paris 1927, pp.212-215.
    (c)   London Cambridge Economic Service Special Memorandum No.48 in South-Eastern Europe, A Political and Economic Survey, The Royal Institute of International Affairs, London 1939, p.164.
[33] Freris to Xeno, pp.13-14.
[34] Haritakis, Oikonomiki Epaitiris for 1937, pp.493-590.
[35] Angelopoulos, Ai Dimosionomikai, pp.11 &12. These estimates are confirmed by a cross reference to Haritakis (Ed.), Oikonomiki Epaitiris 1929, p.268 where it is estimated that the percentage of state revenues necessary to service the National Debt (domestic & external) stood at 26.3% for 1929-30. During the late 1930s, this percentage dropped to about 15%, split almost equally between the foreign and domestic components following Greece's fourth default on its external obligations in 1932.
[36] Freris, To Xeno p.14.
[37] Istoria, Vol.16, pp.335-338.

[38] Anotaton Oikonomikon Symvoulion, <u>To Exoterikon</u>, pp.26-29.
For a general introduction to Greece's foreign trade during this period with special emphasis on trade with the USA see M.Dorizas, <u>The Foreign Trade of Greece</u>, <u>The Economic and Political Factors Controlling</u>, Philadelphia, 1925, esp pp.96-105.

CHAPTER TWO

THE 1930s DEPRESSION : CONSOLIDATION AND
RETRENCHMENT

2.1 MANAGING THE INEVITABLE : FINANCIAL CRISIS
AND DEFAULT

The foundation of the Bank of Greece was seen as a
new chapter and beginning in the troubled
financial history of Greece to that date. The
pegging of the drakma to sterling and the
reintroduction of convertibility ushered in a
brief period of respite and stability. The second
report of the Bank of Greece stated soberly:
'During the last year (1929) we followed the same
guiding principle that directed our activities in
the first period of the operation of the Bank,
namely the stabilisation of currency' [1]. As the
depression began to make itself felt, the Bank of
Greece espoused the then prevailing view that any
expansionist policy would not have had any effect
on output, and therefore, on employment. The
following quotation coming from a publication more
than half a century old sounds all too familiar in
the context of the monetarist thinking of the
1980s. The Bank of Greece is commenting here on
the fall of the note issue during 1929-30. (See
also the data in Table 1.9, p.54 of this book).

'The reduction in the circulation is
perfectly normal and reflects the
structure of our economy which is faced
with the consequences of the current
economic conditions. The fall in the
international level of prices and the
economic crisis could not but affect the
credit activities of our banking system
and circulation. Against this trend,
the central bank could respond by
widening its credit activities, reducing

discount rates and increasing loans. These measures, however, which thankfully very few people recommend, would have had as a temporary result an artificial increase in production and also in prices, via the increase in the stock of money. This would be not only ineffective in dealing with the crisis, but on the contrary, would damage our economy permanently.'
(Ekthesis epi tou Isologismou tou Etous 1930, Trapeza tis Ellados, Athens 1931, p. X)

Despite these precautions, the deflationary policy of the Bank of Greece was not sufficient to stave off the crisis. Since 1928 when the drakma became again fully convertible in terms of foreign exchange, the Bank of Greece had experienced a continuous drain of reserves and of gold. In September 1931 when sterling was devalued, the link with gold was removed. The Bank of Greece was then faced with an additional problem as approximately 25% of its reserves were held in sterling funds which were now worth less in terms of gold or other currencies. The Government decided immediately to continue maintaining the drakma on the gold exchange standard and linked it instead to the dollar with the new official exchange rate being set at $1 = 77.05 drakmas. In addition to this, the state decided that the Bank of Greece would assume a monopoly over all foreign exchange transactions thus abolishing the flourishing open market in foreign currencies. This effectively opened up the possibility of limiting the convertibility of the drakma. The first step was to freeze all the foreign exchange accounts of Greek residents. The next step was the general abandonment of convertibility which came on April 26, 1932. In May 1932 the final step was taken by declaring a moratorium on interest and capital payments due overseas. Greece had defaulted again for the fourth time in its history [2].

The events leading up to this crisis, and the policy measures that the Government took, both before and after the default, paint a vivid picture of the financial and economic thinking of the time and of the state of the Greek economy. Following the break with the sterling standard in September 1931, the drakma immediately came under

heavy selling pressure. The gold and foreign
exchange reserves of the Bank of Greece had been
declining continuously since 1928, but between
1931 and 1932 the fall became precipitous. The
authorities reacted by raising the discount rate
but they were acutely aware that this step, plus
the credit squeeze they had imposed, did little or
nothing to reverse the outflow of reserves. Their
policy reactions were more an affirmation of
their will to maintain the stability of the
drakma as long as possible rather than a
realistic reaction to the situation. Table 2.1
summarises these developments.

TABLE 2.1   Reserves (gold and foreign exchange) of
the Bank of Greece, ml drks and
discount rate (%) 1928-1932

Year	Reserves	Discount Rate
1928 (May)	3,964	10
1928 (December)	4,240	9-10
1929	3,115	8
1930	3,011	10
1931	1,916	9-12
1932	180	9-11

Sources: (a) A. Angelopoulos, Dimosionomikai
Meletai, Tefhos A, Athens 1931, p.90.
(b) Vouros, Ta Deka, p.24.

The continuous deficit in the balance of
trade increased the pressure on the reserves and
so did investment overseas by Greek residents.
This investment took the form of purchasing Greek
state bonds traded in the foreign exchanges of
London and Paris. Apparently the National Bank of
Greece took a leading role in this undertaking
which is estimated to have led to a drain of some
L2-5 million in 1930. The least charitable interpretation of the actions of the National Bank is

that it wanted to take revenge on the new and rival institution of the Bank of Greece. Its own explanation was that this was not investment overseas but investment in Greece because, in a sense, it repatriated the external debt [3]. Irrespective of the interpretation of these actions they did constitute a drain on the foreign exchange resources. The Bank of Greece had a legal obligation to maintain a 40% cover of the note issue in gold and foreign exchange. In September 1931, when the drakma was linked to the US dollar, the reserves stood at 53.6% but by August 1932 they were down to 20.7%, well below the legal minimum. Despite the fact that the Bank of Greece had since September 1931 a legal monopoly on all foreign exchange transactions, there was a flourishing black market in foreign currencies which the Bank itself observed and followed very closely. The official dollar-drakma rate in September 1931 stood at $1 = 77 drakmas. In October 1931 the black market rate was 86 drakmas, in March 1932 111 drakmas and in April 1932, when convertibility had to be abandoned, it had fallen to 120 drakmas [4].

In addition to suspending convertibility in April 1932, the Bank of Greece introduced a battery of controls which ushered in a period of extreme protectionism and extensive state intervention in financial affairs. For a start all foreign exchange debts payable to foreigners or to Greeks were compulsorily converted to drakmas. The same rule applied to all foreign exchange deposits with Greek banks. These particular deposits had become of considerable importance because during 1928-32, a period of relatively free foreign exchange markets, they rose to about 34% of all the deposits held in Greece. Given the arbitrariness of this policy step, in order to ensure an even spread of both the gains and losses, a special conversion exchange rate for debts and deposits was introduced indexed to the current official one but set originally at $1 = 100 drakmas, a level considerably lower than the ruling rate. The Bank in the next few months did not attempt to fix the drakma rate completely but used instead its monopoly in the market to manipulate it. For example, during 1933 it allowed the drakma to appreciate in the hope of encouraging the dishoarding of foreign exchange holdings and to maintain a downward pressure on the domestic price level [5].

Throughout the period following the uncoupling of the drakma from sterling and the abandonment of convertibility in April 1932, the Venizelos government tried to drum up international support in two areas. Firstly, an application was made to the League of Nations and to the International Commission of Economic Control (ICEC) for permission to suspend payments on foreign loans and for a $50 million loan to be used to stabilise the foreign exchange rate. The League of Nations was extremely sceptical on both proposals and sent in February 1932 Sir Otto Niemayer, the deputy governor of the Bank of England, to report on Greece's financial affairs. His report was largely negative emphasizing the fiscal irresponsibility of Greek Governments. In the event, the League of Nations agreed to a one year moratorium only. But developments overtook this decision because in April 1932 Greece left the gold exchange standard and a month later it had declared a unilateral moratorium on all interest and capital payments.

The Bank of Greece at the time had estimated the total external debt of Greece at $514 million with public loans at $382.8 million accounting for 74.5% of the total, followed by loans to banks and commercial undertakings at $87.7 million and finally loans to individuals and other private sector concerns at $43.3 million. In arguing its case for a moratorium, the Greek Government pleaded that almost 80% of all export earnings and 40% of the state budget were being spent on servicing the external debt.

As the unilateral moratorium was in direct breach of the rules under which the ICEC operated, the Greek Government started immediately negotiations with the foreign bondholders which dragged on until 1935. A settlement was then arrived at which involved the payment of about 43% of the interest rate due. The outbreak of the war and occupation disrupted any further payments [6].

In the report for 1930 the Governor of the Bank of Greece stated: [7]

"The attention of the population of our country must be turned towards work and productivity. I do not think that people should expect everything from the state and its organs. Protectionist regimes encourage laziness, ruin initiative

and are the poison that lead to the
destruction of society."

Harsh words indeed, and perhaps a little
prematurely spoken because by 1933 Greece had
introduced another comprehensive package of
tariffs, trade restrictions, and quotas to rival
those of the tariff increases of the 1880s.
Tariffs over a wide range of goods increased by
70% to 200%. Quotas were also introduced using as
a basis the level of imports in 1931. These
quotas were expected to reduce imports by up to
66%. Greece's external trade, which had always
exhibited a deficit in both the current and
capital accounts, entered a period of extensive
controls not only by quotas but also by the
widespread use of bilateral clearing arrangement
especially with the Fascist regimes of Italy and
Germany.

2.2 THE BALANCE OF PAYMENTS AND EXTERNAL RELATIONS

Balance of payments figures for Greece before 1928
are relatively scarce. After the establishment of
the Bank of Greece a more concrete effort was made
to collect and publish these data. Table 2.2
summarises the overall balance of payments
situation between 1929 and 1938. The data in this
table are not expressed in drakmas but in gold
French francs or sterling. No explanation is
given for this in the official statistics.
Exchange rate instability could have hardly been
the reason because, even after 1932,the exchange
rate of drakma remained relatively stable. The
only likely explanation is that the Bank of Greece
reported all the foreign exchange transactions in
terms of gold French francs and hence it made
sense to express the rest of the flows in a
similar manner.

Although the value of imports and exports is
recorded in different monetary units between
1929-30 and 1931-38, the effects of the depression
are obvious insofar as between 1929 and 1933 the
trade deficit declined as international trade
slumped. The current account deficit fell as
well, although this did not make the financing of
the overall deficit any easier. The data in Table
2.3 allow for a more detailed exploration of
capital flows during this period especially in
relation to other components in Greece's

TABLE 2.2 Balance of Payments 1929-1938
Figures for 1929-1931 in thousand gold sterling, 1932-1938 in thousand gold francs.
All current prices.

	1929	1930	1931	1932	1933	1934	1935	1936	1937	1938
IMPORTS	35400	28935	588377	341861	246743	251800	305270	334406	417422	415238
EXPORTS	18717	15782	280166	183334	154576	156700	202952	207243	269038	292613
Trade Balance	-16683	-13153	-308211	-158527	-92167	-95100	-102318	-127163	-148384	-122625
NET INVISIBLES TOTAL: of which(+ inflow - outflow):	+7355	+5027	+190475	+98855	+126267	+63420	+68273	+37805	+108775	+85674
(a) Emigrants' remittances (+)	7815	8359	177100	72520	77595	45500	32331	55377	91245	74052
(b) Shipping (+)	955	872	31250	22776	19155	25000	22684	26705	25008	31056
(c) Interest and profits of Greek capital abroad (+)	4682	3795	138075	50788	36260	30000	35000	30000	26500	25000
(d) Interest and profits on foreign capital in Greece (-)	500	650	18950	22779	26395	25000	17000	16000	16000	7121
(e) Service of National Debt (-)	4600	4776	124000	30598	20113	37652	18899	34200	22516	28387
CURRENT BALANCE	-9328	-8126	-117736	-59672	+34100	-31680	-34045	-89358	-39609	-36951
CAPITAL MOVEMENTS NET: Including changes in foreign exchange reserves and balances from bilateral clearing trade agreements	+9328	+8126	+248523	59672	-34100	+31680	+7963	+6576	+7653	-12836
BALANCING ITEM	*	*	-130787	*	*	*	+26082	+82782	+31956	+49787

(*) Not given separately

Sources: Based on completely reworked and cross-checked data from Haritakis, Oikonomiki Epaitiris for 1931, p.432 and for 1938 pp.246-247.

international transactions.

A number of observations can be made on the data presented in Tables 2.2 and 2.3. Firstly, the importance of remittances from Greeks emigrants, primarily in the United States, helped to finance more than 50% of the deficit in the trade balance during this period. Shipping was making a considerable impact as well. The large losses suffered due to enemy action in the First World War had been rapidly made up, so much so that the gross tonnage almost doubled between 1919 and 1924 and it continued to grow until the Second World War disrupted shipping again [8]. Both the receipts from shipping and emigrants were to remain extremely important sources of foreign exchange for Greece in the post-Second World War period as well. The second observation concerns the role of capital flows. The picture here becomes rather complicated because of the existence of significant balancing items in the statistics. Where the statistics give an explicit number for the balancing item this tends to be quite large in proportion to the deficit in the current account. Specifically for the years 1931, 1935, 1936, 1937 and 1938 the balancing item was 26%, 76%, 92%, 80%, and 134% of the current deficit indicating a massive under-recording of foreign exchange inflows. These inflows must have been the outcome of private transactions rather than official borrowing or running down of reserves because the Bank of Greece would have recorded those. Other flows, however, such as the servicing of overseas national debt and the repatriation of interest and profits of foreign capital invested in Greece are far more clearly recorded after 1929. It is important to stress at this stage that the role of the foreign capital invested in Greece in worsening the deficit of the balance of payments was at best minor (less than 20% of the deficit in five years during 1929-1938) and only in two years did it account for more than 50% (1934-1935). By far the most significant outflow was the servicing of national debt held overseas. This reinforces the conclusion that foreign investment in Greece during the interwar period played a relatively secondary role in the dynamics of the balance of payments. This still leaves however the contents and origin of the balancing item largely unexplained. A number of educated guesses and estimates have been put forward by Greek economists and commentators of

TABLE 2.3 Financial flows and the deficit in the trade and current account 1929-1938 (All figures in %)

Year	As percentage of deficit in trade balance		Capital outflows as percentage of the deficit in the Current Account	
	Remittances from emigrants	Receipts from shipping	Interest and Profit on foreign capital	Servicing of National Debt
1929	46.8	5.7	5.3	49.3
1930	63.5	6.6	7.9	58.7
1931	57.4	10.1	16.0	105.3
1932	45.7	14.3	38.1	51.2
1933	84.1	20.7	(*)	(*)
1934	47.8	26.2	78.9	118.8
1935	31.5	22.1	49.9	55.5
1936	43.5	21.0	17.9	38.2
1937	61.4	16.8	40.3	56.8
1938	60.3	35.3	19.2	76.8

Source: Data from Table 2.2
(*) Current account balance in surplus

the time [9].
    The most comprehensive analysis has been put
forward by G. Haritakis [10]. In examining the
balance of payments data for 1929 he calculated a
balancing item of Ł11ml. This was explained as
follows:-

    "From the unrecorded inflows the most
    important one ... is the interest rate
    received from Greek-owned capital
    abroad. The calculation of the exact
    sum of the Greek owned capital abroad
    and therefore the estimate of interest
    received, is very difficult ... The sum
    total of this capital, despite its
    decline during the last few years, must
    have been quite significant because for
    several decades it financed the deficit
    of our trade account which has always
    been quite high."

    Haritakis also claims that a significant
proportion of the payments for the servicing of
the national debt held overseas was ultimately
received by Greeks. The proportion for 1929 was
estimated to be at least 20%.
    Another estimate by A. Diomidis [11] covers
the period for 1928-31. He calculated a total
outflow of Ł160ml consisting of imports, invisibles and capital movements offset by Ł61ml of
exports, emigrant remittance of Ł4ml, interest,
profits etc. of Ł10ml, shipping Ł3ml, reparations
Ł1.9ml, and official and private loans overseas of
Ł20.3ml. These, plus some items, give a total of
Ł125.6ml inflows leaving a balancing item of
Ł34.4ml. Diomidis calculates that foreign
exchange reserves were reduced by Ł5.4ml leaving
some Ł29ml. This sum, he claims, was covered by
trade credits, primarily because of the growing
overseas confidence in the stability of the Greek
monetary system.
    The structure of Greek exports changed very
little during this period compared with the 1920s
except for the decline in the role of currants and
the relative increase in the importance of tobacco
(Table 2.4).
    There were, however, significant and impor-
tant changes in the direction of trade. Germany
came to dominate both the import and export trade
of Greece and tobacco exports in particular. This
change in the direction of trade was not unrelated

TABLE 2.4   Composition of Exports 1926-1938
            (Average value of selected items,
            percentage of total exports)

Products	1926-30	1931-35	1936-38
Tobacco	55.5	42.7	47.6
Currants	13.2	18.1	10.5
Sultanas	2.7	5.1	4.9
Olive oil	2.3	5.6	4.0
Wine	7.3	3.5	2.3
Skins	2.3	2.0	3.2
Yarns and Textiles	1.0	1.0	1.0

Source: Haritakis, Oikonomiki Epaitiris for 1938,
          p.38-39.

to the protectionist measures adopted by the Greek
Government in the wake of the financial crisis.
They also, of course, reflected the international
contraction of foreign trade and the rapid spread
of bilateral agreements. Table 2.5 summarises the
changes in the direction of trade between 1929-39.
     The export of tobacco makes an excellent
example and illustration of the problem that faced
Greece's external trade during this period. By
the end of the 1930s just three countries
Germany, Italy and the US absorbed about three
quarters of the total value of tobacco exports
from Greece. Two of these three countries, Italy
and Germany, had signed clearing trading
agreements with Greece. Almost two-thirds of the
exports of tobacco yielded no foreign currency,
just trading credits which had to be spent on
German and Italian goods. The situation was
becoming extremely serious because one simple
product, which accounted for only 4% to 5% of the
total cultivated area, was providing 50% of the
potential foreign exchange revenues, enough to pay
for the whole import bill for food. However, only
one third of the foreign exchange receipts from
tobacco exports were freely available in the form
of cash or bank balances. But even so, this one
third contributed more to the total export
earnings than all the other agricultural exports
added together, including currants. Greece's

The 1930s Depression

dependence on tobacco exports and in particular
exports to Germany was becoming all-pervasive.
Indeed there was talk of a second currants crisis
given this dangerous development of a 'one crop
economy' [12].

TABLE 2.5 Destination of Imports and Exports
            1929-1939 (% of totals)

Imports from	1929	1933	1938	1939
US	16.7	5.8	7.2	7.0
UK	12.7	14.3	13.0	12.0
Germany	9.4	10.2	28.8	29.9
Italy	5.6	5.6	3.3	5.3
Exports to				
US	16.0	12.5	17.0	21.6
UK	11.6	18.9	8.3	13.6
Germany	23.0	17.8	38.4	27.5
Italy	18.2	14.0	5.0	6.3

Source: Anotaton Oikonomikon Symvoulion,
         I Oikonomia tis Ellados, kata to Etos
         1939,
         Athens 1940, pp.64-65.

By 1936, 76.5% of exports from and 52.5% of
imports to Greece were subject to clearing
arrangements. Germany played a leading role in
these arrangements [13]. Greece was the partially
willing victim of the so-called Schacht technique,
named after Hitler's foreign trade minister. This
involved purchasing from primarily agricultural countries their surplus produce at above
world market prices. Payments were effected in
reichmarks, rather than foreign exchange, but in
frozen accounts which could only be used to
purchase German goods. In particular Germany was
keen to sell armaments, usually at non-competitive
prices. In 1932 Greece signed an appropriate
agreement with the Reichbank. Initially Greece
had a surplus in its transactions with Germany and
this continued to be so, but as it turned out, at
Greece's expense. By 1936 Greece had accumulated
in trade credits 34.5 million reichmarks, a sum
88

representing several times the import surplus of
Germany's trade with Greece. The Greek authorities
grew concerned enough to negotiate an agreement
with Germany whereby these trade credits were
guaranteed against future depreciation of the
reichmark and steps were to be taken to stop them
from accumulating any further [14]. Politics were
soon to enter the picture as the tension increased
between Germany and the UK. Greece attempted to
use the accumulated German trade credits as
collateral in raising a loan in the international
market, but it met with stiff opposition from
Britain and had to withdraw the plan. In turn,
Greece put pressure on the UK to purchase more of
its tobacco in order to lessen the dependence on
Germany, but to little effect. British smokers
preferred the Virginia type American tobacco to
Greece's Eastern-Turkish produce. When war broke
out between Germany and the UK, Greece signed an
agreement with the UK whereby in return for the
Royal Navy not interfering with Greece's seaborne
trade to Germany, Greece would limit the exports
to Germany and the UK would make an extra effort
to buy Greek goods. The scheme was never put to a
real test as Greece was soon involved in war with
Italy and then with Germany [15].

Greece's external trade and international
commercial and financial relations reflected both
the realities of the domestic economy and of the
international situation. The financial crisis of
1929-32 led to a range of policy measures that
restricted trade in various ways. Tariffs, quotas
and clearing arrangements were used, in addition
to a push towards greatest autarchy in the
production of food. The already small and
restricted industrial sector was encouraged to
concentrate on the domestic market and to lessen
its dependence on imported inputs. As the
quotation from the report of the Governor of the
Bank of Greece in 1930 testified, the Greek
Government was initially averse to involving
itself with the direct management of the economy
other than in external financial matters. The
depression and the establishment in 1936 of a
dictatorship with corporatist aspirations was soon
to change all that.

2.3 DEVELOPMENTS IN INDUSTRY AND AGRICULTURE

Section 1 of Chapter One of this book analysed the

impact of refugees on the industrial sector of the Greek economy. The trends described there continued more or less unchanged in the decade leading up to the war. Spinning, textiles, food processing and chemicals remained the mainstay of the industrial sector. The level of industrial output and employment did not escape the consequences of the depression and both fell continuously between 1930-1932 (Table 2.6). The effects of the depression were more obvious on employment. Part of the explanation must rest with the level of wages. Lack of data do not allow accurate computation of real wages, but using the retail price index as a guide, real wages grew by an average of 4.9% between 1935-39.

In 1922 and then again in 1926 the Greek government took a number of policy measures in order to encourage industrial activity including tax concessions and reductions of import duties on capital equipment. In 1932, however, as part of

TABLE 2.6   Indexes of industrial output, wages and employment (1928 = 100), 1921-1939

Year	Industrial Output	Employment	Wages
1921	61.3	-	-
1922	70.5	-	-
1923	62.7	-	-
1924	80.7	-	-
1925	88.8	-	-
1926	84.5	-	-
1927	94.4	-	-
1928	100.0	100.0	100.0
1929	101.7	107.9	-
1930	105.2	104.6	100.2
1931	108.8	101.9	-
1932	102.6	86.7	96.8
1933	111.7	94.3	-
1934	127.4	94.9	102.3
1935	143.1	99.9	102.9
1936	141.7	102.3	107.5
1937	153.8	118.3	120.4
1938	164.2	123.7	124.5
1939	179.0	124.8	129.8

Sources: (a) Haritakis, Oikonomiki Epaitiris for 1938, p.283.
           (b) Anotaton Oikonomikon Symvoulion, I Oikonomia, for 1939, p.41.

the emergency measures the government introduced a truly comprehensive set of tariffs and quotas, which in combination with the increasing spread of bilateral clearing agreements, threw a tight protective cover over the industrial sector.

Given that Greece's trading partners were behaving in a similar manner it is not surprising that Greek industry turned inwards and supplied an increasing percentage of the industrial goods consumed at home. Indeed there is even some evidence that sectoral interrelationships increased during this period. In 1928, 43% of raw materials used in industry were imported, whereas by 1938 they had declined to 25% [16]. Table 2.7 shows the increasing dependence on domestic industrial output. This development, however, did not stop industrial imports from accounting, on average, for more than 40% of all imports during 1931-39.

TABLE 2.7   Share of domestic and imported manufactured goods in consumption 1928-1939 (1928 = 100, quantity based index)

	1928	1936	1937	1938	1939
Domestically produced	58.6	72.8	74.4	78.8	81.6
Imported	41.4	27.2	25.6	21.2	18.4

Source: Anotaton Oikonomikon Symvoulion, I Oikonomia for 1939, p.48.

It is interesting to observe, however, that throughout this period of relative rise in industrial output, state authorities and well-informed commentators had no illusions about the strength and the potential future role of industry in Greece. X.Zolotas, who became the most influential governor of the Bank of Greece in the postwar period, writing in 1936 pointed out that the rapid expansion of industry was built on sand and was totally dependent on protectionism and the devaluation of the drakma which diminished the pressures of international competition [17]. This view had been expressed earlier in a much more blunt manner in the report of the governor of the Bank of Greece for 1931. In examining the reasons why Greece had been relatively immune from the full effect of the depression he pointed to:

"... the purely local character of our industry which is dedicated to supplying the total of all the domestic needs. This is a characteristic that we should not wish the industry to lose .... but industry should not push itself further than the appropriate limits basing itself on the illusion that the current situation might have created, nor continue the pursuit of protectionist policies which are not always to its best interests".
(Ekthesis epi tou Isologismou tou Etous, for 1931, Athens 1932, p.VII)

Another source quotes a speech made by the Finance Minister in the early 1930s, to a group of Greek industrialists in which he stated that:- [18]

"I am completely indifferent towards industry and I consider that its sole usefulness lies in that it allows the existence of a set of tariffs which contributes more than half of the revenues of the Government budget. Indeed industry causes problems in the balancing of the budget for the simple reason that it causes fewer goods to be imported and therefore less tariff revenues for the state".

This rather cynical view of the role of industry was perhaps also a realistic one, except that it overlooked one important factor. The fiscal needs of the state may well have created the protectionist environment in which industry developed and hence created also the circumstances under which the state took a more active role in the management of the economy.

State intervention in industry continued to expand , especially during the period of the Metaxas dictatorship (1936-1940). A system of compulsory arbitration was introduced whereby all collective bargaining took place under the auspices of the state. So for example between 1936-38, 106 national and 545 local agreements were concluded and registered. Trade Union activities, long dominated by the communist party, were strictly

The 1930s Depression

controlled if not by the fact that the majority of
communist party members were either on the run, in
prison or in exile. An extensive programme of
public works was instituted including forti-
fication of sectors in the northern border, rather
boastfully called the 'Metaxas Line', presumably
after Maginot. The Government fostered the
creation of a nascent war industry particularly in
the production of munitions and of servicing and
repairing aircraft [19]. But in terms of
diversification or of the creation of new lines of
activity there was little or no change in the
structure of industrial output in 1938 compared to
the early 1920s except for the decline in tanning.
In over eighteen years (1921-38) the same four
industries; textiles, food, chemicals and tanning
accounted for more than 65% of the total
industrial output. Electricity generation was by
the end of this period contributing about 10% to
total manufacturing output. Table 2.8 shows the
composition of industrial output in 1938. In
Chapter One, Table 1.9 gives the relevant data for
the major sectors between 1921-1938.

TABLE 2.8   Percentage contribution of industrial
            sectors to the total value of
            industrial output, 1938.

Sector	Percentage
Textiles & Spinning	27.1
Chemicals	21.7
Food processing	17.3
Electricity generation	8.5
Tanning	7.5
Engineering	4.5
Timber processing	3.9
Building Materials	3.9
Paper	3.2
Tobacco processing	1.6
Metal processing	0.5
Clothing	0.3

Source: Haritakis, Oikonomiki Epairtiris for 1938,
          p.281.

During this period Agriculture underwent a
rapid transformation, partially along the lines of

the changes already established in the 1920s.
Perhaps the most important developments were in
the structure of output. Percentage-wise, cotton
and wheat output rose approximately fourfold and
threefold respectively between 1929 and 1939. The
output of currants which had long dominated the
sector remained relatively stationary. Tobacco
production increased rapidly but since most of the
output was destined for export it was subject to
the vagaries of the international market. There
was a particularly significant fall between
1931-32 caused both by natural and market forces
but output continued to fluctuate right down to
the outbreak of the war. (See Table 2.9)

But perhaps the success story of state
intervention in agriculture during this period was
the encouragement of wheat production in order to
ensure Greece's self sufficiency in bread. The
Metaxas regime gave this programme top priority in
view of the growing prospects of another world
war. The key instrument of the policy was a
comprehensive system of price support and
intervention established and supervised by the
Central Committee for the Protection of Domestic
Wheat Production (KEPES from the Greek initials).
As international commodity prices collapsed, the
price support system became particularly
important. For example between 1929-33 the prices
of a key number of Greek export commodities such
as tobacco, currants and olive oil declined by
more than 60%, even after making allowances for
the devaluation of the drakma [20]. This would
not have been much of a problem for the domestic
wheat producers, because little wheat was
exported, except that the state wished to ensure
that the price enjoyed by farmers was equal to
that of imported wheat, but at the same time it
provided an adequate return.

KEPES was established in 1927. Its main
function was to purchase wheat from farmers at a
fixed price. The wheat was then resold to exporters or to domestic millers. Importers of wheat
had also to purchase a given quantity of wheat
from KEPES. As import prices (inclusive of
tariffs) fell, the support prices increased and
vice versa. Between 1928-37 KEPES maintained the
average domestic price of wheat at 8.1% higher
than international prices, allowing for any import
duties [21]. In the first five years of operations, 1927-31, KEPES purchased on average about
5% of the total wheat output. This percentage

TABLE 2.9 Index of volume of agricultural output 1920-1939(1920 = 100)

Year	Currants	Wheat	Tobacco	Cotton
1920	100.0	100.0	100.0	100.0
1921	92.6	92.3	73.7	87.4
1922	146.5	80.6	81.3	136.0
1923	115.1	78.4	182.3	180.6
1924	141.4	69.0	158.7	230.0
1925	135.7	100.3	191.9	237.2
1926	133.1	110.8	193.7	288.8
1927	130.5	115.9	199.5	204.1
1928	127.3	116.9	185.3	241.5
1929	103.1	102.2	216.9	247.8
1930	123.6	86.7	207.8	262.2
1931	65.3	100.3	139.5	222.0
1932	130.7	152.5	92.3	357.0
1933	107.6	253.7	173.2	517.0
1934	140.2	229.5	131.8	587.5
1935	140.8	242.9	145.3	794.0
1936	119.1	174.6	255.5	947.5
1937	125.6	268.5	218.7	1226.1
1938	119.9	321.9	151.7	1067.4
1939	103.8	342.2	174.5	1101.1

Source: Based on data from Haritakis, Oikonomiki Epaitiris for 1929, pp.45-106, and for 1938, p.71. Also Anotaton Oikonomikon Symvoulion, I Oikonomia for 1939, pp.5-25.

increased rapidly so that in the last three years
just before the war KEPES handled more than a
quarter of the total output [22]. The state
encouraged wheat production further by technical
assistance, education, training schemes and
loans. Indeed, given the dependence of Greek
farmers on bank loans and the legacy of mortgages
and other loans from the resettlement of refugees,
the Metaxas dictatorship declared a moratorium or
allowed for delayed repayments on a large number
of agricultural loans. The overall results of
these programmes were quite impressive. The
percentage of land devoted to growing wheat rose
from 2.8% of the total in 1920 to 4.3% in 1930
[23]. Average annual production, which during
1919-27 stood at 282,000 tons, rose to 532,500
tons in 1928-37. Domestic production, which
supplied 30% of the total wheat consumed in
1920-24, was supplying more than 60% in 1935-39
[24].

A further important aspect of agricultural
policy during this period was the establishment of
the Agricultural Bank of Greece in 1929 which took
over the agricultural loans functions of the
National Bank of Greece. For a long time the
credit operations of the National Bank in the
farming sector were subject to continuous
criticisms, primarily because the bank preferred
short term loans, whereas the farmers really needed
long term capital funds. The newly formed
Agricultural Bank encouraged the establishment of
agricultural cooperatives and channelled the
credits preferably through them rather than
directly to individual farmers. A law passed in
1914 had established the legal framework for the
operation of cooperatives, encouraging in particular the formation of rural credit unions in
order to lessen the influence of local money
lenders on the smaller farmers. By 1936 more than
80% of all the cooperatives were of the credit
type [25].

Agriculture in Greece made significant progress during this period, both in terms of the
overall increases and changes in the composition
of output. The 1929 census showed that 80% of the
farmers owned their land and almost 75% of them
tilled very small units. The animal husbandry side
of agriculture was still very underdeveloped with
heavy emphasis on sheep and goats rather than on
the more lucrative but relatively more capital
intensive beef and dairy products [26]. The

country however could feed itself, and the land
redistribution problem had been solved at the
expense of efficiency as it caused a great deal of
fragmentation, but to the satisfaction of the just
aspiration of the indigenous peasants and their
refugee cousins.

2.4 GREECE AT THE THRESHOLD OF THE WAR

The first half of the decade leading up to the war
was dominated by the monetary and fiscal effects
of the depression on the Greek economy. The
memories of the events in 1922-26 were still fresh
in the minds of the public and of the Government.
This was evident by the tenacity with which the
authorities stuck to their stabilisation programme
of the drakma so that they pursued it to the point
that resulted in yet another official default on
the external debt.

The rise of John Metaxas to power and then to
dictatorship in 1936 opened a relatively calmer
period for the Greek economy. State inter-
ventionism that had begun with the problem of
resettling the refugees, accelerated during this
period and was aided and abetted not only by the
collapse of the international economy and trade,
but also by the corporatist views and ideology of
a regime that aped the German and Italian
prototypes. Metaxas took great pride in the
establishment of compulsory arbitration in labour
disputes and in the foundation of the first
comprehensive scheme of social security in
Greece. The latter was something of a mis-
appropriated claim since there was already a law
passed in 1922 which established a state pension
scheme for tobacco workers, bakers, millers and
printers. A further extention of the scheme in
1932 led to a final revision of the existing
arrangements and the introduction of general
health and pension schemes during the Metaxas
dictatorship [27].

The debate about the overall progress and
development of the Greek economy in the 20 years
from the Asia Minor debacle to the outbreak of the
Second World War can be partially settled by an
appeal to the existing quantitative evidence. The
Appendix to this chapter summarises some of it in
terms of the size and composition of the national
income. Where there are available statistics the
coverage extends before 1920. But overall, the

data and the methods of computation are incomplete and primitive. The more reliable evidence covers the 1928-39 period. What limited conclusion can be drawn from this particular set of data can be summarised as follows.

Firstly between 1929 and 1931 GNP almost definitely declined but from then on sustained an average rate of growth of about 3.6%. This is partially confirmed by the average annual growth rate of the index of general economic activity which stood during the same period at 4.8%.

Secondly, the share of industry in the GNP is given by various estimates as 18.2% in 1923, 10% in 1924, 17% in 1934, 17.5% in 1938 and 16.1% in 1939. Given the diversity of the sources and excluding the smallest of the estimates it looks as if industrial output did not increase its share significantly between 1923 and 1939. This is partially confirmed by the relatively static share of industial exports, although an allowance must be made for the overall decline in international trade. Furthermore industrial output during this period grew by 5.5% whereas agricultural output rose by 10.9%. So even if the estimates of the share of industry in the GNP are inaccurate it is unlikely that industrial output would have risen fast enough to equal or overtake the share of agriculture in the GNP.

Greece's economic development in the two decades up to the Second World War exhibits all the signs of the limitation and constraints that the legacy of the nineteenth century had left it with. The financial burden of the external debt caused partially by the fiscal irresponsibility of the state and by the balance of trade deficit imposed a continuous constraint on the exercise of fiscal and monetary policy and was a drain on the meagre foreign exchange earnings of the economy. But perhaps this is an unduly harsh judgement. Capital accumulation by the state in Greece was continuously constrained by the insufficiently large tax base from which to draw financial resources and the fact that any form of capital investment would have to involve imports. Herein lay the seeds of the growing dependence on capital from abroad. An additional factor that did nothing to lessen this dependence was the official encouragement of peasant smallholdings and the deliberate break-up of large estates. Although the social and political merits of this policy are not under dispute, in the context of economic

development within a market economy this policy
eliminated a source of potential capital
accumulation. Given , however , that some of the
biggest landlords before the 'tsiflik' system was
abolished were expatriate Greeks, even this possibility is doubtful. The Greeks of the diaspora,
with few exceptions, were mainly interested in or
involved with trade, and had their large land-
holdings not been broken up, it is most unlikely
that they would have started to invest in industry. Even when some capital investment took
place, such as Trikoupis' extensive expenditures
on infrastructure, it too was of doubtful
importance in terms of Greece's industrial
development.

Finally, and most importantly, the state
budget was permanently saddled with defence expenditures. The collapse of the Ottoman Empire
and the territorial claims of Greece and its just
desire to ensure that most Greek communities lived
under Greek jurisdiction within a Greek state,
meant repeated wars. The Asia Minor campaign was
aberration, a criminally irresponsible undertaking. The economic consequences however were
peculiar in the sense that they did not revo-
lutionise the economy or push it in a different
direction than the one it had already embarked
upon. The political consequences though were far
more radical. The liberal-republican movement was
consolidated and the majority of Greece's
territorial claims settled for good.

Greece's economic dependence on countries
such as the UK, France and Germany was primarily
financial. The external trade links were important
but not vital. Indeed in the 1930s and specifically during the Mataxa's regime the dream of a
self-sufficient and self-contained Greece was
developed a long way. Greece could feed itself,
industrial output was geared to domestic needs and
Government intervention was more of a paterna-
listic type rather than an attempt to fashion or
change the structure of the economy. Had the war
not intervened or had Greece stayed neutral, then
even the outstanding financial obligations would
have been eventually settled. As it happened, the
war and then the civil war after the occupation
changed all this. The external financial dependence was prolonged and it was now coupled with
more active state intervention but no coherent
industrialisation policy.

The 1930s Depression

NOTES

[1] Ekthesis epi tou Isologismou tou Etous 1929,
     Trapeza tis Ellados, Athens 1930, p.IV.
[2] (a) G.A. Pyrsos, Symvoli is tin Istoria tis
          Trapezis tis Ellados, Vol. B,
          Typoekdotiki, Athens 1946, pp.32-133.
     (b) A.N. Kyrkilitsis, I Ethnini Trapeza tis
          Ellados 1928-1934, Kyklos, Athens 1933,
          pp.61-72.
[3] Istoria, Vol. 16, pp.327-342.
[4] (a) Ekthesis epi tou Isologismou tou Etous
          1932, Trapeza tis Ellados, Athens 1933,
          passim.
     (b) For a general discussion of developments
          in the banking sector up to that date
          see T. Galanis, Trapezikai Meletai,
          Papazisis, Athens 1946, passim.
[5] (a) Ekthesis epi tou Isologismou tou Etous
          1933, Trapeza tis Ellados, Athens 1934,
          pp.VIII-X.
     (b) Istoria, Vol. 16, p.329.
[6] (a) Markezinis, Politiki, Vol. 3, pp.351-368.
     (b) For a lucid exposition of the political
          background and the repercussions of
          these developments see G. Dafnis, I
          Ellas Metaxi dio Polemon, 1923-1940,
          Vol. II, Ikaros, Athens 1955, pp.100-142.
[7] Ekthesis epi tou Isologismou tou Etous 1930,
     Trapeza tis Ellados, Athens 1931, p.VIII.
[8] Istoria, Vol. 16, p.300.
[9] For a summary see A.F. Freris, Elliniko
     Isozygio Pliromon 1920-1975, in Oikonomikos
     Tahydromos, 7/10/76.
[10] Haritakis, Oikonomiki Epaitiris for 1929,
     pp.27-28. His calculations do not appear
     explicitly in Table 2.2 because of
     considerable adjustment and correction of the
     data presented.
[11] A. Diomidis, Meta tin Krisin, Kaufman, Athens
     1934, pp.38-41.
[12] A. Mantzaris, Georgiki Paragogi kai Kapniki
     Politiki, Athens 1939, passim. This is an
     abridged reprint of Report No. 24 of Anotaton
     Oikonomikon Symvoulion Athens, 1938, which
     contains additional material.
[13] Anotaton Oikonomikon Symvoulion, To
     Exoterikon, passim.
[14] (a) The London-Cambridge Economic Services
          Special Memorandum No. 48, reprinted in

100

South Eastern Europe: A Political and Economic Survey, The Royal Institute of International Affairs, London 1939, pp.163-165.

(b) A. Toynbee and V.M. Boulter, Germany's Economic Drang Nach Sudosten in A.Toynbee (Ed.), Survey of International Affairs for 1936, Oxford University Press, Oxford 1937, pp. 526-533.

(c) A.G.B. Fisher, Germany's Economic Policy in South Eastern Europe in A. Toynbee (Ed.), Survey of International Affairs for 1937, Vol. I, Oxford University Press, Oxford 1938, pp.459-467.

[15] (a) D. Kitsikis, I Ellas tis 4is Augoustou kai ai Megalai Dynameis, Ikaros, Athens 1974, pp.40-58.

(b) J.S. Koliopoulos, Greece and the British Connection 1935-1941, Oxford University Press, Oxford 1977, pp.128-129.

[16] Vergopoulos, Ethnikismos, p.74.

[17] X. Zolotas, Kateuthynseis tis Oikonomikis mas Politikis, Athens 1936, pp.17-23.

[18] Vergopoulos, Ethnikismos, pp.79-80.

[19] N. Psiroukis, O Fasismos kai i 4i Augoustou, Epikairotis, Athens 1974, pp.88-89 & 92-94.

[20] X. Evelpidis, I Georgia tis Ellados, Logos, Athens 1944, p.132.

[21] Anotaton Oikonomikon Symvoulion, Report No. 26, Epi tou Georgikou Provlimatos tis Horas, Athens 1939, pp.177-179.

[22] Anotaton Oikonomikon Symvoulion, I Oikonomia, for 1939, p.12.

[23] Anotaton Oikonomikon Symvoulion, Report No.7, Metra pros Epafxissin tis Eghoriou Sitoparagogis, Parts I & II, Athens 1934, p.36.

[24] (a) Anotaton, Report No. 26, p.177.

(b) Evelpidis, I Georgia, p.45.

[25] (a) P.S. Avdelidis, To Agrotiko Synetairistiko Kinima stin Ellada, Papazisis, Athens 1975, pp.49-52.

(b) P. Papagarifalos, Oi Georgikoi Synetairismoi en Elladi, 1821-1940, Papazisis, Athens 1973, pp.165-185.

[26] Anotaton Oikonomikon Symvoulion, Report No. 28, To Ktinotrofiko Zitima tis Ellados, Athens 1940.

[27] S. Linardatos, Tetarti Augoustou, Thamelio, Athens 1966, pp.117-119.

APPENDIX TO CHAPTER 2

ESTIMATES OF NATIONAL PRODUCT IN PREWAR GREECE

PRESENTATION OF DATA

There have been few systematic attempts at estimating the level of national product and its components in prewar Greece. This makes any discussion of growth rates or of sectoral developments either very difficult or impossible. The main aim of this Appendix is to present a survey and a summary of a number of these estimates. They are presented in roughly chronological order of the time period they cover. The estimates for the 1928-1939 are cross checked for consistency and accuracy against a set of comprehensive sectoral or general indexes that exist for the same period. This comparison allows the drawing of a number of conclusions concerning economic growth during this period although it still leaves unresolved a number of issues. Where the authors quoted explain their methodology or source of statistics, this is discussed or commented upon. Otherwise only their data and calculations are presented. There is also no clear differentiation between GDP and GNP estimates, but under the circumstances this distinction is rather academic.

1. P. Goulielmos: <u>Neoelliniki Pragmatikotita</u>, Neoi Sosialistes, Athens 1974, pp.183-195.

This is one of the very few systematic attempts at reconstructing and estimating Greek national income data. There is a major problem, however, in that Goulielmos makes seemingly arbitrary assumptions in his estimates and an inexplicable arithmetic step. The methodology used was to assume that Government expenditures and exports were a constant percentage of the national product. As statistics on foreign trade and state expenditures are available (despite any doubts over their accuracy) then this assumption allows a first approximation of GNP. Goulielmos used some existing GNP estimates to start with and then projected his own either forward or backwards. In order to cross-check the data and smooth out any divergences from decade to decade, he averaged out the estimates based on exports and on government expenditures and also calculated them on a per capita basis and then as aggregates. This was done presumably in order to incorporate some kind of time trend from point estimates to projected time series.

There are however three major difficulties with these projections:-

Firstly, the arbitrary assumption that exports and government expenditure stayed at a constant 15% of the GNP throughout 1860-1910.

Secondly, in order to move from point estimates of single years to successive decades Goulielmos assumed that exports and government expenditure grew at about 20% per decade, an unwarranted assumption as there are plenty of data for exports and government expenditures for all the years throughout this period. (See for example X.Zololas, Nomismatika, the statistical appendices)

TABLE A.1   GNP in million drakmas 1820-1940. Data from 1920 onwards on a constant price basis although this is not stated explicitly in the source.

Year	GNP	Year	GNP
1820	60	1900	721
1830	45	1910	930
1840	80	1920	1900
1850	110	1930	2180
1860	149	1940	3000
1870	241		
1880	338		
1890	529		

Average growth rate : 1910-20 = 9.5% p.a.
                       1920-30 = 1.3% p.a.
                       1930-40 = 3.4% p.a.

Finally, and most inexplicably, some of the calculations that are expressed in gold francs or drakmas, are then added together and averaged. This hybrid is then called an indexed drakma estimation (see p.189).

Goulielmos' estimates are set out in Table A.1.

The 1930s Depression

2. (a) Moskof: I Ethniki, p.167.
    (b) Tsoukalas: Koinoniki, p.42.

    Both these studies quote estimates of a
    number of earlier Greek authors. Tsoukalas
    also summarises some of the data presented by
    Goulielmos and Moskof. Some of the data are
    expressed in gold drakmas, others not. This
    can lead to some discrepancies because in
    1848, 1868-70, 1877-84 and from 1885 until
    effectively 1928 the drakma was not freely
    convertible to gold and also was frequently
    devalued, hence altering its gold content.

TABLE A.2   Various estimates of National Product
            1830-1895, ml drakmas

Year	GNP					
1830	60	or	50	or	45	
1840	80	or	45	or	60	or 80
1850	105	or	50	or	110	
1855	140	or	60			
1860	70	or	150	or	149	
1865	200					
1870	205	or	239			
1880	275	or	350	or	338	
1890	529					
1895	400	or	600			

Source: Tsoukalas, Koinoniki, p.42.

3. Evelpidis, I Georgia, p.169.

    Evelpidis sets out a table of the share of GNP
    accounted for agriculture from which it is
    possible to calculate the actual GNP level at
    current prices. This is done in Table A.3. He
    also gives detailed data for the level and
    composition of GNP for 1939. The latter data
    are presented in Table A.4 in combination with
    another set of estimates in order to allow for
    some comparisons.

4. (a) S. Nikolaidis: Ta Vari tou Kratous kai i
         Isfora ton Prosfygon, Eleftheron Vima,
         5th and 6th January 1930. Reprinted in
         Oikonomikos Tahydromos, No. 992, 26 April
         1973, special issue on the Asia Minor
         Refugees and their contribution to

TABLE A.3 National income and agricultural output 1927-39, million drakmas, current prices.

Year	National Income	Growth rate over previous year, %	Agricultural Output	Agric. Output as % of National Income
1927	44092.4		15256	34.6
1928	46310.5	5.0	16255	35.1
1929	44389.0	- 4.1	13006	29.3
1930	42737.2	- 3.7	12522	29.4
1931	39481.2	- 7.6	11568	29.3
1932	43637.6	10.5	15535	35.6
1933	47089.9	7.9	18318	37.9
1934	52668.4	11.8	19698	37.4
1935	54751.2	3.9	21353	39.0
1936	59161.6	8.0	21594	36.5
1939	67239.8	13.6	29720	44.2

Greece's economy, p.44. His estimates are set out in columns 1 and 3 of Table A.4.

(b) G.L. Nikolaides, Grece, L'Effort de Dix Ans 1924-1934, Athens 1935, p.7. His estimates are set out in columns 2 and 4 of Table A.4.

(c) X. Evelpidis, I Georgia, p.169. His data are shown in column 5 of Table A.4. There are some discrepancies in this estimate for 1939 and the one presented in Table A.3 mainly due to aggregation.

A number of points and caveats must be entered here in relation to these data. For a start, all the authors' classifications of sectors or activities have been slightly rearranged or (dis)aggregated in order to make the presentation uniform. But, in general, Agriculture includes animal husbandry, forestry and fishing. Industry includes handicrafts and construction. Financial services cover banking and insurance. Other services cover the public sector, professions, commerce, distribution, and rents, when not shown seperately.

Secondly, S. Nikolaidis calculated both Gross and Net National Income by adding together the value of output of agriculture and industry and then all the incomes derived from services including profits and rents. His estimates are thus a hybrid and are suspect of extensive double-counting as no mention is made of value added. Furthermore, he actually added rather than subtracted the deficit in the balance of trade. The figures given here are gross (i.e. his depreciation allowance of 3% of the value of agricultural and industrial output is added back) and the balance of trade is excluded since the figures refer to output and income rather than expenditures.

Evelpidis (Column 5) included in his figures remittances from emigrants and interest payable on state loans. As S.Nicolaidis' estimates (Columns 1 and 3) do not make any attempt at measuring net income from abroad and Evelpidis does not specify whether these interest payments were made for externally or domestically held loans, these two items were left out. In any case, leaving them in the estimates would have only compounded the already existing double-counting.

TABLE A.4   National Product and its composition for 1923, 1924, 1927-28, 1934 & 1939 in million drakmas, current prices.

Sectors or source of Income	1 1923	%	2 1924	%	3 1927-28	%	4 1934	%	5 1939	%
Agriculture	11,501.2	47.0	13,500	36	21,400	52.0	20,450	38	29,870	46.5
Mining & Salt Production	200.0	-	-		350	-	-		670	-
Industry	4,467.6	18.2	3,700	10	5,000	12.1	9,500	17	10,330	16.1
Transport	1,500.0	6.0	1,300	3	2,300	5.6	2,100	4	3,930	6.1
Financial & Commercial Services	-	-	6,200	16	-		8,600	16	2,600	4.1
Other Services	6,850.0	28.0	9,300	25	12,100	29.5	8,100	15	16,780	26.1
Rents	-	-	3,600	10	-		5,200	10	-	
Total	24,518.7		37,600		41,150		53,950		64,180	

The 1930s Depression

5. Estimates quoted in B.R. Mitchell, <u>European Historical Statistics 1750-1975</u> (2nd Ed.), Macmillan, London 1981, p.822. These are shown in Table A.5. The figures that Mitchell quotes are based on UN publications.

TABLE A.5   Estimates of GNP 1927-1939, Thousand ml drakmas.

Year	Current prices	At Constant 1929 Prices	Real Rate of Growth(%)
1927	44	47	
1928	46	47	0
1929	45	45	- 4.2
1930	43	49	8.8
1931	39	45	- 8.1
1932	44	48	6.6
1933	49	49	2.0
1934	53	52	6.1
1935	55	54	3.8
1936	59	56	3.7
1937	68	61	8.9
1938	67	59	- 3.2
1939	67	60	1.6

6. Assorted briefer or less detailed estimates.

(a) Diomidis, <u>Meta tin krisin</u>, p.213, estimates at constant prices (no base year given).

GNP, thousand ml drks.
1930   41
1931   37
1932   28-30
1933   32-33

(b) Haritakis, <u>Oikonomiki Epaitiris</u>, for 1929, p.265.

1929   GNP 45,000 ml drks.

(c) Anastasopoulos, _Istoria_,   p.1581

>   1937   GNP 64,401 ml drks of which
>   15,182 ml drks industry or
>   23% of GNP

(d) S.   Gregoriadis   (Ed.)   Oikonomiki   Istoria
    tis   Neoteras   Ellados,   Interview,   Athens
    1975, p.51.   The estimates are based   on   UN
    data.   No   indication   is   given whether the
    estimate are at current or constant prices.

National Income in 1938	72.342 ml drakmas of which (%)
Industry and Handicrafts	17.5
Agriculture	37.1
Transport	18.5
Profits	14.4
Services	11.9

(e) M. Malios,   I   Syhroni   Fasi   Anaptyxis   tou
    Kapitalismou   stin   Ellada,   Syhroni   Epohi,
    Athens   1975 p.37.   No   source   or   other
    details are given.

National Income in 1939	78,000 ml drakmas of which (%)
Industry	18
Agriculture	40
All other sectors	42

7. The rest of the data   presented   consists   of   a
    number   of   indexes   of   Industrial   and
    Agricultural Output   and   an   index   of   General
    Economic   Activity.   The   rates   of   growth   of
    these   indexes   are   then   compared   to   either
    sectoral or aggregate growth rates of   the   data
    already   presented   in   order   to   establish any
    areas   of   overall   consistency   and   draw   some
    conclusions.
    The   Index   of   Industrial   Output   is   quantity
    based   and   covers   food   processing,   textiles,
    metal   working,   machinery   and   engineering,
    building   materials,   chemicals,   tobacco
    processing,   wood,   leather   and   paper   and   the
    generation   of   electricity.   The   Index   of
    Agricultural Output is also quantity   based   but
    no   details   are   available   as to its coverage.
    The Index   of   General   Economic   Activity   con-
    sists   of   a   set   of   twelve   weighted   indexes
    namely: Wheat   output, exports of agricultural

products, industrial output, exports of
industrial products, imports, consumption of
beer, spirits, cigarettes, sugar and fuel,
transport and communications. All the indexes
were based on volume except for agriculture
production and imports which were value based
but estimated at constant prices. The source
does not offer any explanation of the
differences, if any, between the volume and
the constant value index.
These indexes are set out in Table A.6

TABLE A.6   Indexes of general economic activity,
industry and agriculture 1928-1939,
1928 = 100.

Year	General Index	Industrial Index	Agricultural Index
1928	100.0	100.0	100.0
1929	103.5	101.7	96.9
1930	99.8	105.2	100.0
1931	95.2	108.8	95.0
1932	91.5	102.6	132.0
1933	97.3	111.7	165.0
1934	102.2	127.4	156.3
1935	116.4	143.1	162.6
1936	115.3	141.7	160.2
1937	132.9	153.8	214.0
1938	140.1	164.2	220.0
1939	138.0	179.0	230.0

Sources:(a) General Index from Anotaton
Oikonomikon Symvoulion, Report No.
11, Oi Deiktai tis Oikonomikis
Drastiriotitos tis Ellados 1928-1934,
Athens 1935. Updated for 1935-39
from Anotaton Oikonomikon Symvoulion,
I Oikonomia, 1939, p.4.
(b) Industrial and Agricultural Indexes
from Haritakis, Oikonomiki Epaitiris
for 1938, p.41, and from the reports
of Anotaton Oikonomikon Symvoulion,
I Oikonomia, for 1937 and 1939.

TABLE A.7   Comparisons of GNP growth rates with those of various indexes 1928-1939 (% over previous year).

Year	Growth rate of real GNP	Growth rate of General Index	Growth rate of Industrial Output	Growth rate of Agricultural Output
1928	0	-	-	-
1929	- 4.2	3.5	1.7	- 3.1
1930	8.8	3.5	3.4	3.1
1931	- 8.1	- 4.6	3.4	5.0
1932	6.6	- 3.8	- 5.6	- 38.9
1933	2.0	6.3	8.8	25.0
1934	6.1	5.0	14.0	18.4
1935	3.8	13.9	12.3	4.0
1936	3.7	- 0.9	- 0.9	- 1.4
1937	8.9	15.2	8.5	33.5
1938	- 3.2	5.4	6.7	2.8
1939	1.6	- 2.1	9.0	4.5

Source: Tables A.5 & A.6.

111

Using now the data for the rate of growth of real
GNP from Table A.5 and calculating the growth
rates of Indexes from Table A.6 a composite
picture can be presented in Table A.7. Although
Table A.3 does give a run of estimates for the GNP
over the same period, the calculations are based
on current prices. No attempt was made to deflate
these because not only is there no GNP deflator
for this period, but also the only price index with
a reasonable time span starts much further back in
1914 and covers cost of living only.

COMPARISONS AND CONCLUSIONS

The data from Tables A.3 and A.4 and sections 6(d)
and 6(e) give the share of industry, on average,
between 1923 & 1939 at 16.4% although there are
two extreme values of 10% and 23%. The share of
agriculture appears to have fluctuated quite
considerably, but this is based on the data of
Table A.3 which are estimates based on current
market prices. It is interesting to note that the
share of agriculture fell when national income
fell and rose again when GNP increased. Domestic
market prices of agricultural goods suffered
heavily between 1929-32 and commodities, such as
tobacco and currants, had also to face the
pressures of falling prices abroad. This then
may well explain the decline in the share of
agriculture in GNP between 1929-31. It is also
important to note that the 10.9% growth rate of
agriculture, was on average much higher than that
of industry's which stood at about 5.5%. But
then the standard deviation of the growth rate of
agriculture was almost three time as high as that
of industry. Despite the wide fluctuation of
agricultural output, the higher growth rate of
that sector is likely to have ensured that its
share in the GNP stayed at a constant level or
even increased between 1928-1939.
    The real problem, however, arises with esti-
mates of GNP at either constant or market prices.
The figures in Tables A.3 and A.5 (first column)
do not differ significantly, but the rest of the
estimates, especially for the last years of the
1930s, do show quite considerable discrepancies.
What is more serious, however, are the discrepancies
between the rate of growth of real GNP and those
of the General Index and of Agricultural and
Industrial Output. The three instances of

negative growth rates in real GNP, 1929, 1931 and
1938 coincide only once with the index of General
Economic Activity (1931), twice with the index for
agriculture (1929 and 1931) and none at all with
that for industrial output. As these three
indexes were calculated on a consistent volume
basis over more than 12 years, it is tempting to
put greater credence on them rather than on the
GNP estimates. What can he said with a degree of
certainty is that GNP must have fallen
considerably between 1929 and 1931, but staged a
substantial recovery between 1932-35 spearheaded
by the agricultural sector. This can be partially
confirmed by examining the growth rates of four
important products; currants, wheat, tobacco and
cotton in Table A.8. Here again the evidence is
far from conclusive in view of the lack of any
data on the percentage composition of the output
of agriculture.

TABLE A.8   Growth rates of agricultural pro-
             ducts, based on volume indexes
             (1920=100), percentage increase over
             previous year, 1929-1935.

Year	Currants	Wheat	Tobacco	Cotton
1929	- 19.0	- 12.5	17.0	2.6
1930	19.8	- 15.1	- 4.1	5.8
1931	- 47.1	15.6	- 32.8	- 15.3
1932	100.1	52.0	- 33.8	60.8
1933	- 17.6	66.3	87.6	44.8
1934	30.2	- 9.5	- 23.9	13.6
1935	0.4	5.8	10.2	35.0

Source: Table 2.9.

Chapter Three

WORLD WAR II, OCCUPATION AND ITS AFTERMATH

3.1 WAR AND OCCUPATION

Greece entered the Second World War on 28 October
1940 when the dictator J.Metaxas refused an
ultimatum by Italy to allow free access for its
troops through Greece. Against great odds the
poorly equipped Greek army delivered the first
victory against the Axis by pushing the invading
Italians back through its frontiers and on into
Albania. However, when the Germans invaded
through Yugoslavia it was inevitable that Greece
could not fight a two-front war, especially
against the mechanised German troops who overran
the mainland and arrived in Athens within a few
days.

As the war lasted for about six months and
was mostly confined to Greece's northern and
mountainous frontiers, there was no extensive war
related damage as such. Some ports had been
bombed but the Germans entered Athens completely
unopposed. Crete resisted but was also occupied
by airborne troops after relatively localised
fighting. The Greek Government and the King were
evacuated to Egypt by the Royal Navy together with
all the gold bullion of the Bank of Greece. A
government in exile was set up. At the start
Greece was occupied by three forces: the Germans
who controlled mostly urban areas, and the
Italians and Bulgarians who opportunistically
invaded sections of Macedonia and Thrace. With
the collapse and surrender of Italy in September
1943 the Germans disarmed the Italian troops and
extended their occupation across the country.

The Government, which was installed by, and
collaborated with the Germans, was expected to
contribute towards the cost of the occupying

114

forces. Initially the occupiers kept up the pretence of paying for whatever goods or services they used. To that effect both the Germans and the Italians issued their own 'occupation marks' and 'Mediterranean drakmas' which were then switched into Greek drakmas at fixed rates of exchange. This created considerable confusion in transactions and these currencies were withdrawn by August 1941.

The occupying forces, and primarily the Germans, used four methods to finance themselves whilst occupying Greece[1]. Firstly, they extracted payments from the Greek Government as its contribution towards occupation costs. Progressively these contributions were met by having recourse to the printing press, and the subsequent rapid increase in banknotes was the main cause of the hyperinflation at the end of the occupation. Secondly, they purchased goods on credit via official banking channels. This method was used extensively to pay for Greek exports to Germany during the war. Since all foreign trade with the allied powers had stopped, and indeed Greek shipping trade was blockaded by the Royal Navy with the exception of Red Cross supplies, the only effective customer for Greek goods was Germany. Exports were routed by rail via Yugoslavia and the rest of occupied Europe. There was some additional trade with Italy and neutral Turkey. But these flows were insignificant. As we have already seen in Chapter Two, Greece and Germany had developed extensive trade relations based on a clearing system well before the outbreak of the war. This system was revived and extended during the occupation. In September 1942 the Germans even established a special agency called Degriges to handle these transactions. As the rate of exchange between the drakma and the reichsmark remained fixed throughout the occupation, Greek domestic prices increased rapidly and this made the few imported German goods extremely cheap. Conversely the prices of Greek exports increased rapidly in terms of reichshmarks. The Degriges agency was expected to levy a counterbalancing tax on imports in order to raise their prices to an equivalent level and use the proceeds of the tax to subsidise the prices of Greek exports to Germany. The remaining part of the tax` was added to the contributions of the Greek Government towards the costs of occupation. Since, however, there was very little that Germany could or would export to Greece during wartime, trade became completely one-sided with the Greek state accumulating large clearing credits which to all intents and purposes were unusable[2]. Thirdly, the Germans requisitioned goods which they paid for at prices that either they themselves fixed or were fixed by the collaborationist government. As inflation accelerated these payments became all but notional. Finally, when the Greek drakma became worthless because of the hyperinflation, the Germans took to selling gold sovereigns and gold twenty francs in the open market in Athens. With typical Nazi efficiency, however, they credited their own clearing balance with Degriges with the market value of the imported coins! This gold coinage added to the ones circulated by the British undercover operations, since gold was a compact and transportable method to finance the growing resistance movement. Gold coins became a major asset held by the population during the occupation and this contributed greatly to the post-war difficulties in weaning investors away from gold and back into financial assets and bank deposits.

One particular guerilla group, EDES, received from British sources more than quarter of a million gold sovereigns. Other resistance groups received around 1.2 to 1.5 million sovereigns. To these sums must be added another half a million sovereigns in the hands of the public at the start of the war as well as the sales of gold coins by the Germans.

TABLE 3.1: Indexes of note circulation and cost of living in Athens 1940-1944.

Year	Index of Note Circulation	Cost of Living Index
1940	100	100
1941	310	625
1942	1,891	13,210
1943	13,769	34,864
1944	49,845,000,000	163,910,000,000

Source: Based on data in D. Delivani: I drakmi apo tou Fthinoporou 1939, Papazisis, Athens 1946, pp.147-156. All the yearly figures relate to October-November.

The outcome of all these financial arrangements was predictable. At the outbreak of the war the Bank of Greece had in circulation 12,598 million drakmas. By November 1944 when Greece was liberated this had grown to 6,279,943,102,000 million drakmas and prices had responded accordingly. Table 3.1 summarises the consequences.

Under the wartime conditions it is not surprising that the fiscal system of the Greek state broke down altogether. During 1941-42, 67% of all government expenditures were absorbed by the cost of occupation with 78% of all expenditures being financed by printing notes. The relevant figures for 1942-43 were 65% and 81%, for 1943-44, 56% and 95% and for April-November 1944, 56% and 99% respectively. The relative decline of occupation costs to total government expenditure took place not because of German charity but because the Greek state was forced to take over the financing of public utilities and banks as the monetary system collapsed[3].

TABLE 3.2: Public Finances during the German occupation, billion drakmas at current prices, 1941-1944.

	1941-42	1942-43	1943-44
Receipts	15.2	123.2	607.9
Expenditures:			
(a) General Government	20.1	225.1	2,331.1
(b) Army of Occupation	38	290.8	3,391.1
(c) Other state organs	9.9	139.3	4,787.0
Total Expenditures	68.0	655.2	10,509.2
Deficit	52.8	532.0	9,901.3
Percentage of receipts to expenditures	29 %	18 %	6 %

Source: Ekthesis for 1941-47, p.98.

Greece's hyperinflation towards the end of the occupation ranks amongst the three worst ever recorded, the other two being Germany's during the 1920s, and Hungary's after the Second World War[4].

The inflationary situation was aggravated by the Germans, who by requisitioning all the available means of transport and purchasing or confiscating on the spot agricultural produce, created an artificial shortage thereby depriving Athens of essential food supplies. This resulted in a terrible famine during the winter of 1941-42 which contributed greatly to the total of 260,000 deaths by starvation or malnutrition recorded during the occupation. It was only after the Germans allowed Red Cross supplies to come through that the situation in the capital improved [5].

The Germans evacuated Athens on 12 October 1944. Three days later British troops entered the capital. The country was prostrate after almost four years of war and occupation. The destruction of physical and human capital was on an enormous scale. Accurate data, especially on industrial and agricultural statistics for the period of the occupation, are either non-existent, or by necessity, inaccurate. Drawing from a number of sources it is possible however to outline the toll that the war exacted from the Greek economy and people.

Loss of human life as a direct or indirect result of the war and occupation puts Greece, on a proportional basis, amongst the worst hit. Some 260,000 people died of hunger, 70,000 were executed by the occupying forces, 60,000 Greek Jews were deported to their death in concentration camps and 100,000 other people died during imprisonment, deportation, fighting with the resistance forces or with the Greek army that escaped and fought with the British in North Africa. Finally, some 30,000 died during the Italian and German invasions including the victims of air bombardment. Out of a pre-war population of 7,344,000 more than half a million perished, or over 7% of the total population[6].

Agricultural output fell precipitously reflecting the inability of farmers to produce and their unwillingness to bring goods to a market dominated by compulsory purchases at derisory prices by the forces of occupation. Villages reverted back to basic autarchy. Dairy produce, wool and egg output declined by the end of the war to less than 50% of their pre-war levels and the stock of cows, horses and pigs suffered losses between 30-50%. A similar large fall was recorded in industrial output primarily as the result of lack of raw materials, spare parts and outright

World War II

confiscation. Transport equipment suffered severely with 84% of all motor transport lost, 82% of
rail engines and 91% of all rail carriages
destroyed and 73% of all cargo and 94% of all
passenger ship tonnage sunk. Some 10% of the
housing stock was either damaged or destroyed[7].
Delivanis has estimated that the GNP which stood
in 1941 at 23 billion drakmas fell to 20 billion
by the end of 1942[8]. Estimates for the rest of
the years became impossible both because of the
lack of data and because hyperinflation had almost
eliminated monetary transactions. Table 3.3
summarises in index form some of the available
information on occupation and wartime losses.
    At the reparations conference in Paris in

TABLE 3.3   Index numbers of agricultural and
industrial output,1940-1947.

Sectors and Production	1940	1941	1942	1943	1944	1945	1946	1947
Industrial Output (1939=100)	70	30-40	13-25	15-20	-	33	54	67
Agriculture(*)								
Wheat	73	54	33	35	-	44	86	-
Barley	74	55	26	32	-	39	79	-
Maize	79	61	70	53	-	43	100	-
Tobacco	93	21	7	16	-	-	-	-
Potatoes	120	87	60	48	-	-	-	-
Total Cereals	-	-	-	-	-	46	81	-

Sources: Based on reworked data from:
    (1) Ekthesis for 1941-46, Part II, p.70.
    (2) Bakalbasis, Oikonomia, pp.31 and 94.

(*) The 1940-45 data on agricultural output
exclude the areas occupied by Bulgaria in
northern Greece and Ionian Islands, and is
based on 1939=100. For the rest of the data
1936-39 or 1938 is taken as the base year.
Figures have been rounded up. A dash indicates
data not available.

1950, Greece's claim for war restitution was set
at $4,391 ml, based on 1938 dollar prices. The
claim was apportioned as follows: $2,268 ml for
lost capital equipment, $1,200 ml for damage
caused by neglect and non-depreciation and $923 ml
for output foregone. The Greek Government had put
forward an estimate of $14,000 ml for overall war
damages both in terms of actual losses and also of
reduced output potential[9].

Estimates of the war damage are, by necessity, approximations, especially when relating to
losses of production potential and human lives
[10]. With the benefit of hindsight, possibly the
most damaging and long-lasting effect of the war
on the Greek economy was the virtual destruction
of the monetary and fiscal system. It is perhaps
indicative that most of the efforts in the
economic field of the immediate post-war Greek
governments were centred around re-establishing
the trust of the population in the national
currency and the elimination of gold coins both as
a means of exchange and store of value in preference to deposits or other financial assets.

3.2 THE IMMEDIATE POST-WAR PERIOD: PROBLEMS WORSEN

The Greek Government in exile arrived back in
Athens on 18 October 1944. It was immediately
faced with dual problems of alleviating the
shortage of food and other basic goods and of
sharing of power with the popular resistance
movement under the aegis and direction of EAM
(National Liberation Front from its Greek
initials). The resistance movement that had grown
during the occupation had assumed by the time of
liberation more than just a military role. As the
Germans had concentrated their occupation efforts
in a few urban centres, the EAM was effectively
the government of the rest of rural Greece. It had
organised its own transport and supply system,
schools, law courts and cultural activities. Its
popularity and grass roots support were undoubted,
but so was the fact that the Greek Communist Party
(KKE), outlawed and persecuted during the Metaxas
dictatorship, was in full command of EAM. A
conflict between EAM and a government including
right-wing politicians was likely. There was also
the question of the return of the King, who had
installed the Metaxas dictatorship before the
war. The actual events leading to the outbreak of

Civil War are truly Byzantine in their complexity.
Matters were not made easier by the open hostility
of the British Government towards EAM. When Left
wing forces rose in Athens during December 1944 it
was mainly British troops that suppressed them
after prolonged and bloody fighting and drove them
out of the capital. The ensuing civil war that
lasted until October 1949 bled an already
exhausted country even further, causing additional
material damage and some extra 150,000 deaths[11].
Agricultural production suffered as a direct
outcome of hostilities and because of the
extensive and forced movements of population as
areas of the country changed control and the
general collapse of an already severely damaged
transport system [12].
    The civil war ended with the complete defeat
of the Left wing forces, a feat which was made
possible by extensive US economic and military aid
to Greece. It is important to keep in mind that
throughout 1945-49, in addition to efforts
directed towards economic reconstruction, the
Greek Government was fighting a fierce war, with
the country divided politically and with most of
its resources directed towards the war effort. The
civil war left an enormous scar on Greek society
which took more than one generation to close since
the military dictatorship of 1967-74, coming only
eighteen years after the end of the civil war,
opened up again all the old wounds and raised the
ghosts and emnities of the fratricidal struggle.
    The economy and social structure of Greece
would have been completely different today had it
not been for the intervention of civil strife. It
is perhaps illustrative to consider that since the
Metaxas dictatorship of 1936 the Right had ruled
Greece almost continuously until 1981. This
excludes the years of occupation when, of course,
a pro-Nazi collaborationist government was
installed and a brief two-year interregnum when a
centrist government was elected in 1963 only to be
dismissed by the King in 1965 in preparation for
the military coup of 1967. Almost half a century
of monopoly of power by one group left its mark
both on the economic and social development of the
country.
    One of the first acts of the Greek Government
in exile upon its return to Athens was to
introduce a new drakma in place of the old and by
now worthless currency, and to fix a new rate of
exchange. In November 1944 one new drakma replaced

50 billion old ones, with the rate of exchange set at one British Military pound to 600 new drakmas. As the BM pound was fully convertible to normal sterling, the new rate of exchange was also effectively fixed against sterling as well. The dollar rate was also set at $1 = 150 drakmas and a support price for the gold sovereign was declared at 2,850 drakmas. The new drakma was made legal tender with the immediate effect of wiping out all private and public debts and, of course, savings with banks. There was considerable controversy at the time over the equity of this move, but there was very little that the Greek Government could do if it was to make a determined move against inflation. Legislation to offer indexed compensation would have been too complicated and, given the non-existence of an effective administrative system, unenforceable. Undoubtedly the new drakma caused a considerable redistribution of wealth and led, perversely, to greater reluctance of the public to entrust their wealth or savings to financial institutions. As a result the flight into gold continued with greater determination than before [13].

The battle of Athens in December 1944 and skirmishes in the countryside that were the slow beginnings of the civil war upset the monetary stabilisation plans because the Government had to continue to rely on printing notes to finance its activities. In June 1945 a far more concentrated and carefully thought-out effort was made at establishing financial stability. This was the so-called Varvaresos Plan, named after the Governor of the Bank of Greece who was also its architect.

The plan was, in essence, counterinflationary. Price controls and rationing were introduced for a variety of goods, especially those that were being distributed by the United Nations Relief and Rehabilitation Administration, (UNRRA). Imports were curtailed and the drakma devalued to Ł1 = 2,000 drakmas and $1 = 500 drakmas. The plan assumed that a negotiated increase in the aid flowing from UNRRA plus the recovery of domestic output would balance aggregate demand and supply. In order to ensure that the burden of this deflationary package was evenly distributed, a special set of taxes was imposed on industrialists, businessmen and professionals whilst wages and salaries of lower-paid employees were increased by 50%. The Bank of Greece summarised the main points of the plan as follows:

> 'Via a series of policy measures an attempt was made to balance the state budget, to adjust wages and salaries to the capacities of the economy, to enforce a strict policing of the flight to gold and of foreign exchange transactions that contravened the restrictions imposed and (to encourage) the gradual fall of prices of goods by imposing state controls on demand and supply and, in general, restricting surplus purchasing power so as to equilibrate demand towards the reduced supply and thereby stabilise the prices of goods'.
> (Ekthesis for 1941-47, p.38)

The Varvaresos plan was well-intentioned but perhaps misguided in viewing inflation at that time as mainly deriving from demand and thus to be countered by spending reductions. There was during this period an acute shortage of goods which was made worse by frozen prices and a poor harvest during the summer of 1945. Within three months of its introduction the plan was abandoned, Varvaresos resigned and "complete monetary anarchy prevailed till January 1946" [14].

Upon liberation the British Military Liaison provided immediate aid, primarily food and repairs to the transport system. By the time it handed over its functions to UNRRA in April 1945, it had distributed some 387,000 tons of supplies. UNRRA took over and handled aid until the end of June 1947. Its main task was to raise the calorific intake of the population. It also supplied industrial and agricultural equipment, raw materials, clothing and medical supplies. In all, UNRRA provided $415 million of aid over the period of its activities. The programme's importance in feeding the population whilst domestic supplies recovered cannot be overemphasised. There were, however, frequent conflicts with the Greek Government which insisted on it being responsible for the distribution of goods. UNRRA was reluctant, suspecting corruption or just plain incompetence in the allocation mechanism, and continued to insist on its own supervision and alternative methods of distribution. Specifically, there were three separate areas of problems.

Firstly, food was rationed but sold at a uniform
price. For the poorest sections of the population
even the relatively low prices of rationed food
were still too high. As a result people either
borrowed to buy food or sold part of their ration
coupons for cash on the black market and used the
proceeds to repay those loans or to buy food. For
the richer sections it also became a matter of
expediency to sell their unused or unwanted
coupons on the black market. UNRRA pressed for a
system of sliding prices with the better off being
charged more. Secondly, industrial supplies sold
via Government agencies were hoarded and when
prices rose resold for a profit. As inflation
accelerated this became a certain way to profiteer
from UNRRA's activities. Finally, the inflow of
aid induced inertia in decision-making especially
where imports and scarce foreign exchange were
concerned because the Government could always hope
that the required goods would be supplied by UNRRA
rather than through its own efforts [15].

Whilst aid provided a respite from pressing
problems, the Greek Government made yet another
attempt at normalising its fiscal and monetary
affairs. In January 1946 an Anglo-Greek agreement
was signed. It provided for loans and technical
assistance by the UK Government, and it waived the
repayment of UK wartime loans to Greece worth some
£46 ml. It also provided for the opening of an
account with the Bank of England in favour of the
Bank of Greece which would contain some of the
reserves of the Bank of Greece and £10 ml for the
UK Government. The use of that account was subject
to the consent of the Bank of England. In return
the Greek Government agreed to control wages and
prices, to cut the budget deficit and to set up a
much tighter administrative system over its credit
and monetary policies. Futhermore, together with
France and the UK, Greece was to negotiate the end
of the International Commission of Economic
Control which had remained in uninterrupted
existence since the disastrous Greco-Turkish war
of 1897 and the subsequent default of the Greek
state on its loans. The drakma was devalued again
to £1 = 20,000 drakmas with the dollar at 5,000
drakmas. The Bank of Greece undertook, yet again,
to stabilise the price of gold sovereigns by open
market operations. Import controls were
liberalised in order to alleviate some of the
domestic shortages [16].

Perhaps the most important innovation of the

Anglo-Greek agreement was the setting up of the
Currency Commission (Nomismatiki Epitropi). This
was effectively a supra-governmental body as it
included in its membership the Governor of the
Bank of Greece, the ministers of Finance and of
Co-ordination and one American and one British
member appointed by the Greek Government. The
functions of the Commission were to supervise the
activities of the Bank of Greece, the control of
the issuing of banknotes over which it had a veto,
and the allocation of bank credit in general. The
Commission could check through its inspectorate
the degree of compliance of the commercial banks
to its instructions and could impose penalties in
the form of additional reserve requirements or
even fines. At the earlier stage of its operations
its decisions required unanimity by its members
thereby leaving open the possibility of a US-UK
veto on the overall exercise of monetary policy in
Greece. The Commission was abolished in April 1982
although its Anglo-American membership had lapsed
well before then [17].

The outcome of the Anglo-Greek agreement was
far from encouraging. The liberalisation of
imports was followed by an outflow of foreign
exchange from the reserves of the Bank of Greece.
A similar situation developed with gold sovereigns
where the Bank had to sell in order to keep the
price down. Most of the dollars sold went into
speculative hoardings rather than imports.
Controls over prices were ineffective and the
escalation of the civil war brought the Greek
economy yet again to the brink of financial
collapse.

3.3   A REVIEW AND SUMMARY

It was perhaps Greece's greatest misfortune to
have as a follow-up to the harsh German occupation
a bitter and long drawn-out civil war which
delayed reconstruction and added to the already
extensive war damage. Whatever the criticisms of
the immediate post-war economic policy it must be
accepted that the options open to the Greek state,
farmers and businessmen were extremely limited,
especially after the outbreak of the civil war.
The immediate post-war policies with famine relief
as priority and some restoration of order in the
monetary sector were appropriate and inevitable.
Varvaresos's plan, despite its internal logic,

touched on too many powerful interests, especially those of the already threatened middle classes. Even if it had been given a chance, the civil war preoccupations would have swept it away. The next chapter will examine and outline the various programmes and policy measures directed at a longer-term reconstruction and redirection of the economy. The background, however, to these policy developments was the continuing civil war that had divided the country both socially and politically and diverted its meagre resources away from peaceful pursuits.

NOTES

[1] Bank of Greece: <u>Ekthesis tou Dioikitou tis Trapezis</u>, 1941, <u>1944, 1945 and 1946</u>, Athens 1947, esp. pp.24-28.
[2] A.F. Bakalbasis: <u>I Oikonomia tis Ellados</u>, Sideris, Athens 1944, pp.108-114.
[3] Delivanis, <u>I Drakmi</u>, pp.65-93.
[4] P. Cagan: 'The Theory of Hyperinflation' reprinted in R.J. Ball and P. Boyle (Eds.), <u>Inflation</u>, Penguin, London 1967, pp.118-119.
[5] On the food situation in general, see E.I.Tsouderos: <u>O Episitismos 1941-44</u>, Papazisis, Athens 1946, passim.
[6] D. Gatopoulos: <u>Istoria tis Katohis</u>, Melisa, Athens, no date, p.608. Another estimate puts the overall number killed at 405,000 but most authors seem to accept the higher estimate. See also note [7] below.
[7] S.N.Gregoriadis: <u>Istoria tis Synhronou Ellados 1941-67</u>, Vol. II, Kapopoulos, Athens 1973, pp.352-3.
[8] Delivanis, <u>I Drakmi</u>, p.78. For the effects of occupation on industry in general see N. Sideris, <u>I Elliniki Viomihania (1945-47)</u>, Athens 1948, passim.
[9] S. Gregoriadis, <u>Oikonomiki</u>, pp.55-56.
[10] For a comprehensive survey of war damages and claims, see A. Th. Angelopoulos: <u>Oikonomika</u>, Vol. I, Papazisis, Athens 1974, pp.137-161. This book also summarises a detailed, but somewhat heroic estimate of the war damage made by Bakalbasis in <u>I Oikonomia</u>, pp.230-246.
[11] There is an extensive and frequently highly partisan bibliography in Greek on the civil war. For a balanced exposition in English of the events and personalities of this period,

see C. Tsoukalas: The Greek Tragedy, Penguin, London 1969, Chs. 4-7 and D. Eudes: The Kapetanios, New Left Books, London 1972, passim. See also H. Richter, Dio Epanastaseis Kai Antepanastaseis stin Ellada 1936-1946, Volumes A and B, Exantas, Athens 1975.

[12] For estimates of the damage to the economy by the civil war, see S.N. Gregoriadis, Istoria Vol. III, Athens 1974, pp.385-395 and also F.N. Gregoriadis: Emfylios Polemos, Vol.X, Neokosmos, Athens 1975, pp.420-22.

[13] (a) B. Sweet-Escott: Greece, Political and Economic Survey 1939-53. Royal Institute of International Affairs, London 1954, pp.93-103. This is an essential reference in English for the immediate post-war period.
(b) V. Damalas: Syntomi Istoria tis Drakmis 1833-1953, Spoudai, Nos.9-10, Vol.1958-59.

[14] (a) W.O. Candilis: The Economy of Greece 1944-66, Praeger, New York 1968, pp.28-29.
(b) Delivanis, I Drakmi, Ch.7, passim.

[15] Sweet-Escott, Greece, pp.96-99.

[16] (a) Sweet-Escott, Greece, pp.101-103.
(b) Candilis, The Economy, pp.32.

[17] (a) D.I. Halikias: Dinatotites kai provlimata pistotikis politikis, Bank of Greece, Athens 1976, pp.12-20 and 35-58.
(b) Candilis, The Economy, p.33.

Chapter Four

RECONSTRUCTION AND DEVELOPMENT: A FRESH START AND
THE LOST CHANCES 1949-1960

4.1 MARSHALL AID AND THE PLANS OF RECONSTRUCTION

By February 1947, just over one year after the
Anglo-Greek agreement, the situation for the Greek
Government became extremely precarious. Elections
were held in March 1946 but growing polarisation,
simmering civil war and the mistake of the Left in
abstaining from the elections returned a
Right-wing government. A plebiscite followed on
the issue of the return of the King. This was
important as King George II had associated himself
with the pre-war dictatorship. The plebiscite
secured a substantial majority for his return. The
division now in the country was complete and the
civil war started in earnest. At that precise
moment the UK decided to withdraw both its
military and financial support for Greece. The
wartime resistance movement had now regrouped and
was waging both guerilla and occasionally full
tactical offences against the forces of the Athens
Government. The vacuum left by the British was
promptly filled by the United States. In March
1947 the announcement of the Truman Doctrine made
explicit the determination of the US to aid any
country threatened by a potential Left-wing or
communist takeover. Three hundred million dollars
were initially allocated to aid Greece, roughly
half of it to be spent on military aid, the other
half for economic development. Initially the aid
was to be administered by the American Mission for
Aid to Greece (AMAG). This body had a dual
function in overseeing defence expenditure and,
through a team of experts, to pursue agricultural,
industrial, transport and public health
programmes. Although the American intervention
sounded the death knell for the Left-wing forces

in Greece, it also meant that Greece's future economic and developmental policies would come under increasing American influence and direction. This was not an unnatural outcome in view of the fact that the US Government would be footing most of the defence expenditure, and aid would play a crucial role in the internal finances of Greece well into the 1950s [1].

Three months after the declaration of the Truman Doctrine, General Marshall, US Secretary of State, announced the intentions of the US to aid Europe's recovery in a comprehensive and systematic manner. In July 1947 sixteen countries met in Paris and established the Committee of European Economic Co-operation (CEEC) whose main aim was to channel and administer the US aid. The CEEC put forward a four-year plan based on the principle that post-war reconstruction would be founded on the increased production effort of European countries. This effort would include economic co-operation amongst them and free trade in the context of a stable monetary and fiscal framework. The exact modus operandi of the CEEC, now renamed Organisation for European Economic Co-operation (OEEC) was finalised in April 1948. Greece was a signatory of all these agreements.

Upon the announcement of the Marshall Aid Plan, AMAG's responsibilities as far as reconstruction and development were concerned were taken over by the mission to Greece of the Economic Co-operation Administration (ECA). The ECA was set up by the US in order to co-ordinate its aid effort and later on to administer Marshall Aid [2].

The terms and conditions of Greece's own agreements under the Truman Doctrine and Marshall Aid are worth some detailed examination as they set the background against which Greece's economic policy and reconstruction efforts were to be formed and developed for more than a decade [3].

In January 1947 an ECA commission headed by P.Porter arrived in Greece to examine first-hand the situation and assess the needs. One of the main conclusions of its report was that without any foreign aid and strict controls by the Greek Government, there was every likelihood of another bout of runaway inflation with all the potential disastrous consequences. The commission was highly critical of the policies pursued by the Greek Government since the liberation, and especially the lack of urgency by which raw materials and

Reconstruction and Development

equipment imported by UNRRA were being utilised.
The Truman Doctrine was announced before the
commission had completed its report. Its
recommendations, however, were incorporated in the
agreement that Greece and the United States signed
on 20 June 1947 under the Truman Doctrine
provisions [4]. A commission of ECA to Greece was
to supervise the utilisation of all aid. The
commission had extensive powers not only to advise
but also to direct the Greek Government in using
the aid and helping it to plan and dispose of
domestic resources. In general, the Greek
Government undertook to keep both the commission
and the US Government informed of any developments
or plans that would affect the aid flows. Indeed
the provisions of the treaty that the commission
would have supervisory role in the use of domestic
as opposed to US aid resources, reflected the
recommendations of the Porter report that the
Greek Government's budget should be submitted for
approval to ECA before it was put into effect.
Separate provisions related to military aid under
the Mutual Security Agency. On 2nd July 1948 the
Greek Government signed another treaty relating to
Marshall Aid. This agreement was meant to
complement rather than substitute the Truman
Doctrine treaty. In essence it required that in
using US aid the Greek Government would do its
best to stabilise prices and exchange rates, to
balance its budget and to re-establish confidence
in the domestic monetary system as well as
enforcing law and order [5].

Both these treaties ensured that no economic
or military decision of any consequence could be
taken by the Greek Government without the prior
approval or consent of the US Administration or
its representatives in Athens. This was the
outcome not so much of the servile attitude of the
Greek Government as of the realities of its total
dependence on US economic and military aid.

It was soon after signing the Marshall Aid
agreement that the Greek Government drafted the
first of a number of truly comprehensive medium to
long-term reconstruction and development plans.
The significance of these plans laid in that they
represented, for the first time since liberation,
a systematic scheme for the development of all
sectors of the economy and also for a comple-
mentary financial plan. Although these plans were
never really put into action and were subjected to
numerous amendments and revisions, they none-

130

the-less encapsulated both the attitudes of the
Greek and American Governments as to the future
directions of the Greek economy and the comparative role of the state and of private
enterprise in these developments. The first plan,
covering 1948-49 to 1952-53, was submitted by the
Greek Government in November 1948 to OEEC, after
consultation with ECA. As the OEEC was the
European co-ordinating counterpart of the Marshall
Plan in Europe it had required its members to
draft plans in conjunction with the aid they would
be receiving [6].

The aims of the plan were as follows:
(a)   to restructure the monetary, fiscal and
      credit system on a sound basis;
(b)   to make further use of the productive
      resources of the economy;
(c)   to maintain, and where possible to increase
      to tolerable levels, the standard of living
      of the population;
(d)   to eliminate the deficit in the balance of
      payments.

The plan, however, laid heavy stress in
shifting the centre of gravity of the planning
effort of the state from agriculture to industry.
The preamble of the plan indicated that shortages
of domestic investment funds before the war made
Greece's industrialisation impossible. Foreign
investment could not be relied on because the
expected returns were too low. Now, however,
Marshall Aid would provide Greece with the breakthrough that was needed. Once the take-off was
achieved, new industries could be financed by
private investment, both domestic and foreign.
Private capital would then have every incentive to
move in and continue and complete the
industrialisation of Greece once the Marshall Aid
Plan was completed [7]. The role of the state in
the Plan was seen as an initial co-ordinator. In
discussing domestic sources of investment, the
plan stated explicity that any intervention by the
state was meant to be temporary and would be
removed as soon as circumstances permitted:

> 'Let it be noted that the Government
> despite all the planned interventionist
> policies is certain that private enter-
> prise will move fast and effectively so
> as to become the main agent of the
> reconstruction of the country' [8].

The Plan went on to detail, sector by sector, all the proposed developments. Emphasis was laid on the mechanisation of agriculture and the greater exploitation of Greece's ample hydro-electric and lignite potential for the production of energy, an absolute precondition for the expansion of industrial output. The industrial plans allowed for the establishment of an oil refinery, a small steel mill and expansion of the production of chemicals, especially those of fertilisers. Total investment expenditure ran to $1,186.6 ml over four years. Of this total $572.8 ml would be spent on imported goods and the rest at home. The Plan estimated that $475 ml would be found from foreign aid, the rest would come from domestic sources. To cope with these extensive demands made upon the domestic financial system, the plan stressed the need for the complete reorganisation of the banking, financial and fiscal systems in order to ensure the maximum flow of saving and the effective collection of taxes.

Within seven months of submitting this plan to OEEC, the government had to withdraw it and revise it extensively. The continuing civil war, the poor harvest of 1948 and shortages of foreign exchange had disrupted the economy to such an extent that it would have been impossible to fulfil any of the Plan's targets by 1952, the year up to which Marshall Aid was supposed to run. A revised version of the plan was submitted to OEEC in June 1949 covering the 1949-50 period and a further version was issued in January 1950 covering 1950-51 and 1951-52[9]. The planned foreign exchange expenditures for 1948-52 had originally been set at $572 ml but were now scaled down to $375 ml. Although the aim of the plans remained the same, there were drastic reductions in the planned expenditures in most areas. The revised plan concentrated on industry, agriculture, land reclamation and refugee resettlement at the expense of public health, education, sanitation and water supply programmes[10]. The Plan, however, made it abundantly clear that any further progress would depend on the continuation of US aid, despite the fact that this was meant to end in 1952. So, for example, the projected deficit in the current account of the balance of payments for 1950-51 which stood at $300.1 ml was to be covered by at least $263.6 ml of aid and that for 1951-52 of

$221.9 ml by $181.6 ml of aid. The rest of the funds would be found from war reparations from Italy and Germany and from direct investments. The Plan stated, rather forlornly, that:

> '... there are well-founded hopes that foreign capitalists will begin to exhibit active interest in investment in this country. It is also highly probable that Greek-owned foreign funds and capital will also be attracted. It seems, however, that it will also be necessary to find a way to continue for a while foreign aid to Greece, even at a reduced scale after June 1952.'
> (Ypomnima, p. 9)

An additional problem in the execution of these plans was not just the shortage of foreign exchange necessary to finance capital imports, but also the difficulties of raising the appropriate amount of drakmas for domestic investment expenditure. As the memory of the wartime inflation was still fresh in people's minds, both the Greek Government and the ECA were reluctant to resort to excessive credit creation. Domestic savings and faith in drakma-denominated financial assets were still minimal. Indeed the original plan submitted in November 1948 made it unequivocally clear that the drakmas necessary for domestic investment expenditure would be found via the Counterpart Fund [11]. The Bank of Greece used the dollar aid to sell foreign exchange to the importers of goods. The drakma proceeds were then deposited in a blocked account, the Counterpart Fund, and could not be used or released without ECA's permission. Great care was exercised in using these funds because of the potential inflationary effect this may have had on an economy with an extremely inelastic domestic supply response and a virtually blocked imports sector. Needless to say, these drakma funds were used not only for investment expenditures but also to help finance the large deficit in the current expenditures account of the government budget. The dependence of the Greek economy on US aid during this period cannot be overemphasised. A quantitative appraisal of this dependence is given in Section 4.3 below.

The following quotation is taken from the 1952 annual report of the governor of the Bank of

Greece. The excerpt fully illustrates the realisation by the highest policy-making bodies in the
country that the task and direction of the
reconstruction was now resting completely with the
United States:

> 'Greece, like all other European
> countries, put forward a long term plan
> of economic reconstruction requiring a
> total of $1200 ml. Greece received
> during 1948-52 economic aid worth
> $976 ml and spent about half of it on
> reconstruction. The main factors that
> stopped Greece from fully utilising the
> American aid were, amongst others, the
> ... (civil war) ..., and the undertaking
> of excessive military expenditures by a
> country with already a low level of
> national income.... Finally, the firm
> monetary policy pursued was an addi-
> tional deflationary factor as it
> precluded the channelling into recon-
> struction of all the drakma proceeds of
> aid .... The reduction of the US aid to
> Greece to completely insufficient levels
> generates problems for the completion of
> the effort of reconstruction. The
> demand that Greece should be aided in
> order to finance and complete all the
> investments necessary to exploit the
> resources of the country is a supreme
> demand soundly justified ... We hope
> that this just request of Greece will be
> finally fulfilled by the powerful
> American ally. It is essential to use
> all the means and ways available to
> raise finance for these investments from
> abroad. But the most secure venue will
> be offered by the provision of
> sufficient American aid ....' [Bank of
> Greece, Ekthesis tou Dioikitou, 1952,
> Athens 1953, pp.(XXII-XXIII)].

4.2 THE 1953 DEVALUATION

The outbreak of the war in Korea in June 1950,
hardened America's attitude towards the European
recovery programme in general and Greece's
performance so far in particular. The civil war
had ended in the summer of 1949, with the complete

defeat of the Left but the country's dependence on US aid was undiminished. In September 1950, P.Porter, the head of ECA's mission to Greece, announced a reduction in the planned Marshal Aid to Greece for 1950-51 and made it abundantly clear that the US was not pleased with the progress made by the Greek authorities in increasing taxation revenues, decreasing budget deficits and lessening their dependence on aid. Further recommendations were made during February 1951 by ECA on credit restrictions, price controls, rationing and a further and more drastic revision of the already revised long-term reconstruction plan. Finally, US aid was to be cut back even further. The Greek Government was faced yet again with a severe crisis. It was at this particular point that a clean break was made with even the pretence of attempting a radical and long-term restructuring of the Greek economy with a shift away from agriculture. There were four basic reasons why this change in the course of economic policy took place.

Firstly, the successive reductions in American aid imposed an effective imports constraint and therefore limited the extent by which industry could be re-equipped with capital and machinery.

Secondly, despite the successful conclusion of the civil war, defence expenditure was now absorbing an inordinate amount of both the government's budget and of the GNP. For the 1948-52 period it absorbed 47% of the state budget and 9.4% of GNP[12]. This development reflected the outcome of the cold war climate, given that three out of the four neighbouring countries of Greece, Albania, Yugoslavia and Bulgaria, were now under communist rule. There was also explicit pressure by the US Government, especially in the February 1951 ECA's economic recommendations, that stressed the financing of projects of military importance over all others.

Thirdly, there was also a shift in the willingness of the Greek state either to resist US pressures or to make a truly determined effort to break the financial deadlock, reduce military expenditure and press on with the plan for industrialisation. A clear indication of this change in official opinion and direction was the second Varvaresos plan of 1952[13]. This plan outlined the options available to the Greek economy in view of continuing reductions in US aid. It concluded that as long as the reduced US aid was used to finance defence a thorough revamping of the domestic monetary and fiscal systems would produce enough finance to close the balance of payments deficit in four years. In the context of the Varvaresos plan any proposals for industrialisation were abandoned in favour of using the available resources for the immediate increase in the standard of living by spending more on municipal housing projects, agriculture and so on. Sweet-Escott summarised the essence of the plan thus:

> 'What was in doubt at the time the [Varvaresos] report was issued, was what was to happen next as the result of the change since 1950 in the American attitude to Greece's economic problems. The change was due mainly to the conviction that rearmament must be put before an improvement in the standard of living.' (Greece, pp.115-116)

This change in emphasis was made even more explicit by the dissolution in early 1952 of ECA's mission to Greece and the assumption of its responsibilities by the Mutual Security Agency which had been established under the provisions of the Truman Doctrine treaty.

Fourthly, and finally, there were some instances of actual hostility and direct interference by international organisations or by the US towards the industrialisation plans of Greece. The evidence is by necessity anecdotal and hardly conclusive. Taken in conjunction however with the declared change in the emphasis of US policy, it does not contradict the main thrust of the argument:

> 'For the foreign economic missions not only did not encourage industrialisation but even fought against it. When in 1949 a steel mill was given to Greece by the Germans as part of war reparations, P.Porter, chief of the US economic mission, imposed his veto. The machinery never left Hamburg and was eventually sold on behalf of the Greek Government as scrap. According to the former representative of Greece to the OECD, Professor Nicolaides, industrialisation

> met with unrestrained reaction mainly
> because of its effects on the foreign
> trade of the interested countries, but
> also largely because of the economic
> self-sufficiency of Greece which would
> have resulted from it in a few year's
> time.'
> (Tsoukalas, The Greek Tragedy, p. 129)

Since 1947 when US aid started to flow, the Greek
monetary authorities had been faced with the
double task of maintaining strict credit control
so as to dampen inflation and simultaneously to
ensure that the available finance was channelled
to industry and agriculture but within the
confines of the foreign exchange reserves. As the
commercial banks had no funds since the public
mistrusted deposits, the Bank of Greece supplied
them with direct deposits. The Bank of Greece, in
its turn, obtained funds from public corporations
and from the contributions to the social security
schemes, all of which had to hold deposits with
it. Until 1950 these compulsory deposits were
held with the National Bank of Greece which,
strictly speaking, was a private bank. As from
1950, however, all available public sector funds
had to be deposited with the Bank of Greece which
then redeposited a substantial proportion of them
with commercial banks thus supplying them with a
source of lending funds. The commercial banks in
their turn had to maintain considerable reserves
with the Bank of Greece, usually 10-20% of their
deposits[14]. By 1953 almost a quarter of bank
loans were derived directly from the redepositing
activities of the Bank of Greece. Given the
potentially inflationary effects of the direct
financing of the private sector by the central
bank, matters were not made better by the
existence of nearly 12.5 million gold sovereigns
in the hands of the public. At the current price
of gold in 1951 this represented nearly 8% of the
total stock of money (banknotes plus deposits).
The Bank of Greece had continued its intervention
policy by selling gold in order to stabilise its
price and hence help reduce inflationary
expectations. These operations were also viewed
as counter-inflationary because they withdrew from
circulation banknotes as the Bank of Greece sold
sovereigns to the public. At the same time,
however, gold sovereigns were being used not just
for hoarding but to effect transactions [15].

137

Until the late 1950s, the prices of land, houses and flats were quoted in gold sovereigns and their purchase and sale was also undertaken for cash in gold. Even the ever-present 'proika' or dowry that Greek brides were expected to bring into the marriage was frequently expressed and given in gold.

The drakma meanwhile had been devalued in January 1946 from its June 1945 price of $1 = 500 drks to $1 = 5,000 drks. To avoid further devaluations an ingenious scheme of foreign exchange intervention was developed. Exporters of goods upon selling their foreign exchange proceeds to the Bank of Greece, received a certificate from the Bank testifying to that transaction. Importers of goods or other purchasers of foreign exchange needed these certificates before they could obtain permission to purchase dollars from the Bank of Greece at the official fixed price. A booming secondary market developed for these certificates, with the official blessing of the Bank of Greece, which also intervened actively in the market in order to manipulate or control their prices. By June 1948, and taking into account the open market price of these certificates, the drakma stood at $1 = 10,000 drks. But the devaluation was inevitable and it did take place in September 1949 when the price was set at $1 = 15,000 drks.

Throughout the period of relatively fixed exchange rates but high domestic rates of inflation, the state subsidised exports directly but also devised another indirect scheme which became widely open to abuse. Exporters of goods in addition to the marketable certificates of foreign exchange they received from the Bank of Greece, were also allocated saleable rights (permits) to import non-essential or luxury goods. There was a secondary market in these permits as well. Thus the officially declared rate of exchange was in essence irrelevant, as there were a number of different effective exchange rates for different classes of imports. During 1952-53 this complicated system of direct and indirect export subsidies was either abolished or considerably streamlined. By this time, however, there was a widespread feeling that the drakma was still overvalued vis-a-vis the dollar. This did inhibit the opening up of the Greek economy to international trade and of course delayed or postponed the readjustment of domestic prices to

138

Reconstruction and Development

those of the international markets. Given the
continuing dependency of the Greek economy on
overseas sources of funds it was by now becoming
imperative to attempt a long-term solution, which
by definition would have involved an internal
price readjustment to the international prices.

Calculations using the movements of American
British and Greek retail and wholesale price
indexes with 1938 as the base year, and
comparisons of their relative movements to the
movements of the official price of the dollar and
sterling, showed that by February 1953 the drakma
was overvalued by 49.5% compared to the dollar and
about 72% against sterling [16]. Another estimate
set the drakma overvaluation against the dollar in
March 1953 at 33%:

'Measured in terms of relative changes
in the purchasing power (and on the
assumption of equilibrium position in
1938) the drakma was overvalued versus
the dollar by 33% in March 1953. This
suggested that official exchange rate
should be adjusted from 15,000 drks to
22,500 drks per US dollar. But by their
very nature such calculations cannot be
reliable, particularly when the price
statistics available are inadequate. In
particular for the post-war drakma, the
wide divergence between the movements of
the prices of Greek exports and of other
prices makes it necessary to use the
utmost caution in interpreting the
results of such calculaticns. The dollar
prices of the three main Greek export
staples, which account for about 60% of
total exports, were estimated in 1952 to
be only approximately 40% higher than
before the war, while the dollar prices
of other goods had increased, on the
average, by more than 125%. This does
not, of course, mean that the world
prices of Greek exports were to be taken
as a basis for determining the extent to
which the drakma ought to be devalued.
It was a factor, however, to be given
serious consideration when making the
decision. Since no mathematically
accurate estimate was possible, it was
probably safer to err, if at all, on the
side of caution, by choosing a rather

high percentage for exchange adjustment
in preference to a rather low percentage.' (Eliades, Stabilisation, p.51)

In sum, all these estimates of the overvaluation were by necessity approximations in view
of the effective multiple exchange rates in
existence, the inaccuracy of the Greek price
indexes used and the potential secondary, and
offsetting effects, of the rises in the domestic
price level once the devaluation had taken place.
To some extent, however, the proposed devaluation
was an act of faith. Given that tobacco, raisins
and currants accounted at the time for more than
50% of the value of Greek exports and given the
low price elasticity of demand in general for
agricultural products, it was unlikely that the
devaluation would have made a significant impact
on Greece's exchange earnings. There were,
however, five important considerations that had to
be taken into account in deciding to devalue.
Firstly, as Table 4.1 indicates, the economy was

TABLE 4.1   Indexes   of   economic   activity   and
inflation 1945-1954

Year	Index of Industrial Production 1939=100	Index of Agricultural Production (Crops and animals) 1957-59=100	Cost of Living Index(% increase over previous year, 1938=100)
1945	33	36	664.0
1946	54	47	20.2
1947	67	55	41.6
1948	73	52	14.7
1949	87	66	7.8
1950	110	60	12.5
1951	125	63	5.1
1952	124	65	-
1953	141	83	-
1954	172	82	-

Sources: Candilis, The Economy,pp.49, 65 and 69.
L.   Shaw,   Post-war   Growth   in   Greek
Agricultural   Production,   Centre   of
Planning   and   Economic   Research,   Athens
1969, p.50.

showing signs of recovery and the rate of inflation was on a downward trend. Industry had reached by 1950 its pre-war level of activity and agricultural output following a fall in 1949-50 was exhibiting a healthy upward trend. Indeed, as Table 4.2 shows, by 1952 most of the important food products had achieved their pre-war levels.

These data and those of Table 4.1 are not comparable because of differences in the base years, but at least they offer some broad perspectives of changes and movements in important economic magnitudes. It was therefore expected that the economy could respond to any changes in aggregate demand caused by the devaluation.

TABLE 4.2   Index of agricultural output as percentage of 1935-38

Output	1949	1952
Wheat	109.3	136.8
Oats	97.1	100.0
Maize	87.3	90.3
Barley	99.6	108.1
Rye	75.5	100.0
Potatoes	266.3	293.9
Tobacco	75.4	68.9
Olive Oil	199.3	62.1
Currants	56.9	48.7
Raisins	101.4	127.6
Cotton	108.4	173.4

Source: Candilis, The Economy, p.64.

Secondly, the low official rate of exchange meant that the sum of drakmas realised by selling the foreign aid dollars was proportionally reduced thus limiting the capacity of the state to expand the investment programme or just to cover its budget deficit. Thirdly, the effective subsidisation of imports resulting from the overvaluation did not necessarily benefit the Greek consumers. Total lack of competition from domestic suppliers and the overall level of excess demand meant that the importers of goods could increase their prices thereby cancelling any of the beneficial effects. Fourthly, the government was either unwilling or unable to capture this monopoly profit via taxes and redistribute it. So domestic prices increased because of lack of competition and excess demand, importers' income increased proportionately whilst income taxes did not, thus adding to the inflationary pressures. Finally, the state lost some revenue by handing out saleable certificates of foreign exchange or importing rights to exporters. Although this was a deliberate policy decision rather than the direct outcome of foreign exchange overvaluation, it allowed profits to be made that the state did not share in. All this was the direct outcome of excess demand for dollars reflecting not only the excess demand for imports caused by the deficiencies in aggregate supply in Greece but also the artificially low prices of foreign exchange [17].

The devaluation did take place in April 1953 with the new rate set at $1 = 30,000 drks. At the same time in a symbolic attack on the memories of the wartime hyperinflation, three zeros were excised from the existing banknotes and prices in general so that the new exchange rate was $1 = 30 drks.

4.4   THE AFTERMATH: OPPORTUNITIES FOREGONE

The immediate impact of the devaluation was expected to be on domestic prices, and according to calculations made at the time, they rose during the following year by 25%. In 1953 there was no systematic and countrywide retail price index in existence. The first one to be calculated in the post-war period was in 1959. The Bank of Greece estimated a cost of living index based on prices in Athens. As the base point was 1938 the intervening hyperinflation of the war made systematic year to year comparisons meaningless. But irrespective of the inaccuracies of the data, prices did rise by a considerable amount following the devaluation. The Government did take some transitional measures to cushion the effect of the devaluation on the standard of living including some subsidies on imports and on the prices of essential goods. At the same time, however, the complicated system of import restrictions and export subsidies was progressively dismantled. The liberalisation of the import regulations did, of course, cancel some of the beneficial effects of the devaluation. In fact the deficit in the balance of trade increased in 1954 from $109.2 to

$167.5ml. Invisibles, however, also increased and
so did private capital inflows leading to a fall
in the overall deficit, including capital transactions, from $56.2 ml in 1953 to $15.8 ml in 1954
(see Table 4.3).
    The long-term effects of the 1953 devaluation
have been the subject of discussion and controversy. Certainly in terms of foreign exchange
earnings its effects were limited. It did not
lessen the dependence of Greece on imports neither
did the structure of primary agricultural exports
change for several years. Perhaps its most
important effect was a shifting of gear towards
greater freedom of private enterprise, an opening
up of the Greek economy to internatinal trade by
dismantling most of the complex import controls
and export subsidies, and by eliminating some of
the price and income distribution distortions
caused by the extensive use of multiple exchange
rates. D. Halikias summarised the overall effects
thus:

'The devaluation of the drakma in 1963
was a landmark in the post-war economic
history of Greece. It was combined with
the liberalisation of imports and gave a
push towards a gradual liberalisation of
economic activities from various state
rules and regulations.'
(Dinatotites, p.43)

    As Table 4.3 indicates, the balance of
payments right through this period exhibited a
deficit which was covered by capital movements
deriving almost exclusively from the US aid and
war reparations. The agricultural sector still
dominated economic activity and fixed capital
investment accounted for a small percentage of GDP
and most of it, anyway, was directed towards
housing (see Table 4.4). The move of private
sector investment activity towards housing and
construction was to remain a characteristic of
capital accumulation in post-war Greece down to
the present day. It has caused an enormous amount
of discussion and concern precisely because right
from the post-war period the private sector
shunned investment in industry or agriculture and
concentrated instead on housing. This issue will
be examined in greater detail in Chapter Five. But
perhaps the most important characteristic of the
Greek economy during this period was its

143

TABLE: 4.3 Balance of Payments 1947-1960, million
dollars, current prices.

Year	Trade Balance	Invisible Balance	Current Account Balance	Net Capital Movements
1947	-278	32	-246	127.5
1948	-298.7	35.2	-263.5	256.8
1949	-282.8	26.2	-256.6	270
1950	-309.2	30.4	-278.8	299.5
1951	-324.1	37	-287.1	297.3
1952	-162.1	48.8	-113.3	133.5
1953	-109.2	84.4	-24.8	81
1954	-167.5	94.1	-73.4	89.2
1955	-158.3	117.8	-40.5	95.1
1956	-255.7	143.2	-112.5	115
1957	-286.1	186	-100.1	89.1
1958	-267.8	169.9	-97.1	91.6
1959	-237.8	182.3	-55.5	110.2
1960	-296.3	207.7	-88.6	47.2

Source: Bank of Greece, In Elliniki Oikonomia
kata to Etos 1966, Athens 1967,
pp.108-9, Monthly Statistical Bulletin
of Bank of Greece, various issues.

continuing complete dependence on external aid as
a means to finance the deficit in the balance of
payments and as the key source of government
revenue, and by extension, of state investment. A
detailed examination of this dependence will put
into perspective the devaluation of 1953 and also
the fiscal policies followed throughout this
period.
    Until the late 1950s, the commercial banking
system was thoroughly and tightly controlled by
the Bank of Greece and the Currency Commission.
All the banks were obliged to maintain extensive
reserves with the Bank of Greece. In the early
1950s, these stood at 10-20% of their deposits,
but they were gradually reduced in 1956 to 8% and
then to 5% by 1961. There were additional and
complicated rules concerning the size, type and
distribution of loans, all of which required prior
notification and/or permission by the monetary
authorities. Furthermore, the banks were expected
to place a fixed percentage of their assets in
government bonds. This percentage stood at 5% in

TABLE 4.4 Sectoral composition of GDP at factor cost as percentage of total 1948-1960. Fixed capital investment (FCI) as percentage GDP, and dwellings as percentage of FCI. Rate of growth of GDP (change over previous year). All at 1958 constant prices.

Year	Agriculture	Industry	Services	FCI as % of GDP	Dwelling Construction as % of FCI	Rate of Growth of GDP %
1948	28.6	10.7	55.6	14.1	33.3	-
1949	33.2	11.0	50.9	13.4	34.0	19.3
1950	28.8	13.7	51.2	20.1	30.3	0.3
1951	30.3	13.6	50.5	16.6	30.5	7.9
1952	28.5	13.4	52.2	15.7	33.6	-0.2
1953	31.9	13.5	48.5	14.6	43.1	12.9
1954	30.9	14.7	47.7	15.6	39.5	2.9
1955	30.1	15.1	48.2	15.4	43.0	6.7
1956	29.2	15.7	47.9	17.6	39.5	6.0
1957	30.7	15.6	46.6	16.4	34.8	7.6
1958	27.6	16.5	48.0	21.4	31.2	2.5
1959	27.8	16.2	47.5	23.6	25.5	4.2
1960	25.0	17.3	48.2	29.7	21.2	3.0

Source: (a) National Accounts of Greece 1948-1970. National Statistical Service of Greece, Publication No. 21, Athens 1972, various tables.
(b) Monthly Statistical Bulletin of the Bank of Greece, various issues.

NB: Agriculture includes fishing and forestry. Industry covers manufacturing only. The rest of the sectors adding up to 100% include mining, electricity, gas, water and construction. Throughout this period dwellings accounted for about 50% of total construction.

1957, 10% in 1958, 18% in 1961 and 20% in 1963. Interest rates charged on loans and paid on deposits were also tightly controlled with an extensive system of differentiation in order to favour certain sectors or activities, especially loans to exporters and agriculture [18]. In addition to all these controls, as has already been indicated, the Bank of Greece provided the commercial banks with a considerable proportion of their funds and therefore became indirectly an important source of loans. This was absolutely necessary during the early post-war years because the investing public had scant faith in bank deposits, and commercial banks were unable to attract any because of the extensive controls on their activities. The consequences of these redepositing activities of the Bank of Greece meant that until the mid-1950s more than one-third of all credit and loans in the economy originated from the Central Bank (see Table 4.5).

TABLE 4.5 Direct and Indirect financing by the Bank of Greece as a percentage of the total finance extended by the banking sector, 1948-1957.

Year	Credit Supplied by Bank of Greece	
	Total	of which Directly
1948	70.2	12.8
1949	67.2	11.8
1950	69.0	12.0
1951	69.8	14.0
1952	66.3	14.5
1953	45.3	8.3
1954	43.3	10.1
1955	41.1	7.8
1956	34.2	7.21
1957	32.8	7.1

Source: Bank of Greece, I Elliniki Oikonomia kata to Etos 1957, Athens 1958, pp.125-130.

It is important to note, however, that this direct dependence on finance from the Central bank diminished rapidly after 1955. This was due to no small part to a savings campaign that was launched during 1956 accompanied by a sharp increase in interest rates offered on deposits from 7% to 10%. The timing of the campaign and of the interest rate rise must have been unusually good as it caught Greek savers during a period when they were reappraising their attitudes towards financial assets in general and bank deposits in particular. The falling inflation rate must have contributed to this change in attitudes [19]:

> '... From 1950 until 1956 the real return on M_2 (banknotes plus sight deposits plus saving and time deposits) was negative, because the nominal rate of interest was lower than the rate of inflation ... during this period the propensity to save in the economy was exceptionally low whilst the demand for money per unit of income stayed at a low level. The falling rate of inflation during 1957-58 had as a result the actual increase in the real rate of return, which must have acted as a strong incentive for savers to demand money and encouraged the rate of saving for the whole economy.'

The growth in savings and bank accounts continued well after the 1956 rise in interest rates as Table 4.6 shows.

TABLE 4.6   Deposits of the private sector with banks 1951-1959, million drakmas.

Year	Total	Sight	Time
1951	901	697	69
1952	992	748	82
1953	1,579	1,175	141
1954	2,250	1,608	298
1955	3,102	2,093	523
1956	4,319	1,898	1,757
1957	7,611	2,287	4,102
1958	10,032	2,460	5,771
1959	13,627	2,928	8,543

Source: Zolotas, Nomismatiki, p.82.

TABLE 4.7 US aid to Greece and its utilisation and role in Government finance 1944-1962

(a) Outright aid $1,918.3 ml
     Loans $224.2 ml
     Military aid $1,600.5 ml
     Total $3,743.0 ml
     These figures include aid, USA's share of UNRRA donations, donations by USA charities, donations of military equipment and loans.

(b) Greek Government finance and US aid, million drakmas, current prices.

Financial Year	1 Current Deficit (-) or Surplus (+)	2 State Investment Expenditure	3 Total Deficit (1+2) (*)	4 US aid	5 US aid as % of 2	6 US aid as % of 3
1947-48	-1,062	518	1,580	1,578	304.0	99.8
1948-49	-980	1,166	2,146	1,969	168.8	91.7
1949-50	-1,684	1,950	3,634	1,968	101.0	54.1
1950-51	-1,383	2,439	3,822	3,534	144.8	92.0
1951-52	-817	1,716	2,533	2,008	117.0	79.2
1952-53	-221	1,458	1,679	808	55.4	48.0
1953-54	-530	1,275	1,805	1,622	127.0	89.8
1954-55	-689	1,397	2,086	1,378	98.0	66.0
1955-56	-501	1,792	2,293	1,736	96.0	75.7
1957	+193	2,209	2,016	1,261	57.0	62.5
1958	+1,044	2,600	1,556	674	25.9	43.0
1959	+657	3,374	2,717	975	28.8	35.8
1960	+848	4,144	3,296	825	19.9	25.0
1961	+1,497	5,056	3,559	987	19.5	27.7
1962	+1,550	5,853	4,303	482	8.2	11.2

Source: Karavias, I Voithia, pp.203, 219-220.

TABLE 4.7 continued

In part (b) of the table the data for 1955-56 cover 18 months. From then on the state budget apparently switched to a calendar year. The source gives separate figures for the portion of US aid that was used for investment purposes rather than current expenditure coverage. In the table, the figures are aggregated together. The source does not make clear whether the figures include military aid. This, however, is unlikely as military aid was given mostly in kind.

(*)   The figure for column 3, Total Deficit or financing requirement, is given by adding together state investment expenditures and the current deficit. When the current deficit becomes a surplus then investment expenditures are substracted, rather than added, to give the overall financing requirement.

_____

This surge in savings helped to release the Bank of Greece from the task of being the main source of finance for industry and commerce. The situation, however, with respect to the financing of the budget deficit, remained quite serious until the late 1950s. As Table 4.7 shows, until 1957 US aid contributed more than 75% to the overall budget deficit requirements, including investment expenditures. Similarly, Table 4.8 shows that in terms of capital accumulation and coverage of the balance of payments, US aid was also an extremely important contributor to the resources available to the Greek economy.

The year 1957 appears to be a hiatus both for the financing of the Greek budget and the overall financial situation of the country. For a start, as can be seen from Table 4.7 (b) the budget yielded a surplus in the current account for the first time in the post-war period thus providing a source of finance for investment expenditures. Secondly, the surge of private savings after 1956 supplied the banking sector with the necessary funds to channel into investment and other projects, and finally there was a rapid falling off in US economic aid which slowed down to a trickle and all but stopped after 1962. Military aid, however, continued to flow as part of the Mutual Security Agreement under the Truman

TABLE 4.8 The role of US aid in the GNP and current balance of payments, 1948-1962.

Year	US aid as % of GNP	US aid as % of Gross Fixed Capital expenditures	US aid as % of the Deficit in the Current Balance of Payments
1948	2.9	42.0	74.0
1949	10.8	83.3	100.0
1950	14.9	76.5	95.0
1951	11.5	78.7	90.9
1952	7.0	54.5	88.4
1953	3.3	26.8	327.0
1954	3.0	20.8	78.4
1955	3.0	19.8	214.0
1956	3.0	19.4	79.5
1957	1.9	12.4	34.8
1958	0.9	4.7	29.1
1959	1.1	5.8	53.3
1960	1.1	5.5	48.1
1961	0.9	4.4	43.3
1962	0.5	3.9	22.9

Source: Karavias, I Voithia, pp.221 and 223.

NB The GNP data are at factor cost, current prices in ml drks. Those for the Balance of Payments in current dollar prices. Where the percentage exceeds 100, presumably the aid was accumulated as foreign exchange reserves or used to repay loans. The source does not specify whether the sum of the US aid refers only to that used for capital expenditure, although by inference there is reason to believe that this is not so, i.e. the data refer to the sum total of US aid.

Doctrine and as part of NATO obligations.

4.4 CONCLUSIONS

The developments in the Greek economy during the period can be summarised under four broad headings. Firstly, there was an all too brief period of reconstruction with emphasis on re-establishing faith in the monetary system and national currency. Secondly, an attempt was made at a systematic and long-term plan for restructuring the economy with a shift towards industrialisation. The finance for that plan had to be found from abroad, and primarily from the United States. The on-going civil war and the cold war climate meant that the US became far keener to see Greece pursue an anti-communist struggle than devote its efforts to industrialisation. There is no doubt, however, that the intransigence of the Greek Right, and the repeated political and strategic errors of the Left, ensured that the shift in US policy was not resisted by the Greek Government, which by the late 1940s was eager to deal with the threat from the Left once and for all. Thirdly, the 1953 devaluation was an indication that a policy of opening up the Greek economy to international trade was to be pursued. This diminished the chances, if any, of pushing forward with the plan of domestic industrialisation under the protection of tariffs and of an overvalued currency. Finally, the continuing dependence until the late 1950s on US aid in order to cover and pay most of the essential activities in the economy diminished both the will and the economic ability of the Greek Government to follow policies of which the US might have disapproved.

Subscribers to a conspiracy theory may well interpret the American post-war policy towards Greece as a deliberate attempt to create a client state. A more realistic but cynical view would take the line that given the initial dependence of the Greek economy first on Britain and then on the US for its sheer survival, and then for its continuing existence and gradual development, it would have been too much to expect that the donors would have approved policies that ran counter to their economic or global political aims. With a completely defeated and prostrate Left the Greek Right would have no reason to bite the hand that fed it, and indeed rescued it from a powerful and, initially, extremely popular Left movement. The post-civil war governments were not purely the simple instruments of the US Government, but followed a pragmatic but perhaps short-sighted policy in the context of the political and financial situation in Greece at that time. Any serious attempt at planning in the sense of the state determining the direction of investment and limiting the influence of the private sector could have led to conflict with US aid agencies which monitored, commented on, and where appropriate, approved Government action [20].

The role of private enterprise and initiative in the development of post-war Greece and that of foreign direct investment in particular became a hotly debated issue in the 1960s. As was pointed out in Chapter Two, the role of direct foreign investment in Greece before the war was quite significant but was dwarfed by the state foreign debt. Under Marshall Aid and the Truman Doctrine a number of loans were extended to the Greek Government, one of which issued by the Manufacturers Hanover Trust helped to establish the Public Electricity Corporation (Dimosia Epihirisis Ilectrismou, DEI). The Corporation spearheaded the electrification of the country and became one of the success stories of recon- struction. At the early stages of its foundation in 1948 and until 1955 DEI was managed directly by an American firm, Ebasco Services Inc. [21]. In the early 1960s there were numerous and highly controversial agreements concerning direct foreign investment in Greece, the terms and effects of which are still a matter of dispute. Economic development, state planning, private enterprise and continuous direct dependence on a foreign state made for odd partners indeed, and these conflicts left deep traces and marks on the course of the Greek economy in the 1960s and 1970s. But the uneasy feeling persists that had the Greek Right showed greater determination in taking on the risk of lessening Greece's dependence on aid, and if necessary confronted both the Americans and the Greek electorate on that issue, then the policy switch on industriatisation need not have been so drastic. Similar considerations also apply to the issue of defence expenditures once the civil war was over.

NOTES

[1] Sweet-Escott, Greece, pp.104-106.
[2] Sweet-Escott, Greece, pp.105-107.
[3] (a) Th.Karavias, I Voitheia ton Inomenon Potileion pros tin Ellada kata tin Periodon 1944-1962, Epitheorisis Oikonomikon kai Politikon Epistimon, Nos.3-4, Vol. 19, July-December 1964, pp.197-226.
    (b) Angelopoulos, Oikonomika, pp.128-133.
[4] A full copy of the text appears in Bank of Greece, Ekthesis tou Dioikitou, 1947, Part B, pp.79-82, Athens 1948.
[5] A full copy of the treaty is published in Bank of Greece, Ekthesis tou Dioikitou, 1948, Part B, pp.164-178, Athens 1949.
[6] Prosorinon Makroprothesmon Programma Oikonomikis Anorthoseos tis Ellados, Ypourgeion Syntonismou, Publication No. 6, Athens 1949, passim, but especially pp.9-21 and pp.89-91 on the foreign exchange requirements for the execution of the plan.
[7] Prosorinon, pp.2-3.
[8] Prosorinon, p.98.
[9] (a) Anatheorimenon Programma Oikonomikis Anorthoseos tis Ellados 1949-50, Ypourgeion Syntonismou, Publication No.5, Athens 1949 (The June 1949 Plan).
    (b) Ypomnima pros ton OEOS epi ton Programmaton 1950-51 kai 1951-52, Anotaton Symvoulion Anasygrotiseos, Athens 1950 (The January 1950 Plan).
[10] Sweet-Escott, Greece, p.112.
[11] Prosorinon, p.90.
[12] Angelopoulos, Oikonomika, p.304.
[13] Sweet-Escott, Greece, pp.114-115.
[14] Halikias, Dinatotites, pp.39-43.
[15] E.P. Eliades, 'Stabilisation of the Greek Economy and the 1953 Devaluation of the Drakma', IMF Staff Papers, Vol. IX, September 1954, pp.22-72.
[16] M.N. Goudi, 'I Anaprosarmogi tis Timis tou Synallagmatos', Meletai Oikonomikis Analyseos, No.7, Papazisis, Athens 1953, pp.12-13. This study also explores in some detail the potential shortcomings of these estimates and the differences in the cross-exchange rates in estimating the overvaluation of the drakma.
[17] Goudi, I Anaprosarmogi, pp.14-16.

[18] (a) X. Zolotas, <u>Nomismatiki Issoropia kai Oikonomiki Anaptyxis</u>, Bank of Greece, Athens 1964, pp.78-96. An English translation of this important work was published under the title , <u>Monetary Equilibrium and Economic Development</u>, Princeton University Press 1965. All references are from the Greek edition.
(b) Halikias, <u>Dinatotites</u>, pp.39-57.
[19] I.M. Papadakis, <u>I Politiki ton Katefthinomenon Epitokion</u>, Institouton Oikonomikon kai Viomihanikon Ereunon, Athens 1978, p.24.
[20] For a balanced analysis of the political and economic factors at work during this period see J. Maynaud, <u>Politikes Dynameis stin Ellada,</u> Athens 1974, pp.406-428. It is perhaps indicative of the situation in Greece at the time, that one of the earliest and most comprehensive post-war plans for the industrialisation of Greece was authored by D. Batsis who was later tried and shot for his alleged participation in the activities of the outlawed Greek Communist Party. His work laid great emphasis on the development of the energy sector as a precondition for the creation of heavy industry. His analysis and recommendations, however, take a clear stand on the side of a planned economy. See D.Batsis, <u>I Vareia Viomihania stin Ellada,</u> Nea Vivlia, Athens 1947, passim.
[21] D. Benas, <u>I Eisvoli tou Xenou Kefalaiou stin Ellada,</u> Papazisis, Athens 1976, pp.38-41.

CHAPTER FIVE

THE TAKE OFF THAT NEVER WAS : THE GREEK ECONOMY IN
THE 1960s and 1970s

5.1 INTRODUCTION

Much has been made by both politicians and
economic commentators of the monetary stability
that was achieved by the post civil war
governments in Greece. The rate of inflation as
measured by the changes in the cost of living
index (1952 = 100) fell from a high of 15% in 1954
to just over 2% in 1959. But the return of
confidence in the national currency, and a
political environment dominated by conservative
administrations was not sufficient to provide the
incentives for the kind of private sector
investment necessary for the solution of the
structural problems of the Greek economy. Perhaps
it would have been unfair to expect that domestic
resources alone would have created the conditions
for a take-off into an industrial economy. But,
as it will be shown later on, foreign investment
and a permanent deficit in the trade balance did
not help either. Significant progress was made
however, in a number of fronts. The share of
industry in the GDP increased from about 14% to
almost 19% between 1960 and 1970 and fixed capital
investment continued to absorb 25% of GDP (See
Table 5.1). The growth of the industrial sector
was counterbalanced by the relative decline of
agriculture, but the service sector continued to
account for almost 50% of the GDP not only during
the 1960s, but right down to the 1980s. It is
therefore important to stress, that although the
structure of the GDP changed, the contribution of
each sector to its growth did not necessarily
reflect that sector's relative position. As the
data in Table 5.2(a) indicate, although the
average percentage increase of manufacturing

TABLE 5.1 Sectoral Structure of GDP at factor costs as % of total (1961-1980). Fixed Capital Investment (FCI) as % of GDP, and dwelling construction as % of FCI. Rate of growth of GDP over previous year. All data in ml drks at constant 1970 prices.

Year	Agriculture	Industry	Services	FCI as % of GDP	Dwelling as % of FCI	Rate of growth of GDP
1961	26.3	13.8	48.7	22.5	28.1	11.2
1962	22.7	14.4	51.3	23.5	30.3	0.5
1963	24.8	14.2	49.7	22.6	31.2	10.0
1964	23.0	14.9	49.9	25.3	31.5	7.5
1965	23.1	15.0	49.5	26.2	31.5	9.2
1966	22.1	15.5	50.4	25.6	30.9	5.3
1967	21.4	16.1	50.9	24.1	28.0	4.6
1968	18.5	17.0	51.3	27.7	32.1	5.6
1969	18.0	17.8	50.4	30.0	32.3	9.3
1970	18.2	19.0	50.3	27.3	27.9	8.3
1971	17.4	19.5	49.9	28.9	29.3	7.9
1972	16.9	19.3	49.5	30.5	32.3	9.1
1973	15.5	21.0	49.7	30.3	30.5	8.3
1974	16.6	20.8	51.9	23.0	21.3	-1.8
1975	16.9	20.8	51.6	21.9	27.4	5.1
1976	15.5	21.6	51.8	21.1	27.4	6.0
1977	13.9	21.3	52.8	23.1	30.7	2.9
1978	14.4	21.3	52.3	23.0	33.0	6.4
1979	13.1	21.7	52.9	24.2	31.8	3.6
1980	14.4	21.3	53.0	22.2	29.4	2.0

NB: Agriculture includes fishing and forestry. Industry covers only manufacturing. The rest of the sectors adding up to 100% include mining, electricity, gas, water and construction. Throughtout this period dwellings accounted for about 45% of total construction.

Source: a. The Greek Economy in Figures, Electra Press, Athens 1984 various tables.
b. Monthly Statistical Bulletin, Bank of Greece, various issues.

TABLE 5.2   Sectoral growth 1960-1979

(a)	Average annual percentage change in output of industry and services (at constant 1970 prices)		
		1960 - 73	1974 - 79	1960 - 79
	Industry	10.8	4.4	8.8
	Services	7.5	4.8	6.6

(b)	Contribution of sectors to the increase in GDP (= 100)		
		1963 - 73	1974 - 79	1963 - 79
	Industry	25.8	14.7	21.9
	Agriculture & Mining	10.6	4.7	8.6
	Services	50.1	77.2	59.7
	Construction & Energy	13.4	3.4	9.9

Source: Based on T. Giannitsis, Elliniki
Viomihania, Gutenberg, Athens 1983, pp, 52-53.

output was in general higher than that of services, its contribution to the overall growth was by comparison much smaller [Table 5.2 (b)].

The absolute decline of the share of agriculture in the GDP over the 1960s was accompanied by an average growth rate of gross agricultural output of about 4.9%. The structure of output, however, hardly changed, with crops predominating over livestock. This particular issue will be examined in greater detail in section 5.4 [1].

The structure of industrial output, however, did change. Sectors such as food, drink, tobacco, clothing and shoes all declined whilst chemicals increased. But basic capital goods industries such as mechanical and metallurgical changed only marginally (Table 5.3). This was an extremely important development, or lack of, when taken in conjunction with the structure and composition of fixed capital investment. At the risk of over-simplifying the developmental process, an aspect of it involves the growth of sectors that foster both forward and backward linkages in terms of input-output relationships. Greece's industrial structure showed hardly any sign of changes towards greater interdependence. The crucial capital goods sector remained relatively underdeveloped thus shifting the onus of capital formation to imports. Those points will be picked up again and examined in Section 5.3 of this chapter.

TABLE 5.3 Structural changes in the composition of industrial output 1953-1979 (% of total)

Sample of Industrial Branches	1953	1963	1974	1979
Food, drink & tobacco	26.8	22.3	17.8	18.8
Textiles	17.9	14.8	15.9	18.1
Clothing & Shoes	16.8	11.6	9.5	9.1
Chemicals	4.2	7.8	12.5	13.0
Basic Metallurgical	0.6	1.7	7.0	5.9
Mechanical and Engineering (*)	12.3	13.2	13.0	11.1
Transport Equipment	3.8	6.6	5.0	4.2

(*) Includes manufacturing of metal articles, motors, machines and electrical apparatus.

Source: A. Kintis, Anaptyxi tis Ellinikis Viomihanias, Gutenberg, Athens 1982, p.48.

The Greek economy did exhibit a number of structural changes in the 1960s and 1970s, but none of them was sufficient to change its fundamental characteristics or provide the conditions for self-sustaining growth.

5.2 POSTWAR ECONOMIC POLICY AND EMIGRATION

The conservative governments, including a military dictatorship, which ruled Greece until 1981 (except for a brief period in 1963-65) followed the pre-war policy of state intervention in the economy. The Greek state saw itself more as a regulator than a leader, and hence its intervention lacked any element of dirigisme. The government promulgated a multitude of petty regulations for every branch of the economy, the banking system was rigidly controlled and permits were needed even for minor industrial or commercial undertakings. It is perhaps indicative of this obsession with the minutae, that Greece must be the only market economy where a branch of the police is exclusively dedicated to controlling prices of a number of goods. Greek restaurants still exhibit signs to the effect that the 'market police' has approved of their prices. In the old meat and fish market in the centre of Athens housewives can ask the market police to reweigh their purchases in an official scale thus ensuring fair pricing.

Monetary policy was exercised by the Bank of Greece via an extensive system of quantitative controls on banks. Commercial banks were obliged to hold on deposit with the Bank of Greece a percentage of their saving and sight deposits and also a percentage of certain types of loans. In some cases these compulsory reserves yielded no interest at all. The Government directed loans towards exports and certain industries via a system of differentiated additional reserve requirements. Since the monetary authorities also decreed the level and structure of interest rates, there was a double system of controls over the lending activities of the commercial banks [2]. The system became truly byzantine in its complexity with further requirements on banks to keep a percentage of their assets in government securities as well. In some instances that percentage reached 44%, with negative yields adding injury to grievance [3].

This system of controls might have ensured some degree of monetary stability had it not been used as a means of financing the public sector borrowing requirement as cheaply as possible and thus contributing directly to inflationary pressures. Furthermore, the regime of rigidly fixed and controlled interest rates created a situation of continued disequilibria in the money and financial markets and did little or nothing to encourage competition in the banking sector. Given the avowed dedication of postwar govern- ments in Greece to the principles of private enterprise and the market mechanism, monetary policy during this period proved to be an interesting exercise in contradictions.

Fiscal policy in the 1960s and 1970s was characterised by three broad develop ments. Firstly, the share of the public sector in the GDP increased from 21% in the early 1960s to 30% by the 1980s. Surprisingly, however, the private sector continued to provide most of the investment

expenditures. Indeed the percentage of public
sector expenditure directed towards investment
declined from 25% of the total in the early 1970s,
to about 14% in the 1980s. Meanwhile the private
sector accounted for about 67% of the total gross
fixed capital formation during the 1960s, and more
than 75% during the 1970s. Public sector
investment remained heavily concentrated in
construction which absorbed about 70% of the
total. However interventionist the Greek state
had been, it did leave industrial investment
firmly in the hands of the private sector [4].
     The second development concerned the finance
of the budget deficit. The public sector gross
borrowing requirement rose throughout this period
to account for more than 10% of the GDP by the
1980s. Most of the finance was provided by
domestic sources with a substantial proportion
coming from the Bank of Greece itself [5].
Finally, despite its continuing growth and
therefore ability to exercise a leverage effect on
the economy, the public sector expenditure and
fiscal policy in general appeared to be
pro-cyclical and aggravated inflation [6]. Its
role in the overall developmental process was also
negative. This particular point was aptly
summarised by Negreponti - Delivani as follows:

     'Despite the fact that the general
     characteristics of the public sector in
     Greece do not differ significantly from
     those of other countries which are
     roughly at the same level of development
     as that of Greece's, there is no evi-
     dence of any specific directions in the
     exercise of policies during the 1960 -
     78 period. The public sector did not
     contribute to the acceleration of the
     overall effort of the development of the
     country nor to a fairer distribution of
     income. The expansion of its activities
     under these circumstances is not justi-
     fied since in the final analysis it does
     not appear to offer specifically
     differentiated services in total in
     comparison to the private sector, with
     the only possible exception of infra-
     structure .... As for the contri-
     bution of the public sector in economic
     decentralization and the effort of
     regional development, this was

The Take Off That Never Was

nonexistent ....' (Analysis, p. 246)

The last sentence of this quotation touches
on one, perhaps the most serious, shortcoming of
the microeconomic policies of the postwar
administration in Greece: the failure to control
or direct the regional concentration of economic
activity. The movement of rural population to
urban centres, which will be presently examined,
was accompanied by growing concentration of
industry and labour force in two big centres,
Athens and Salonica. Table 5.4 shows the trends.

TABLE 5.4 Regional concentration of economic
activity 1961-1985.

(a) Employment in Industry and Handicraft (% of
active population)

	1961 - 63	1971 - 73
Metropolitan Athens	30.8	31.7
Salonica	32.3	29.3

(b) Distribution of active population in
geographical areas (% of total)

	1961	1971	1985(estimate)
Athens	30.2	34.0	39.02
Salonica	16.9	17.3	17.8

Sources: (a) G.X. Kottis, Viomihaniki Apokentrosis
kai Periferiaki Anaptyxis, Institouto
Oikonomikon kai Viomihanikon Ereunon,
Athens 1980, p.40.
(b) M.Negreponti-Delivani, Analysis,
p.296.

The Greek government used a variety of fiscal
incentives and administrative controls to steer
industries away from major urban centres. Despite
however, repeated zoning efforts, the banning of
issuing of building licences for factories, and
in 1980s, strict controls on emission and
pollution, the trends seemed irreversible. Very
frequently the government found itself in front of
a dilemma of either granting permission for yet
another industrial development near a major city
or no investment at all being undertaken. The
development of infrastructure and communications
did not seem to have made much difference to the
continuing concentration of industry around a few

urban centres. Although there is yet no
conclusive evidence, it would appear that the
relative benefits of producing near major cities,
in terms of the availability of a pool of labour
and the existence of already established local
markets and transport links, outweighed the fiscal
incentives offered by the state.

A survey of all the various Government
policies on incentives to invest away from the
congested urban areas came to the following
conclusions: [7]

'The lack of sufficient theoretical
underpinning but also of detailed
quantitative estimation of the spatial
behaviour of Greek industries and of the
influence of state measures for industrial decentralisation were extremely
important factors in contributing to
the ineffectiveness of these policies
aimed at the geographical dispersion (of
industry) ···· the Greek programmes of
regional development did not show
continuity and consistency. The
repeated changes of the incentives
caused uncertainty in industry and
confusion as to which policy was in
force in each period.'

Even the colonel's seven year stretch in
power (1967-74) did not leave any major
impressions on Greece's economy despite the fact
that it reopened all the political wounds of the
civil war and added few of its own by widespread
jailings, exiling, torturing and numerous deaths.
Perhaps the most lasting effect was the freezing
of the Agreement of Association of Greece with the
EEC until democratic rule was restored. Given the
authoritarian nature of the regime and the
incompetency of its chief ministers it is not
suprising that the period of its rule is replete
with 'knee-jerk' reactions to economic events,
financial scandals and conspicuous public
consumption projects. The latter included the
collection by public subscription of a large sum
of money in order to fulfil, belatedly, an
official promise made to God (!) during the Greek
Revolution of 1821 against the Turks to build a
huge cathedral if Greece was delivered from its
ancient enemy and oppressor [8].

This admittedly sketchy survey of fiscal and

monetary policy in the 1960s and 1970s, cannot be complete without some reference to a number of economic plans that successive administrations announced, occasionally amidst maximum publicity, only to have them later quietly and resolutely abandoned. So for example there have been economic plans for 1960-64, 1966-70, 1968-72 and most recently for 1983-87.

The majority of these plans enunciated a number of usually vague targets, but limited the role of the state in terms of purely indicative planning functions. Most of these plans were not 'executed' or 'fulfilled' in the sense that they involved a specific set of targets that was achieved. Some of them, like the one for 1966-70, were overtaken by political events. In other cases no specific data were made available, especially for some plans during the 1974-81 period. Given the brief but unfulfilled flirting with economic planning in the immediate postwar period and following the developments associated with Marshal Aid, it would have been most surprising if the Greek state had taken on its planning role at all seriously [9].

The first, of the many, signs that all was not well with the post war recovery in Greece came in the early 1960s. As we have already seen in Chapter One, Greece had witnessed massive population movements in the 1900-1920 period which included both the refugees, caused by the various wars and also emigration, particularly to the United States. The second wave of emigration in Greece's history was effectively a continuation of the exodus of labour which had dried up in the 1920s with the imposition of quotas in the United States, the Depression and later with the war. As Table 5.5 shows, the movement accelerated from 1959 and it only subsided with the onset of the international depression following the 1973 oil crisis. Although stock and flow comparisons of population size and net emigration flows are hardly appropriate, it is tempting to note that almost 12.2% of the total population of Greece emigrated between 1951-1981. During the peak period of 1960-1970 more than 800,000 people left Greece representing a net loss of 9.3% of the total average population. What made this large scale loss of people potentially damaging to Greece was the fact that the overwhelming majority of the emigrants were amongst the members of the economically active population. This was a clear

sign of the extent of unemployment and underemployment in the labour force. The contribution
of emigration in alleviating unemployment is
rather difficult to gauge because of the
widespread belief that the official unemployment
statistics underestimate the true extent of the
situation. One study attempted to bypass this
problem by calculating the difference between
actual and potential full employment GDP

TABLE 5.5 Post war emigration 1946-1977

Year	1 Total permanent emigrants	2 Repatriation	3 Net Emigration (1-2)
1946-1955	88,239	-	-
1956	35,349	-	-
1957	30,428	-	-
1958	24,521	-	-
1959	23,684	-	-
1960	47,768	-	-
1961	58,837	-	-
1962	84,054	-	-
1963	100,072	-	-
1964	105,569	-	-
1965	117,167	-	-
1966	86,856	-	-
1967	42,730	-	-
1968	50,866	18,882	31,984
1969	91,552	18,132	73,390
1970	92,681	22,665	70,016
1971	61,745	24,709	37,036
1972	43,397	27,522	15,875
1973	27,529	22,285	5,244
1974	24,448	24,476	-28
1975	20,330	34,214	-13,884
1976	20,374	32,067	-11,693
1977	16,510	12,572	3,938
TOTAL	1,294,746	237,524	1,057,222

Source: Various issues of the Statistical
         Yearbook for Greece, Ethniki Statistiki
         Ypiresia, Athens.
NB: The data for 1977 are for half year
         only. Since 1977 no specific statistical
         information on emigration or repatriation
         have been collected. Repatriation data
         were collected since 1968 only.

over the 1960-1978 period. This yielded a rate of
unemployment of about 9.8% as opposed to the
average official figure for this period at 4.4%.
The study went on to calculate the level of
unemployment that would have occurred if the net
amount of emigration had not taken place. This
raised the level of unemployment to an average of
16.4%. So on the basis of these calculations
emigration helped to reduce unemployment by about
6.6 percentage points or some 40% less than it
would have been in the absence of job
opportunities in Europe and elsewhere [10].

This large scale export of Greece's
unemployed or underemployed labour caused major
upheavals in the demographic and regional balance
of the country. For a start, as the majority of
the emigrants were young there were fears of a
gradual change in the age structure with only the
very young and the very old dominating the labour
markets. As most of the emigrants came from rural
areas in northern Greece this deprived agriculture
of labour and led to major depopulation problems
for whole counties. It is important to note that
the movement of agricultural labour on its own
might have been a blessing in disguise given its
low productivity. But the emigration to Europe
during this period was also combined with a rapid
internal migration movement towards urban areas.
For example the population of Athens in 1951 stood
at 1.37 million; by 1980 it had increased to 3.5
million accounting for almost 40% of the country's
population. Similarly the population of major
cities increased by 3.5 million between 1951-81
whilst the natural increase of population during
this period was about 2 million [11]. The upshot
of these changes was a gradual development of
labour shortages in the countryside. A study of
the labour market in agriculture which was
conducted before the major wave of emigration in
the mid 1960s, explored the question and existence
of 'removable surplus labour' [12]. Its
conclusions were as follows:

'...... we have found that the volume of
removable labour has declined and that
Greek agriculture is reaching a stage of
permanent labour shortage during peak
seasons ...... with regard to seasonal
surplus we have found this continued to
remain relatively high thus presenting a
serious economic problem'.

What perhaps made the overall situation worse
was the fact that most of the emigrants were
employed in their host country in unskilled or
semi-skilled jobs. The arguments that emigration
would provide an inexpensive way of training the
future industrial labour force of Greece rang very
hollow indeed especially as the flow turned out to
be very susceptible to cyclical movements. As
Table 5.5 shows, net emigration for the last years
of the 1970s became an influx rather than an
outflow. Germany, which was the major recipient
of immigrant workers, not only imposed
restrictions to further movements but also started
an active programme of voluntary repatriation.

In the final analysis, the only tangible
benefit to the Greek economy of this loss of human
resources was the remittances sent back home by
these workers. During the 1960s they accounted
for more than 30% of all invisible earnings and
covered about 35% of the deficit in the trade
balance. The alleviation of potential unemployment was an additional benefit but it simply
removed the symptoms rather than provide a cure.

The official attitude towards this serious
development was one of vacillation or inability to
deal with its causes. The arguments for and
against emigration were thoroughly rehearsed, but
other than suggesting that the government should
ban the movement of labour there was no serious
attempt to deal with the problem on a long term
basis [13].

The upsurge of emigration can be seen as the
inability of the private sector in Greece to
generate jobs. But even here the picture becomes
quite complex because in terms of international
comparisons, both the rate of growth of the GDP
and the percentage of it devoted to investment was
not out of line with those of other developed
economies.

5.3 INDUSTRIAL INVESTMENT : DOMESTIC AND FOREIGN

As the data in Table 5.6 show, fixed capital
investment absorbed about a quarter of the GDP
during 1961-80. An exceptionally high proportion
of it however, almost 65%, was accounted for by
construction and on average 45% of construction
was directed to dwellings. Investment in
machinery and other equipment rose in the early
1970s but then towards the end of the decade fell

back to the same level as at the end of the 1960s.

TABLE 5.6 Structure of fixed capital investment
(FCI) 1961-1980, million drks, at 1970
constant prices.

Year	Construction as % of total FCI	Investment in machinery and other equipment as % of total FCI
1961	72.2	17.9
1962	73.5	18.7
1963	73.7	19.7
1964	71.2	21.4
1965	70.7	22.7
1966	68.6	20.9
1967	66.9	23.4
1968	70.5	21.1
1969	67.9	22.8
1970	64.3	35.6
1971	66.4	24.7
1972	68.3	24.0
1973	64.8	24.8
1974	58.1	31.8
1975	62.4	28.0
1976	61.7	26.5
1977	63.4	24.0
1978	63.2	22.0
1979	61.4	23.8
1980	58.3	26.0

Source: The Greek Economy in Figures, various
tables. Construction includes dwellings,
other buildings and other construction.

If nothing else, the data in Table 5.6
show that there was no decisive turning point in
the share of machinery and other capital goods in
the 20 year period under examination. While it is
not surprising that investment was subject to
cyclical factors, the steady preference of Greek
investors towards construction in general, and
housing in particular, does require some
explanation. Public sector investment was
committed to improving the infrastructure of the
country and hence in the earlier part of the
period (1963-72) more than 80% of it was directed
to construction. But it is also important to
remember that state investment in Greece never

accounted for more than 30% of total capital formation. Hence the preference of the private sector towards investment in construction dominated the picture. The overall poor performance of investment in the industrial sector can be examined from a variety of standpoints. In the literature there appears to be a confusion over a number of separate issues. Adequacy of investment funds is one of them. The argument in this case is that relative lack of funds stunted investment in the manufacturing sector. Even if that was the case, it would still not explain the reason why the available funds were allocated the way they were. Shortages of funds could have increased the opportunity cost of investing in manufacturing and thus directed the available resources to higher yielding projects such as construction. This raised the second important issue of the relative returns to investment in different sectors. The evidence on both these questions is not clear cut. For a start, there is some evidence to show that during the earlier postwar period there was no shortage of capital funds. One study covering the 1950s and early 1960s came to the following conclusion: [14]

'All the available statistics have led us to argue against the general belief that the supply of capital in Greece has been inadequate. Thus from 1952 to 1962 the domestic savings ratio increased rapidly from 6.7% of GDP to 21% while the private savings ratio rose from 8.3% of GDP to 17.7%. The contributions of households to financing net capital formation has been increasingly important, rising from 28.1% in 1954 to 58.8% in 1961. Over the same period private savings in money terms were in excess of private investment ex-post.'

Another study, however, covering the 1950-1975 period came to different conclusions: [15]

'The conclusion of the foregoing analysis is that the development of private savings was never sufficient for the financing of the realised private productive investments. A significant percentage of total private savings represented the financing of housing

through internal sources. The rest,
which via the credit system was
channelled to other productive
investment, could not be considered at
all sufficient. As a result the company
sector relied increasingly on internal
sources of finance and depreciation
allowances. Irrespective of the actual
state of long term demand for capital
for private investment, the corresponding supply of funds from private
savings was not sufficiently large
enough to cover it.'

It is important to note that what is disputed
here is the role of private savings in providing
sources for capital investment finance rather than
the overall availability of funds. The crucial
question, however, still centres on the relative
returns to investment in different sectors.
Negreponti-Delivani used the incremental
capital-output ratio as an approximation to
returns on investment in different sectors. For
the period 1961-70 the figures for agriculture
stood at 5.6, industry 1.8, energy 1.0 and
housing 15.5. In other words, investment in
housing required more than eight and half times
the amount of funds invested in industry to yield
the same returns [16]. The preference towards
investment in housing has been explained or
interpreted in various ways. The explanations
that have been offered include lack of alternative
financial assets, the relative underdevelopment of
the capital market, lingering fears of inflation
and of political instability and so on. One
author summarised these explanations thus : [17]

'Several reasons contributed to
(investment in construction) such as the
poor housing level specially after a
decade of foreign occupation and civil
war, the enormous internal migration
towards urban centres, the lack of
alternative means of private
accumulation during a period of rapid
increases in incomes and, possibly above
all, the fact that land and buildings
were widely distributed because of the
historic absence of a feudal class and
landless peasants.'

A systematic comparison, however, of rates of
return on investment in housing compared with
saving and deposit accounts, yielded a net return
to housing both in nominal and real terms. For the
1950-75 period the nominal average returns on
housing stood at 13.8%, for cash plus current
accounts at 1.2%, and for saving and deposit
accounts at 6.8%. The corresponding real returns
were 6.8%, -5.7% and -0.09%. The author concluded
that: [18]

'..... the high percentage of domestic
savings that was channelled to housing
is not due as much to the assumed
psychology or social orientation of the
average Greek citizen nor to lack of
investment opportunities outside the
banking sector, but is a purely economic
phenomenon due to the rational behaviour
of the average investor.'

This conclusion is not perhaps unjustified in
the case of Greece where the relative underdevelopment of the capital market did not offer
many opportunities for portfolio diversification. There is also the additional point that
although construction accounted for 65% of all
the fixed capital investment during this period,
investment in dwellings was less than 50% of all
construction. So to focus on dwellings may well
exaggerate its relative importance, but on the
basis of the evidence presented it does appear
that a mixture of financial as well as social and
expectational considerations directed investment
towards construction rather than industry. It is
also important to note at this stage that
Negreponti-Delivani's study examined relative
returns amongst sectors rather than among assets.
The comparisons of yields between long term
physical and medium term financial assets may not
be highly relevant even in the context of a
limited range of options and assets to invest in.
This now raises the separate issue of interpreting
why industry attracted relatively less investment
than other sectors, despite the potentially higher
returns, rather than inquiring why private
investors chose houses in preference to bank
deposits. One particular interpretation relates
this question to technical progress.
Negreponti-Delivani examined the 1964-78
period and found that in the major sectors of

industry, capital was substituted by labour, in
the sense that the K/L ratio fell. Furthermore,
the contribution of technical progress to
increases in the value added of major industrial
sectors showed an overall rising trend from 28% of
the total increase in 1964-67, to 10.7% in
1968-71, 72% in 1972-75 and 93% in 1976-78. This
particular development taken together with the
slow-down in capital accumulation (hence the
falling K/L) was interpreted as an example of
disembodied technical progress. The industrial
sector was apparently making better use of the
labour resources and therefore moved towards
expansive rather than intensive use of factors of
production. There were three further causes
contributing to the relative slow down in
industrial investment. Firstly, the rate of
increase in demand for manufactured products in
the domestic market was quite slow during this
period because of falling agricultural incomes and
a decline in the real income of the salaried
sector of consumers because of the high rate of
inflation during the early 1970s. Secondly,
demand for manufactured products turned out to be
price inelastic and the possibilities for exports
limited. Under these circumstances industrialists
preferred to restrict output and gradually
absorbed their underutilised capacity by
substituting labour for capital. Finally, this
whole process of labour substitution was aided by
the higher marginal productivity of labour
compared to that of capital [19].
      The explanations offered for the poor overall
performance of industrial investment must now be
examined in conjunction with the rapid increase of
direct foreign investment in Greece during this
period. This particular development turned out to
be quite controversial in terms of politics and
economics. The controversy, in a nutshell, rests
on the proposition that direct foreign investment
in the postwar period altered not only the course
but also the nature of the Greek industrial
sector. Direct foreign investment can thus be
held partially responsible for the relative
underdevelopment of Greece and the absence of a
genuine take off into industrialisation.
      At an early stage in the postwar period the
Greek Government took a number of steps in order
to attract foreign investors. The main instrument
was the 2687/1953 Law which set the framework for
the rest of the policy. The provisions of this

Law gave special tax considerations to foreign
firms setting up in Greece, guaranteed the free
repatriation of capital and profits and prohibited
the confiscation of foreign owned assets. The law
also included special provisions for the registra-
tion of ships under the Greek flag. Although this
was by no means the only set of incentives offered
to foreign investors, the provisions of the Act
did attract a substantial amount of foreign capital. By the early 1960s, foreign investors were
involved with some of the biggest undertakings in
the Greek economy such as the Esso-Pappas refinery
in Salonika, the setting up of Hellenic Steel and
of the Pechiney aluminium projects.

In order to do justice to the complex
question of the effects of this foreign investment
the topic will be examined under three broad
headings. Firstly, the relative importance of
foreign owned firms will be assessed against the
whole industrial sector. Secondly, the effects of
investment on industrial concentration, competition and the balance of payments, will be
examined. Finally, the influence of foreign-owned
firms on the structural changes in the Greek
economy will be evaluated, especially in terms of
sectoral backward and forward linkages.

Between 1954 and 1964 12.5 billion drks were
invested by foreign firms in Greece in the form of
direct shareholdings, loans and credits.
Significantly, however, some 17% of this
investment was accounted for by just three
undertakings, the Esso-Pappas refinery, Greek
Aluminium and Greek Shipbuilders [20]. A number of
studies have attempted to estimate the percentage
of industrial capital either owned or controlled
by foreign firms. By necessity some of the data
used were based on samples and hence these studies
are not strictly comparable. Table 5.7 summarises
the results. It is interesting to note that
throughout the period surveyed the percentage of
foreign control was never less than about 30% of
the total assets involved.

As has already been indicated these
percentages are meaningless unless they can be
correlated with other structural developments
within the Greek economy. A number of different
approaches have been tried.

The simplest one was to estimate the contribution of firms with a high percentage of foreign
control to the balance of payments. From Table
5.7 it appears that petrol products, chemicals,

172

TABLE 5.7 Percentage of capital assets of industrial firms directly controlled or owned by foreign firms, 1961-1979.

Sectors	1961-64	1968	1972	1979
Food processing	5.5	0.6	12.5	3.5
Drink	-	-	11.7	36.9
Tobacco processing		-	26.7	-
Textiles	11.8	6.0	4.3	3.9
Clothing and Shoes		10.5	13.9	15.7
Wood and Cork	8.5	45.1	37.4	34.7
Furniture	-	-	-	-
Paper	59.5	2.2	17.6	14.6
Printing	-	-	0.5	0.5
Leather	-	4.8	6.2	4.8
Plastics and Rubber	60.3	46.2	40.0	22.2
Chemicals	31	22.2	45.1	22.7
Petrol products	70	89.4	95.9	5.2
Non-metal mining	-	11.0	9.4	4.7
Metallurgy	30.5	59.5	56.9	38.2
Metal products		23.4	6.3	7.3
Machinery and Equipment		6.5	8.2	9.2
Electrical goods	43.9	44.7	41.7	45.7
Transport equipment	45.7	-	60.3	2.9
Other		96.3	84.3	65.5
Total	37(*)	24(**)	29.8	14(**)

Source: (a) Data for 1961-64 from Valsamidis, I Ersroi, p.231.
(b) Data for 1968 and 1979 from Giannitsis, Elliniki, p.273.
(c) Data for 1972 from S. Babanasis and K. Soulas, I Ellada stin Periferia ton Anaptygmenon Horon, Themelio, Athens 1976, p.138.

N.B. The exact definition of control varies from source to source. The most comprehensive definition is that of Giannitsis which separates the ownership terms of (i) complete foreign control, (ii) minority foreign control, (iii) expatriate Greek capital in control. The data marked (**) refer to class (i) control only. The significant drop in the percentage between 1968 and 1979 came

about because of a shift in the pattern
of control. If all three categories were
taken together then the data for 1968
would rise from 24 to 36.3% and those for
1979 from 14 to 29.2%. The data marked
marked (*) include Greek Aluminium and
Esso Papas companies.

metallurgical products and transport equipment,
and to a lesser extent tobacco processing have
attracted a high percentage investment. Table 5.8
shows that these sectors contributed significantly
to both imports and exports in 1976.

TABLE 5.8 Percentage contribution to total
imports and exports of sectors with
high participation of foreign capital
(data for 1976)

Branch	Exports	Imports
Transport equipment	3.9	35.7
Petrol and petrol products	11.0	22.2
Chemicals	5.8	8.7
Tobacco processing	8.2	0.1
Total	28.9	66.7

Source: Negreponti-Delivani, Analysis, p. 347

Given that between 1966-78 the overall
imports of manufactured goods (both capital and
consumer goods) was well in excess of 53% of total
imports, then these four sectors were accounting
for almost one-third of the total manufactured
imports bill. Despite the approximate nature of
this estimate it is apparent that these sectors
contributed heavily to imports and little to
exports. Similar results regarding the export
performance of foreign owned firms in Greece were
obtained in an extensive study undertaken by
V. Papandreou [21]:

'The exports of multinational firms
constitute a significant percentage of
the exports of industrial goods ..... A
large percentage of their exports
consists of semi-processed raw
materials. In other words these

enterprises are vertically incorporated in the multinational system and not with the local economy. Most of these multinational enterprises, despite their international link-up and access to the distribution network of the parent company, do not export or export a small percentage of their output; in other words they address themselves primarily to the local market.'

Another issue of the question of the effects of direct foreign investment was to examine its relationship with that of industrial concentration. This particular proposition is hard to quantify because of the problem of causality, i.e. whether direct foreign investment increased concentration or whether foreign investors preferred the relative safety and higher potential returns of an oligopolistic market.

Greek industrial structure exhibited a considerable degree of concentration which tended to increase over time. A study by Tassopoulos used as an index the standard deviation of gross value of industrial output for 1963 and 1973 weighted by five groups of enterprises classified according to the number of their employees. For the first date the standard deviation stood at 3.96 and for the second at 23.6, a sixfold increase. The deviation divided by the average value of industrial output also increased from 0.64 to 0.88. Although these results rely on the grouping of enterprises according to size of employment only, it is interesting that the dispersion around the mean output increased considerably within a very short time period. The Gini coefficient calculated on the basis of value added to the number of industrial enterprises rose from 0.506 in 1963 to 0.534 in 1973, a 5.5% increase [22]. A further survey of 2,680 industrial enterprises used a number of indicators to calculate concentration for the top 100 and top 10 enterprises in the sample. The results are summarised in Table 5.9.

In general, foreign investment was heavily concentrated in some of the biggest firms. In 1973, in 35 of the largest enterprises, employing more than 1,000 workers, eight were completely foreign owned, and in another eight, foreign shareholders had a minority holding. The nineteen which were purely Greek owned accounted for 47.2%

TABLE 5.9 Concentration indexes for the top 100 and top 10 industrial firms (percentages refer to total of firms surveyed) Data for 1977.

Index	Top 100	Top 10
Sales	51	21
Capital employed	46	12
Net profit	62	35
Workers employed	32	5

Source: Tassopoulos, Elliniki p. 145

of the total employment in the sample [23]. Table 5.10 summarises some of the evidence for 1972.

TABLE 5.10 Foreign investment and degree of control of industrial firms on the basis of size of assets. (ml drks), 1972.

Total assets ml drks	Total no. of firms	Foreign-owned firms	Foreign-owned firms as % of number of firms in each category
Up to 9.9	534	39	7.3
10 - 49.9	657	79	12
50 - 199.9	340	78	22.9
200 - 499.9	81	25	30.9
500 - 899.9	22	8	36.4
Over 900	30	20	66.7
Total	1664	249	15

Source: Babanasis and Soulas, I Ellada p.139. The source does not specify the extent of foreign ownership, but it can be taken to mean 50% and over.

The final and perhaps most important aspect of the effects of direct foreign investment in Greece concerns the structural changes and developments in intersectoral links that it might have caused. The following exposition draws heavily from the detailed work of T. Fotopoulos [24]. As the analysis involved is fairly complicated and requires a number of building block and statistical data, it has been divided into a number of steps.

The first step was to identify key industrial sectors in the Greek economy by using input-output tables for 1958, 1960, 1966 and 1969. The aim here was to pick out those sectors which were relatively interlinked or exhibited a higher degree of interdepenence compared to others. This was done by constructing indexes of backward and forward linkages by averaging out the sum total of columns (backward linkage) and rows (forward linkage) of the standard $(I-A)^{-1}$ Leontief inverse. So for an industry with high vertical interdependence, an increase of its output would lead to a relatively large expansion throughout the rest of the sectors. A high degree of horizontal linkage signified that the industry in question would have expanded its output more than other industries for a given increase in final demand.

On the basis of these data six sectors were identified as having relatively high forward and backward linkages in 1969 compared to the rest of the sectors: basic metals, metal products, chemicals (organic and inorganic), paper, textiles (wool and cotton), plastics and petrol products.

Once these key industries/sectors had been identified the next stage was to evaluate their overall contribution to the Greek economy by using a number of different indexes and also to explore the degree of foreign capital participation in these sectors. The following indexes were used:

(1) Overall classification of sectors in order of output expansion by 1973 (1959 = 100)

(2) Labour intensity

(3) Capital intensity

(4) Labour productivity

(5) Degree of concentration

(6) Overall degree of competition

(7) Foreign capital penetration.

The Take Off That Never Was

The four sectors whose output expanded most during 1959-73 were (1959 = 100):

	Output Index
Basic metals	1673
Rubber and plastics	1338
Chemicals	707
Petrol and coal products	679

All these sectors singly or in combination (except rubber) appear in the list of key sectors. It is important to note, however, that the basic metals sector is dominated by aluminium and nickel, which are exported without extensive processing.

The next stage involved the measurement of the degree of labour intensity in these sectors by using the ratio of the index of employment to output from 1959-60 to 1969 and the ratio of the increase in employment to the increase in output for the same period. The four sectors referred to above and the rest of the key sectors (with the exception of oil and coal products) exhibited the smallest ratios which is, of course, indicative of their overall capital intensive technologies.

The degree of capital intensity was measured by the per capita consumption of electricity in these sectors and confirmed the previous findings. The key sectors in general had the highest indexes compared to others. Furthermore, the higher the percentage of total manufacturing output accounted for by a sector, the lower was the percentage of overall employment of industrial labour. So, for example, basic metallurgical industries produced during the period surveyed 5.5% of industrial output but employed just over 1.1% of the industrial labour force. The labour productivity index, which was calculated by using the value added per employee, also placed the key sectors consistently above the rest.

The level of industrial concentration in 1968 was then estimated by using four criteria: the number of workers employed per establishment in each of the sectors, the gross value of output per establishment, the percentage of establishments employing more than ten workers and the percentage of employees in establishments which employed more than ten workers. Once again the key sectors exhibited the highest degree of concentration,

178

although there was considerable variation within them. Similar criteria were used to establish the degree of oligopoly power in terms of total sales and employment accounted for by the largest four firms in each sector.

Finally, the degree of foreign investment penetration and control of industries or firms in key sectors was then examined. It was found that:

(i) production of basic metals and metallurgical processes was dominated by two foreign enterprises, Pechiney in aluminium and Republican Steel. These two companies were the first and third in size respectively in these branches;

(ii) rubber and plastics were primarily produced by subsidiaries of Dow Chemicals, Esso Papas, Goodyear and Pirelli;

(iii) in chemicals, control was exercised not only by direct ownership but also via patents and licences of firms such as Dow Chemicals, Unilever, Abbot, Gobain, Colgate, Ciba etc;

(iv) in petrol products the refinery in Salonika of Pappas-Standard Oil accounted for half the total output of this sector and was at the time the biggest single industrial unit in the country.

The conclusions of this analysis can now be summarized. Key sectors as defined by backward and forward linkages were dominated by foreign firms. The overall contribution of these sectors to macro aggregates was not extensive despite their structural importance. So for example, on the basis of the input-output classification of these sectors they contributed 21% of GDP in 1970, 42% of the total output of the industrial sector, 34% of industrial employment and only 5.1 of the employment of the total active population [25]. Capital goods production in Greece is still unimportant in terms of the criteria employed here. The machinery, electrical machinery and transport equipment sectors were absent from the list:

'The non-qualification of these sectors as key sectors in the Greek case, however, could be explained if we took

179

into account the fact that the import
content in their production is much
higher than that deriving from domestic
supplies. Thus 66% of machinery, 56% of
transport equipment and 32% of
electrical machinery according to the
1966 input-output tables were not
produced domestically, therefore
reducing the degree of interdependence
that is shown in the tables.'
(Fotopoulos, Key Sectors, p.84)

Output of sectors such as food processing,
tobacco, timber, cement, construction etc. did
increase during this period but their relatively
low degree of backward or forward linkages did not
qualify them as Key sectors. The significance of
the key sectors rests precisely in their
structural importance in the sense that they can
foster further integrated development. The data
presented so far indicate that:

(a) These key sectors are dominated by foreign
     capital. The implication here being that
     future developments and decisions will be
     taken outside Greece or without due attention
     being paid to Greece's special problems and
     requirements.
(b) There is a high degree of concentration in
     these sectors thus reducing the overall
     amount of competition in the economy.
(c) Their overall contribution to employment and
     output is relatively small in comparison with
     their dominance of specific sectors.
(d) The contribution of these sectors to exports
     is not significant, especially in terms of
     the value added component of the exported
     goods, whilst these sectors contribute to
     imports and to capital outflows. The latter
     is an issue of considerable controversy. It
     has been claimed that although the
     remittances of profits etc. abroad by
     foreign firms in Greece represents a small
     percentage of the total capital outflow, it
     underestimates the true size by a large
     amount. The reasons for this are either
     outright evasion of foreign exchange
     regulations or their avoidance by overpriced
     invoices for imports and differential prices
     between subsidiaries and the parent companies.

Multinationals and their investment policies do generate political, as well as economically substantive issues. Greece's experience in this area was no different to that of other developing countries [26]. The data and evidence presented here, indicate both the extent of penetration of foreign owned firms in Greece's industrial sector and the possible consequences of that penetration. The expectation that foreign investment would somehow provide the 'starting motor' of industrialisation proved false. This is not surprising because, after all, the business of multinationals is profits and not developmental policies. It was perhaps unfortunate that the inflow of foreign capital and direct investment did nothing to ameliorate the problems and structural weaknesses of the Greek industrial sector.

5.4 AGRICULTURE

As Tables 5.1 and 5.2 show, Greece's agriculture made relatively slow progress during this period. The percentage of active population employed in agriculture fell from 56% in 1951 to 53.3% in 1961 to 40.3% in 1971 and finally to 30.6% in 1980 [27]. Similarly the percentage contribution of agriculture to GDP at constant prices fell from 30.3 in 1951 to 14.4 by 1980. The relative decline of farming did not benefit the industrial sector because agricultural workers either emigrated abroad or swelled the ranks of the service sector. Although the overall agricultural output increased and it contributed about 8.6% to the rise in GDP over 1963-79, this was caused more by greater use of machinery, fertilizers and a withdrawal of marginally productive farms than by restructuring the composition of output or rationalisation of land ownership.

The number of tractors used rose from 24,533 in 1962 to 238,131 in 1981 and fertilizer use from 14.8 kilos per acre in 1970 to 24.8 kilos in 1978. The total amount of acreage cultivated actually declined by about 4% between 1961 and 1981. But land ulitisation and average size of farm remained very small in comparison with EEC or the United States.

In 1973 the average holding in Greece stood at 8.8 acres as compared to 27.2 in EEC and almost 300 acres in the USA. Table 5.11 summarises the situation. This problem is compounded because not only are the average holdings small, but they also tend to be fragmented in smaller scattered strips, a legacy of the land reforms of the 1920s, and of inheritance and marriage laws. The land survey of 1977 yielded some interesting results on land fragmentation. The sample of the 940,000 or so holdings contained more than 5.7 million parcels of land. This gives an average of 6.1 parcels per holding and average size of parcel of 1.45 acres. Even holdings of less than 2.5 acres contained more than one parcel. To the 128,000 holdings of less than 2.5 acres corresponded an average of 3 parcels per holdings with an average size of 0.7 of an acre! [28].

TABLE 5.11 Size of agricultural holdings (sample survey 1977-78).

Size of holdings in acres	Numbers of holdings	Percentage of total	Average size of holdings in acres
less than 1	111,820	11.4	0.24
1.2 to 2.2	128,990	13.5	1.65
2.5 to 4.7	197,860	20.8	3.40
5 to 7	141,020	14.8	5.80
7.4 to 12	175,450	18.4	9.26
12.3 to 24.5	140,470	14.7	16.20
24.5 to 49	42,360	4.4	31.80
49 to over 247	11,780	1.2	156.70
Total	949,750	100.0	8.40

Source: The Greek Economy in Figures, p.141. The original figures are quoted in 'stremas' which were then converted to acres on the basis of 1 acre = 4.046 'stremas'. This accounts for the approximate figures on size distribution.

There has been however a slow movement towards the concentration of land holdings in slightly larger farms although even this development is still insignificant compared with European standards. So, for example, in 1961 rural households with holdings of 0 to 25.5 acres owned almost 80% of all cultivated land. This percentage dropped marginally to 78.3% in 1971 and then to 69.1% in 1977 thus concentrating about 30%

of all land in holdings of over 25 acres which brings it a step nearer to the European average. The small size of farms and extreme land fragmentation will present Greek agriculture with difficult problems of rationalisation especially as increases in output will have to be sought in greater use of machinery or economies of scale. The latter effect is easily exhausted after a certain size but will still require bigger farms than those in existence now. But perhaps the most serious of all the problems has been the unchanging structure of agricultural production in Greece [29].

This particular phenomenon has two key aspects. Firstly as Section 2.3 in Chapter Two indicated, wheat production was strongly encouraged during the decade before the Second World War and came to dominate the production of cereals and the overall output of plant farming. The second aspect concerns the virtually unchanged relationship between livestock and plant output which hovered constantly around a ratio of two in favour of plants throughout this period. Table 5.12 Part (a) shows the broad division of output between animal products and plants and Part (b) illustrates this division in greater detail. For two separate decades, meat and dairy production has been the perennial problem sector in Greece, particularly in the case of beef which accounts for more than a fifth of total of meat output in terms of weight. As figures in Table 5.13 show, the rate of growth of beef and milk declined right through this period. One of the explanations for this slowdown has been the inadequate investment in livestock farming, and to some extent the inherent limitations of land structure and climate. The consequences of this slowdown were quickly felt however. During 1950-60 domestic output satisfied 87% of total consumption of meat and animal products whereas during 1960-70 the figure dropped to 70%. The outcome of this has been a continuing dependence on imports. The situation worsened after Greece's accession to the EEC as this opened up the domestic market to the highly efficient dairy and meat producers of Denmark, Germany and the UK.

In the case of wheat, output rose from 1.66 ml tons in 1960 to 1.93 ml tons in 1970 and then on to 2.97 ml tons in 1980. This increasing trend output had its roots in state intervention. Central purchasing organizations such as KYDEP

TABLE 5.12 Composition of Agricultural Production, 1938-1979, percentage of total value.

(a)

	1938	1953	1960	1965	1970	1975	1979
Farming	65.4	74.1	65.9	63.4	61.9	63.0	65.1
Livestock	30.3	22.2	28.9	30.7	31.5	29.7	30.2
Forestry	2.2	1.9	2.1	2.9	2.9	2.4	2.3
Fishing	1.9	1.6	2.9	2.9	3.5	2.4	2.3

(b) Selected items only

	1951-60	1961-70
Wheat	19.7	17.6
Tobacco	7.6	7.4
Currants	4.7	4.6
Cotton	4.6	5.5
Edible oil	9	8.9
Oranges	1.2	1.8
Animal products	22.6	26.9
Cereals	28.8 (1958-61)	26.1 (1966-69)
Fruit	3.8 (1958-61)	5.3 (1966-69)

Source: (a) Samaras, Kratos, p.64. The source does not indicate whether the data are calculated at constant or current prices.
(b) I Elliniki Oikonomia kata to Etos 1969 and 1970, Bank of Greece, Athens 1970 and 1971. p.15 and p.21 respectively. The data are estimated at 1956 prices which may well explain some discrepancies with those of Part (a).

The Take Off That Never Was

TABLE 5.13 Growth of livestock and milk production
(Data in thousands of tons, percentage
change over previous average output).

Year	Beef	Meat (Total)	Milk
1965-1969	91.6	69.6	21.4
1970-1974	24.6	29.2	20.6
1975-1980	4.7	33.1	14.3

Source : The Greek Economy in Figures, p.194.

handled more than three quarters of all wheat
output [30]. The state guaranteed high support
prices for cereals and frequent attempts to change
the composition of crops resulted in failure. For
example a special agricultural plan for 1961-65
forecast a 16.5% increase in wheat; the actual
outcome was a rise of 28.2%. As long as the
relative support prices of wheat were higher than
those of industrial plants such as cotton, animal
feeds etc, farmers continued to produce it [31].
During 1967-68 there was an attempt to substitute
a simplified system of support prices, especially
those for cereals, with a two tier system designed
to encourage the free trading of wheat. Support
prices for tobacco, cotton and currants were all
reduced. The process of reform was accelerated
with the accession to the EEC since all those
subsidies had to be harmonised with the common
agricultural policy (CAP) [32].
    One of the success stories of diversification
of agricultural production was the introduction of
sugar beet whose output rose from a very low level
in 1961 (52,000 tons) to 2.7 ml tons in 1979. The
establishment of five sugar processing plants,
which bought directly the output of farmers,
encouraged this massive increase. But the
creation of a sugar surplus within the EEC has
meant that Greek farmers are now being encouraged
to cut back their production.
    Another area of production, that of citrus
fruits has experienced an overall growing level of
output but subject to wide fluctuations due to
weather conditions. Between 1968-1980 output
averaged at 615.4 thousand tons with a standard
deviation of 159. Furthermore, fruit exports from
Greece to the EEC met with increasing problems
both in terms of competition and subsidies. These
issues are examined separately in the next chapter.

The Take Off That Never Was

The marketing of agricultural produce and the
relative prices received by farmers have generated
a number of problems all of which are likely to
become more pressing with Greece's accession to
the EEC.
Between 1954 and 1962 the prices paid by
farmers for inputs increased by 25.3% but the
prices received for their products increased by
20%. From 1965 to 1978 the relationship was
reversed. Taking the difference between the two
price indexes over this period the 'scissors'
opened up in favour of farm prices from 100 in
1968 to 121 in 1978. This did not mean, however,
that the personal income of farmers increased in
relation to the rest of the sectors since retail
prices of agricultural goods did not necessarily
indicate the prices received by farmers [33].
Greek farmers have had great difficulties in
controlling the marketing of their produces. One
particular aspect of this problem, which also
relates directly to the issue of land
fragmentation and small farm size, has been the
weakness of the cooperative movement. As shown in
Chapter Two the agricultural cooperative movement
has received state blessing and support since the
early 1900s. Indeed the Agricultural Bank of
Greece channelled most of the credit and loans to
farmers via cooperatives rather than on an
individual basis. It was perhaps because of this
that the cooperative movement in Greece never grew
beyond the confines of a quasi 'credit club' to
become an instrument for the production and
marketing of produce [34]. As late as 1982 only
about 25% of all the cooperatives in Greece were
involved in the production or marketing of goods.
Almost 70% were dedicated to credit functions
only. Of the total agricultural output in 1982
only 5% was channelled, sold or processed by
cooperatives. For individual products the
percentage varied from relatively small (46% of
bottled wines) to derisory (0.14% for wheat)
[35]. Given the extremely developed cooperative
movements in Europe, Greece's farmers have still a
long and difficult way to go. This is
particularly true in the case of the marketing of
fresh vegetables and fruit where the existence of
wholesale monopsonists for products or in
geographical areas deprived individual farmers of
a substantial proportion of the retail price of
their output.
Greece's agricultural development echoed, to

a considerable extent, the lack of structural
change in the industrial sector, both in terms of
size and diversification. Joining the EEC brought
to the fore all these problems and a few more.
These will be given a more extensive treatment in
Chapter Six.

5.5 BALANCE OF PAYMENTS

The current account balance remained in the red
throughout the 1960s and 1970s, with the visible
trade contributing all the deficit (Table 5.14).
Receipts from tourism and remittances from
emigrants made up for about half of the visible
deficit. Shipping contributed another 27% whilst
accounting for about a third of the invisibles
receipts.
    The importance of emigration as a source of
foreign exchange earnings has already been
mentioned in Section 5.2 above. Shipping however
is uniquely associated with Greece primarily
because of the glamour and importance surrounding
Greek shipowners such as Onasis and Niarchos. The
foundations of Greece's merchant fleet were laid
after the First World War. The post Second World
War period however witnessed two significant
events that initiated an explosive growth.
Firstly, in 1946 the US Government allowed 100
Liberty- type ships to be sold to Greek shipowners
under a scheme backed by loans guaranteed by the
Greek state. The buyers deposited 25% of the
purchase price and then paid off the rest over 17
years at 3.5% interest. In addition to this, 36
ships that the Greek state had received as war
reparations were sold off at heavily discounted
prices [36]. Secondly, the 2687/1953 Law
concerning the protection of foreign investment in
Greece contained special provisions for ships
flying the Greek flag. In effect, registering a
ship in Greece was equivalent to investing and
hence the owners enjoyed all the taxation and
foreign exchange privileges afforded to foreign
investors. At the start of 1950, there were some
1.18 million gross tons of ships under the Greek
flag and some 3.55 million gross tons under flags
of convenience, a ratio of about 1:0.3. By the
late sixties the equivalent figures were 7.8 and
11.8 million gross tons giving a 1:0.66 ratio. The
rapid rise in the proportion of Greek registered

The Take Off That Never Was

ships was attributed to the favourable treatment under the existing legislation and the general hostility of major industrialised countries to carriers flyings flags of convenience [37]. By 1960 Greek-owned ships ranked as the third biggest world group and the Greek registered fleet as the sixth biggest in the world.

Except for the growth of invisibles of earnings there was a further development in Greece's external trade.

TABLE 5.14 Balance of Payments 1961-1980:
In current prices, $ mls.

Year	Trade Balance	Invisibles Balance	Current Account Balance	Capital Movements
1961	-332.9	243.5	-89.4	128.8
1962	-397.7	292.0	-105.7	129.8
1963	-435.7	355.3	-80.4	141.3
1964	-555.0	350.2	-204.8	210.3
1965	-685.6	412.6	-273.0	240.1
1966	-745.4	481.3	-264.1	284.3
1967	-696.7	475.0	-221.7	206.2
1968	-771.9	524.8	-247.1	283.9
1969	-883.7	547.5	-336.2	310.3
1970	-1,084.2	682.3	-401.9	368.6
1971	-1,302.3	975.0	-327.3	513.8
1972	-1,571.6	1,203.8	-367.8	889.2
1973	-2,800.3	1,625.1	-1,175.2	1,045.6
1974	-2,888.1	1,675.5	-1,212.6	993.9
1975	-3,035.7	1,960.4	-1,075.3	1,109.5
1976	-3,328.5	2,237.0	-1,091.5	1,146.5
1977	-3,887.4	2,620.4	-1,267.0	1,543.7
1978	-4,339.2	3,383.9	-955.3	1,348.1
1979	-6,177.8	4,296.4	-1,881.4	1,542.1
1980	-6,809.5	4,593.4	-2,216.1	2,270.5

Sources : Monthly Statistical Bulletin of Bank of Greece, various issues.

As Table 5.15 shows, industrial exports as a percentage of the total increased from 3.5% in 1961 to over 50% by 1980, a rise of more than 1450%! Such a spectacular and massive shift in the composition of exports merits closer examination, especially when compared to the relatively static picture of industry. Textiles

188

dominated industrial exports, with the major portion being cotton yarns which accounted for more than 50% of the value. Yarn however is a simple product with low value added. Exports of capital goods such as machinery and transport equipment accounted for less than 4% of industrial exports. Fuel has accounted for some 25% of the value of imports since 1973. At the same time, however, about 25% of all industrial exports are energy intensive which means that increases in exports will not necessarily reduce the trade deficit. Furthermore, five of the eight most energy intensive branches of industry (cement, iron, other metals such as aluminium, building materials, clays and china) are directly connected to the building sector. Given the high proportion of fixed investment which is devoted to construction, it follows that increases in investment associated with an upswing in the business cycle will have an immediate adverse impact on the trade balance [38].

It is perhaps stating the obvious in pointing out that the imbalance in Greece's external trade simply reflected domestic developments or the lack of them. The large increase in industrial exports, although welcome, was focused on a very narrow band of goods highly susceptible to international competition. Indeed the association with the EEC caused immediate problems, especially in connection with the common policy towards imports from third countries. A further development has been that as the absolute size of the trade deficit increased, so did Greece's external indebtedness because private capital flows did not rise proportionately. It is now common practice to express the external debt position of a country as a percentage of the GDP, thereby committing the error of comparing stocks with flows. Keeping that in mind, Greece's Debt/GDP ratio rose from 10.4% in 1978 to 23.8% in 1983 [39]. A final complicating factor has been the justifiably equivocal attitude of Greece's monetary authorities towards the foreign exchange rate of the drakma. Overall, Greece has followed a managed float against the dollar which is likely to be institutionalised once the drakma joins the EMS. Given the extreme dependence on the service sector and particularly on tourism to help cover the trade deficit, it is not surprising that the drakma has been repeatedly devalued against the dollar. The drakma has never been freely

TABLE 5.15   Structure of exports, 1962-1980, Current prices, million of dollars.

Year	Industrial exports as % of total exports	Individual categories of industrial goods exported as % of total industrial exports (selected items)			
		Textiles	Cement	Metal Goods	Aluminum and alumina
1962	6.0	35.0	2.5	-	-
1963	5.8	26.5	4.7	-	-
1964	6.9	27.4	3.4	-	-
1965	10.2	21.7	6.3	-	13.7
1966	13.3	28.0	4.9	-	30.1
1967	17.9	18.5	5.3	-	27.7
1968	23.2	17.8	3.8	-	20.7
1969	32.6	14.8	4.2	-	19.3
1970	36.5	15.3	2.2	-	20.7
1971	33.4	21.2	4.5	-	15.6
1972	37.9	26.6	4.6	-	11.6
1973	40.3	32.5	2.7	7.3	8.6
1974	48.3	24.5	9.7	17.2	6.1
1975	48.3	25.9	13.4	14.1	5.1
1976	52.0	31.8	11.3	12.0	6.8
1977	51.7	33.9	11.9	10.2	6.9
1978	51.4	34.9	11.9	9.7	6.9
1979	49.7	34.4	10.4	10.1	7.0
1980	54.9	34.8	11.0	11.7	6.1

Sources: Monthly Statistical Bulletin, Bank of Greece, various issues. A dash indicates either not applicable or no specific data available. Until 1969 exports of skins and furs were not included in the statistics of industrial exports. The data here have been adjusted to include these as from 1962. The justification for doing so was that during the 1960s a greater proportion of these articles were exported as finished or processed goods rather than as a class of animal products.

convertible in the postwar period and it is unlikely to become so in the foreseeable future. This will create complications as it may conflict with the freedom in capital movements advocated by the EEC.

5.6 THE PROBLEM OF INFLATION

The hyperinflation of the immediate post-war period had left deep and bitter memories in the minds of the Greek public. The 1960s witnessed an era of monetary stability and low rates of inflation which was rudely shattered by the 1973 oil crisis and the international inflationary pressures that followed. Although most industrialised countries began to experience lower rates of inflation in the 1980s, Greece's rates remained quite high (Table 5.16).

TABLE 5.16 Rate of Inflation 1960-1983:

Percentage changes in the consumer price index over previous period (1974 = 100)

Year	Rate	Year	Rate
1960	1.5	1970	2.9
1961	1.9	1971	2.9
1962	-0.3	1972	4.2
1963	2.8	1973	15.5
1964	0.9	1974	26.9
1965	3.1	1975	13.4
1966	4.9	1976	13.3
1967	1.6	1977	12.1
1968	0.3	1978	12.5
1969	2.4	1979	18.9
		1980	24.4
		1981	24.4
		1982	20.9
		1983	20.5

Source: Monthly Statistical Bulletin, Bank of Greece, various issues.

The causes of inflation in Greece is still a relatively unexplored area with conjectures predominating over hard empirical evidence. The dependence of Greece on oil for more than 70% of its energy requirements, makes imported inflation an obvious culprit for the period after 1973. The oil shock may well explain a once-and-for-all effect on prices but not the fluctuations in the price index. The resurgence of inflation in the 1980s, even before the second oil crisis needs further explanation.

Negreponti-Delivani listed some of the factors that contributed to inflationary pressures in Greece in the 1960s and 1970s as follows [40]:

(a) Bank credit increased at an annual average rate of 18.6% compared to the 14.1% growth of money GNP (1964-78). Also bank credit which stood at 3.14% of GNP in 1964 rose to over 27% in 1978. The expansion of bank credit more than covered the needs of capital investment and hence the excess spilled over to consumption adding to aggregate demand.
(b) The overall rise in the stock of money over the 1960-78 period was greater than that of money GNP.
(c) The falling off in the rate of investment generated a decrease in the aggregate supply without a parallel fall in aggregate demand.
(d) The relative rise of the service sector generated additional demand for goods without adding anything to the physical productive capacity.
(e) The monopolistic structure of most industrial sectors generated additional pressures on prices without a concomitant expansion of output.
(f) The public sector added to aggregate demand by incurring increasing deficits.

Although this is a comprehensive list of inflationary factors and causes, it does suffer from a major defect in that it lacks any quantification. Furthermore, these factors do not explain what caused the rate of inflation to vary. It is significant for example that the role of imports does not appear at all in this list and neither does the interaction of the state deficit spending with changes in the stock of money.

There is little hard or conclusive evidence on the influence of monetary factors on the rate of inflation in Greece. Regression models attempting to explain changes in retail prices or in money GNP by changes in the stock of money yielded very poor results [41]. This is not surprising in view of the simplicity of the models but also because of a number of complicating

The Take Off That Never Was

factors. For a start income velocity of
circulation declined almost continuously during
this period, from 5.48 in 1961-64 to 4.9 in
1980-83 [42]. Secondly, the size of the public
sector deficit increased very rapidly as a
percentage of GNP. This on its own might not have
been of significance, except that its increase was
accompanied by a change in its composition and its
contribution to the increases in the stock of
money. The evidence on this issue is quite
complex. Part of it is summarised in Table 5.17.

TABLE 5.17 Public sector deficits and monetary
expansion 1970-1982, ml drks current
prices.

(a) Year	Percentage of investment in public sector expenditure	Public Sector borrowing requirement as % of GNP
1970	23	-
1971	26	-
1972	28	-
1973	27	-
1974	21	-
1975	18	8.3
1976	17	8.9
1977	15	8.2
1978	15	8.2
1979	16	8.8
1980	16	11.6
1981	14	17.1
1982	14	13.3

(b) Year	Average percentage contribution of public sector spending to changes in the stock of money (Ml)
1960-64	75.3
1965-69	152.1
1970-74	89.2
1975-79	171.3
1980-83	418.3

Sources:
(a) The Greek Economy Today, pp.24-25.
(b) Provopoulos, Dimosies, p.239 and updated from
various issues of the Monthly Statistical

<u>Bulletin</u> of the Bank of Greece. Where the percentage exceeds 100 it signifies that the private and the external sectors contributed negatively to the increase of M1.

There are two important conclusions that can be drawn from these data. Firstly, the percentage of government spending on investment declined by 9 percentage points or more than 60%. Transfer payments and public consumption increased proportionally thus adding to demand. Secondly, from the 1960s onwards a growing proportion of the central government deficit was financed, from domestic sources but at an increasing inflationary manner [43]. Whereas up to 1967-72 bond issues available to the general public contributed more than 39% of the deficit finance, since then their contribution has dropped to zero and their place has been taken by Treasury Bills held mostly by banks. Even more disconcertingly, between 1979 and 1982 direct loans to the government from the Bank of Greece increased rapidly from 7% of the total deficit in 1979 to 26% in 1980, 67% in 1981 and 54% in 1982. Given however that the Bank of Greece throughout this period pursued a policy of closely controlled and administered interest rates it may well be true that the changes in the stock of money were accommodating, and thus closely related to, public expenditures and the balance of payments. A detailed study of the influence of money on macro variables in Greece undertaken by Papadakis yielded some important conclusions [44]. The study found a high degree of endogeneity in the monetary base (cash plus the liquid reserves of the banking system) linked primarily to the balance of payments. Given the passive policy followed by the monetary authorities and the continuing disequilibrium in the money market caused by artificially low interest rates, the effects of monetary policy tended to be pro rather than countercyclical. In evaluating the overall effects of monetary policy on inflation Papadakis observed that:

'The regime of directed interest rates created continuous excess demand in the money markets. Under these conditions it cannot be argued that the postwar mone-tary expansion was a cause of infla-tionary pressures. Indeed, looking at

the side of aggregate supply it is
important to note that during the
1950-75 period in the 13 years in which
there was a downturn or a slowdown of
economic growth there were marked monetary restrictions in 9 of these years.'

None of the evidence presented is conclusive,
but all of it points out that inflation in postwar
Greece was a phenomenon that cannot be explained
by changes in the stock of money alone. If any
issues stand out, these must be the effect of
imported inflation, which is largely unexplored
and can only be guessed at, and the role of the
changes in the composition of public expenditures
during the 1970s. The behaviour of the stock of
money under the condition of administratively
fixed interest rates appears to have been
accommodating rather than leading, especially when
taken in conjunction with the methods of financing
of the public sector deficit.

5.7 CONCLUSIONS

The developments in the Greek economy during this
period were in a sense predictable and an
inevitable outcome of the lack of any structural
changes in key sectors of the economy. The state
never attempted to assume a leading role in
establishing consistent policies towards the
growth of industry, the balance of payments
deficit and unemployment. Market forces when
allowed to operate freely, took the economy down a
path that aggravated existing problems or created
new ones. There is an apparent contradiction here
in simultaneously criticising the policy record of
successive governments for not being interventionist enough but then bemoaning the effects
of the operations of markets. This however is not
an inconsistent position, if a number of considerations are taken into account. Firstly, the
hand of the Greek state did lie very heavily
indeed on a number of sectors or activities such
as banking and finance, the foreign exchange
market and price support schemes in agriculture.
But in areas where genuine economic or social
problems did exist or developed, such as in the
case of the massive emigration of the 1960s, the
state did absolutely nothing. Secondly, the record
of industrial policy was extremely poor precisely

because it failed to help generate the jobs that
would have relieved agriculture of the surplus
underemployed and unproductive labour. The growth
of the industrial sector could have generated a
process of potentially self-sustaining development
and by providing alternative employment
opportunities to farmers would have made the
consolidation of agricultural units into bigger
and more efficient undertakings all the easier.
Instead the policy relied primarily on foreign
investment to provide both the funds, the
technology and the overall direction. Foreign
investment in Greece was not the source of
problems as the analysis of Section 5.3 has shown,
but it did little or nothing to change the
structure of industry. Foreign firms ended up
dominating a number of key sectors but they made
little contribution to employment and exports,
they reduced competition and removed control of
the developments in strategic sectors away from
Greece. These conclusions are not necessarily
narrowly 'anti-foreign investment', because if
that investment had not taken place the Greek
economy would have been all the poorer for it.
The main criticism is that government inertia
coupled with existing structural imbalances
perpetuated the weaknesses in industry and
agriculture. So for example when the old problem
of financing the balance of trade resurfaced after
the war, the foreign exchange resources were found
by encouraging an expansion of the service sectors
of the economy and in particular that of tourism
and shipping. Neither of these two activities
could lead to any structural changes, and both
were subject to considerable cyclical fluctuations
and highly sensitive, in the case of tourism, to
income changes in other countries. Furthermore,
shipping was not unlike foreign investment, an
activity where effective control and direction
could easily slip away from Greece's frontiers.
As an additional aggravating factor, tourism
helped to inflate the already overexpanded
construction sector by encouraging further
investment in hotels, holiday complexes and
related amenities.

Perhaps the most characteristic aspect of
this lack of sense of direction and expectation
that solutions would appear from abroad was the
signing in 1961 of the pact that led to Greece's
full membership of the EEC. This in itself could
have been an imaginative move if it had been

accompanied by a coherent and consistent approach to some developmental policy. As the final chapter will show full membership did create opportunities but also made it unlikely that the lost chances of the 1950s were to be made up.

Notes

[1] Shaw, Postwar Growth, p.50.
[2] Halikias, I Dinatotites, pp.33-62.
[3] (a) See an excellent survey of post war monetary and financial policy in Oikonomikos Tahydromos, 9/12/82, pp.40-49.
     (b) G.D. Demopoulos, Monetary Policy in the Open Economy of Greece, Centre of Planning and Economic Research, Athens 1981, pp.39-40.
[4] (a) M. Negreponti-Delivani, Analysi tis Ellinikis Oikonomias, Papazisis, Athens 1981 (2nd Ed.), p.75, p.218 and p.245.
     (b) The Greek Economy Today, Centre of Planning and Economic Research, Athens 1984, p.25 and pp.23-24.
[5] (a) G.A. Provopoulos, Dimosies Dapanes kai Oikonomiki Drastiriotis, Institouto Oikonomikon kai Viomihanikon Ereunon Athens 1981, pp.253-265.
     (b) Dimosies Dapanes kai Plithorismos, Institouto Oikonomikon kai Viomihanikon Ereunon, (no author), Athens 1979, pp.34-54.
         See also the discussion in Section 5.6 in this chapter.
[6] Provopoulos, Dimosies, pp.262-263.
[7] G.Kottis, Viomihaniki Apokentrosi kai Periferiaki Anaptyxi in Proetoimasia gia tin Entaxi kai tin Anaptyxi, Institouto Oikonomikon kai Viomihanikon Ereunon, Athens 1979, p.35. See also B. Ward, Greek Regional Development, Centre of Economic Research, Athens 1962, passim.
[8] For details of the Colonels' economic policy see J Pesmazoglu's contribution in R. Clogg and G. Yannoponlos (Eds.), Greece under Military Rule, Secker & Warburg, London 1972, pp.75-108.
[9] There is a fair amount of literature on this paricular issue. See for example:
     (a) P.K. Eleftheriadis, Sygrisis ton Pentaeton Programmaton Oikonomikis

Anaptyxeos Periodon 1960-64 kai 1966-70 in I Elliniki Oikonomia kata to Etos 1965, Bank of Greece, Athens 1966, pp.167-179.
(b) Candilis, The Economy, devotes a whole chapter to the 1960-64 and 1966-70 plans, pp.168-179.
(c) Ypourgeion Syntonismou, Programma Oikonomikis Anaptyxeos tis Ellados, 1968-72, Athens 1968.
(d) Oikonomikos Tahydromos for 31/5/84, pp.9-12 and 12/7/84, pp.3-4 for the 1983-87 plan.
(e) A.G. Papandreou, A Strategy for Greek Economic Development, Centre of Economic Research, Athens 1962. Although this was not an official plan it did reflect the ideas that the briefly - lived Liberal Government of 1963-65 might have attempted to put in action.
[10] Negreponti-Devilani, Analysi, pp.90-93.
[11] G. Samaras, Kratos kai Kefalaio stin Ellada, Syhroni Epohi, Athens 1982 (4th Ed.), pp.47-48.
[12] A. Pepelasis & P.A. Yotopoulos, Surplus Labour in Greek Agriculture, 1953-60, Centre of Economic Research, Athens 1962, pp.21-22.
[13] X.Zolotas, Metanasteusis kai Oikonomiki Anaptyxis, Bank of Greece, Athens, 1960. See also M. Nikolinakos (Ed.), Oikonomiki Anaptyxi kai Metanasteusi stin Ellada, Kalvos, Athens 1974, passim.
[14] D. Psilos, Capital Market in Greece, Centre of Economic Research, Athens 1964, pp.241-242. See also H. Ellis et. al Industrial Capital in Greek Development, Centre of Economic Research, Athens 1964, pp.39-40 and pp.199-230 in particular where the question of investment in construction is discussed.
[15] I.M. Papadakis, Hrima kai Oikonomiki Drastiriotis, Institouto Oikonomikon kai Viomihanikon Ereunon, Athens 1979, p.260.
[16] Negreponti-Delivani, Analysi, p.39.
For a general examination of the building and construction industry see Oi Oikodomoi kai i Oikodomi stin Metapolemiki Ellada (A group publication), Ergasia, Athens 1975, passim.
[17] T. Scouras, Eisodimatiko Kefalaio kai Anaptyxi, in Oikonomikos Tahydromos, 28/6/84, p.27.

[18] Papadakis, Hrima, p.262.
[19] Negreponti-Delivani, Analysi, pp.107-110.
[20] S.X. Valsamidis, I Eisroi tou Allodapou Epiheirimatikou Kefailaiou eis tin Ellinikin Oikonomian kai i Symetohi eis tas Viomihanikas Epiheiriseis kata tin Periodon 1954-64. In, I Elliniki Oikonomia kata to Etos 1965, Bank of Greece, Athens 1966, pp.222-232.
[21] V. Papandreou, Polyethnikes Epiheiriseis kai Anaptyssomenes Hores, Gutenberg, Athens 1981, pp.283-84, see also pp.241-78.
[22] T. Tassopoulos, Elliniki Viomihania, Tymfy, Athens, pp.132-138.
[23] A. Grigorogianni, To Xeno Kefalaio stin Ellada, Grammi, Athens 1975, pp.61 and 165. See also Papandreou, Polyethnikes, pp.191-213.
[24] T.Fotopoulos, Key Sectors in the Greek Economy, Greek Economic Review, Vol.2, No.1, April 1980, pp.78-86 and also by the same author, Exartimeni Anaptyxi kai Ekviomihanisi, in S. Papaspiliopoulos (Ed.), Meletes gia tin Elliniki Oikonomia, Papazisis, Athens 1978, passim.
[25] Fotopoulos, Key Sectors, p.84.
[26] See Maynaud, Politikes, pp.437-444.
[27] Samaras, Kratos, p.42.
[28] The Greek Economy in Figures, pp.148-149, pp.138 and 142.
[29] For a general survey of these issues see:
     (a) P. Avdelidis, I Agrotiki Oikonomia, Gutehberg, Athens 1975, passim.
     (b) Kamarinou, Georgia, passim.
     (c) Malios, I Syhroni Fasi, pp.90-93.
[30] For the functions etc of KYDEP, see Oikonomikos Tahydromos, 10/5/84, p.57.
[31] N. Xanthakis and I. Kamaras, Ai Exelixeis eis tin Elliniki Georgia kai ai Programmatisthentes Stohoi 1961-65 : Sygriseis kai Symperasmata. In, I Elliniki Oikonomia kata to Etos 1964, Bank of Greece, Athens 1965, p.167.
[32] See (a) I Elliniki Oikonomia kata to Etos 1967, Athens, Bank of Greece 1968, pp.20-23.
         (b) Ekthesis tou Dioikitou tis Trapezis for 1974, Bank of Greece, Athens 1975, pp.39-40.
[33] Negreponti-Delivani, Analysis, pp.48-56.
[34] Avdelidis, To Agrotiko, passim.
[35] See an excellent report in Oikonomikos

Tahydromos, 10/5/84, pp.47-50.

[36] N. Psiroukis, Istoria tis Synhronou Ellados, 1940-67, Vol.I, Epikairotis, Athens 1975, p.290.

[37] See extensive reports in I Elliniki Oikonomia kata to Etos 1960 and 1966, Athens, Bank of Greece, 1961 and 1967, pp.116-135 and pp.244-249 respectively.

[38] Giannitsis, I Elliniki, pp.159-60.

[39] Oikonomikos Tahydromos, 12/7/84, p.84.

[40] Nereponti-Delivani, Analysis, pp.310-328.

[41] A number of regressions of $\triangle LogP_t$ on $\triangle LogM_t$ or $\triangle LogM_{t-1}$ using annual data for 1960-83 yielded R^2s of 0.21 and 0.31 respectively. (P_t being the retail price index and M_t the M1 definition of money stock : cash plus sight deposits). Similar attempts with $\triangle LogY_t$ (GNP at current prices) regressed on $\triangle LogM_t$ or $\triangle LogM_{t-1}$ yielded R^2s of 0.33 and 0.24. More complex lagged models on similar lines did not produce significantly better results. Aside from the simplicity of the models, there is also the unwarranted assumption of the exogeneity of the stock of money, in view of the regime of controlled interest rates followed by the Greek monetary authorities at the time.

[42] Income velocity defined as Money GNP/M1. The five year averages were 1960-64, 5.48, 1965-69, 4.65, 1970-74, 4.57, 1975-79, 4.56, 1980-83, 4.9. The rise in the last four years might have been the result of a resurgence in inflationary expectations.

[43] The percentage of Government finance from domestic sources stood at 44.1 in 1960-64, 65.2 in 1965-69, 64.4 in 1970-74, 60.5 in 1975-79 and 70.4 in 1980-82. Data from the Greek Economy in Figures, pp.283-286.

[44] Papadakis, Hrima, pp.116-122 and 272-289.

CHAPTER SIX

THE EEC, WIDENING HORIZONS AND A RETROSPECTIVE VIEW

6.1 GREECE'S ACCESSION TO THE EEC

Perhaps the most significant event in Greece's postwar economic history , other than the abandonment of a consistent policy towards industrialisation in the 1950s, was the decision to join the European Economic Community. The process of doing so had already been started in 1961 but was interrupted by the military regime during 1967-1974. It was, however, the acceleration of the process to seek full membership by 1981 that refocused the public's attention on the problems involved and forced the government to pay long-overdue attention to the policy and structural issues involved. The whole question of the accession merits a section of its own not only because of its importance but also because it will help to draw together the threads of a number of arguments and questions that have already been raised in the last chapters concerning Greece's postwar economic performance and development.

Under article 238 of the Treaty of Rome, Greece became an associate member of EEC as from 1st October 1962 after signing the relevant agreement in 1961. The provisions of the agreement were as follows: Greece was granted a twenty-two year transitional period before full membership. The EEC member countries reduced immediately the duties levied on imports from Greece to the levels they charged each other, but Greece was allowed to reduce its import duties, subject to detailed provisions, progressively over several intervals. The twenty two year transitional period was to be used to give time to the domestic industries to prepare for the competition they would face once all duties were abolished altogether or brought down to EEC levels. In specific, for imports into Greece for which there were no domestically produced close substitutes the transitional period was reduced to twelve years. For agricultural imports the same twenty-two year period held, except that the duties would be abolished on an ad hoc basis, and subject always to EEC's current agricultural policy. Greece was to remove all quotas and other trade restrictions on EEC goods and was to adopt gradually the EEC common tariff towards third countries [1].

In 1967, following the military coup in Greece all the financial and political provisions of the associate memebership were suspended until Greece returned to democratic rule. The tariff reduction provisions however remained in force. By 1968 Greece had achieved completely duty free access for all its exports to Europe. By 1977 two thirds of EEC's exports to Greece were also duty free and Greece had adopted most of EEC policies towards third countries.

Following the restoration of democracy in the summer of 1974, Greece applied to revive the terms of the agreement and indicated its willingness to accelerate the process towards full membership. In May 1979, the Government signed the accession treaty which became fully effective on 1st January 1981, thus creating the "Europe of Ten" as the Greek press liked to call the enlarged EEC.

Both the original and the final treaties were negotiated and signed by conservative governments. Indeed, the architect of the original application in 1961, C. Karamanlis, was the first post-dictatorship prime minister and was instrumental in speeding up the process of the full accession. This casts some light on the heated discussion which the final agreement had generated concerning the benefits and dangers that full association would have implied for Greece. Both liberal and left parties criticized the terms, and the Panhellenic Socialist Movement (PASOK after its Greek initials), which was the main opposition party at the time, even made veiled threats to withdraw Greece altogether from the EEC if it came to power. Irrespective of party politics however the terms of the agreement merit close examination as they set the background for the economic development of Greece to the end of the 1980s [2].

Firstly, Greece was granted a final five year

transitional period to 1986 during which time it would abolish the rest of the import duties on EEC industrial goods. Over the same period Greece would complete its harmonisation of its tariffs towards third countries with those of EEC including all the relevant provisions of the textile and artificial fibres agreements. Secondly, a transitional period of five years was granted over the liberalisation of capital and investment movement with an extra two years added for the movement of labour. Greece was to join fully the European Monetary System (EMS) by 1988 and introduce a VAT system by 1984. Thirdly, over a variable five to seven year period Greece was to harmonize its agricultural policies and prices with those of EEC by abolishing state subsidies and by introducing the Common Agricultural Policy (CAP) rules concerning support, guaranteed price, etc.

The rapidity of the full accession to membership produced an unpleasant shock for Greek producers and farmers. All the old fears of 'foreign domination' of the Greek economy were revived. This was reinforced by the realisation that the Greek civil service apparatus was insufficiently trained or flexible enough to put into action the massive and complex EEC regulations concerning incentives, trade, finance etc.

Furthermore, Greece's argiculture presented some problems which required special attention. Although Greece's partners were unwilling to concede too much, they still considered Greece a special case, and a particularly useful one at that, as it provided a preview of all the problems that the future accession of Spain and Portugal would present.

At the risk of oversimplifying the issues, full membership confronted Greece with three problems. Firstly, the complete elimination of tariffs on industrial imports by 1986 would generate sudden competitive pressures on Greek industries which would be still unready or unable to compete with their European counterparts. Secondly, Greek farmers could look forward to the higher support prices, but not all sectors would benefit equally. Meat and dairy production, which was traditionally weak, would become an easy target for EEC imports. Furthermore, CAP by 1981 was already under pressure and the high support prices were likely to be phased out as structural reforms and consolidation were encouraged or imposed on farmers accross Europe. The enlargement of EEC with the accession of Spain and Portugal would put further pressures on traditional Greek agricultural exports such as fruit and olive oil. Finally, there was uncertainty over the net effects on Greece's balance of payments, even after taking into account the trade diversion following the removal of tariffs and the income flows from the price support schemes and other funds from EEC.

The PASOK Government led by A. Papandreou that came to power in October 1981 and was re-elected in 1985, presented the EEC in March 1982 with the so-called Memorandum. This contained a number of requests and suggestions modifying to greater or lesser extent the conditions under which Greece joined in 1981. One of the key requests was that industrial imports from the EEC were to be subject to additional controls over a further five year period. Greece, under the terms of the Memorandum, proceeded to impose special taxes and duties on a number of EEC imports during 1984. Another request concerned the postponement of the introduction of VAT until 1986 rather than 1984. This was more than just an organisational adjustment, since Greece's contribution to the EEC budget would have been based on VAT receipts. Furthermore, the VAT would have made some domestically produced import substitutes more expensive, and hence would have aggravated the competitive pressures. EEC's overall response to the Memorandum was cautiously favourable. Emphasis was laid, however, on linking some of these concessions to the Integrated Mediterranean Programmes which envisaged comprehensive development plans of specific regions within the EEC [3].

6.2 THE COSTS AND BENEFITS OF THE ACCESSION : AN ASSESSMENT AND BALANCE SHEET

Not unnaturally the discussion of the reper- cussions on Greece joining the EEC had centered around the future of industry and agriculture. Three years (1981-83) is by no mean a long time in which to assess the effects of such a radical change. There is enough information , however, to throw light on some areas and, in general, to cast doubts on, or at least not to support, the worst fears and predictions of the critics of the

The EEC

accession.

For a start the productivity of Greek farmers compares very unfavourably with that of their EEC counterparts. The average size of a Greek farm is about 8 acres whereas that in EEC is 42. In 1978 the yield of soft wheat per acre in EEC was 1.6 times greater than in Greece and for barley more than 1.5 times. The average milk yield per cow was 3,839 litres in the EEC but 1677 litres in Greece. Similarly unfavourable comparisons held for mechanisation and fertilizer use per acre. In the case of fruit production, especially peaches and citrus fruits where Greece has a climatic advantage over its partners, or goods such as currants, tobacco, and olive oil, which for long have been Greece's staple exports, there are both competitive and structural problems to be faced. The future accession of Spain will create problems for olive oil and fruits. EEC has indicated its unwillingness to encourage the production of goods that may require price support. There is already strong pressure to switch cultivation from olives to other edible oils. Olive trees however have a very slow rate of maturation but also live for a long time and hence represent several generations of investment for farmers. The third country tariff agreement presents another potential problem, possibly in the areas of cotton and tobacco. Greece may find that the production and exports of these goods compete not only for European but also for home markets with imports from outside the EEC [4]. Industry's problems are of a different nature. The structural and organizational characteristics and weaknesses of Greece's industry during the post-war period have already been discussed. Joining the EEC will present however some special problem [5]. The EEC has now become the major importer of Greece's manufactured goods. During 1979-80 the EEC took 43.2% of Greece's industrial exports and this was increased to 52.3% by 1983 [6]. Given,however,that the majority of Greece's manufactured exports consists of food products and textiles, these goods are likely to meet increasing competition from two sources. Firstly, from the highly standardised and heavily advertised (brand image) food products within the EEC, and secondly from third country imports into EEC, especially in textiles [7]. The capacity of the industrial sector to compete both with imports into Greece and in EEC markets will turn out to be a crucial factor for its further development. There is some evidence that the price elasticity of demand for exports of tobacco, electrical goods and some other industrial goods is less than one. The price elasticity of demand for all exports from Greece also appears to be approximately equal to one [8]. Although these findings do not relate specifically to EEC markets, they demonstrate that the Greek exports will have to compete primarily via quality, standardisation and marketing rather than by price alone. The position of textiles appears to be particularly precarious in this respect. Textiles were contributing in the early 1980s well in excess of 30% of all the manufactured exports, and the EEC took on average more than 80% of the exported textiles. Basic cotton yarns accounted for more than 50% of the total of all textile exports. Yarn, however, is a basic, simple product with relatively low value added and subject to import competition from third countries. Similar problems will face the exports of garments and foot-wear industries [9].

In the case of the steel industry, Greece had to face the consequences of the general international surplus of steel capacity and output and had to mothball one of its steel smelters [10].

A better appreciation of the potentially weak areas or sectors of Greek industry can be obtained by comparing Greek industries to their EEC counterparts using a number of different criteria. Thus, for example, using the number of workers employed as an indicator of size, out of a group of 60 Greek industries only 6 (which accounted for 6% of the total value added of the sample) were bigger than their EEC counterparts. Thirty eight other industries which accounted for 26% of the value added of the sample were in general two thirds smaller than the average size of corresponding EEC industries [11]. Relative size however can only offer an impressionistic view of the potential structural problems. A thorough comparative analysis and study of these problems was undertaken by the Institute of Economic and Industrial Research in Athens. The results and findings of this study were most illuminating [12]. Firstly, the overall comparative structure of Greek industry exhibited certain similarities with the industries of other EEC members, although of course the absolute levels of productivity, production, export performance, etc, were very different indeed. But all the similarities

ended with the composition of industrial output
and did not extend to the conditions of
production, factor utilisation or competitiveness. In the case of productivity, Greece had
made significant progress between 1963 and 1973
although it still lagged behind a number of
countries by a factor of 30%-40%. More detailed
comparisons however did bring out further important differences. Returning back again to the
issue of size, the study found that in the case of
enterprises employing less than 10 workers the EEC
- Greece differences were never greater than by a
factor of 20%. But in the case of larger enterprises, where there was a clear correlation
between the size of the firms and their markets,
Greece differed significantly from EEC. The key
characteristic of the Greek industries in this
area was the lack of large units. Furthermore, in
constructing a table of productivity changes over
1963-1975 in Greece, three industries occupied
permanently the bottom position, clothing, shoes,
timber and furniture whereas basic metallurgy,
petrol products and chemicals occupied the top
three spots. There was some evidence that the
explanation for the interbranch differences
rested, in addition to other factors, on the
differences in the average size of firms.

The importance of these findings rests not so
much on the similarities or differences they
revealed but on the possible consequences for
Greek industry of full membership. It appeared
that the basic structure of Greek industrial
production was based to a limited extent on
comparative advantages. The policies of
protectionism and import substitution pursued in
the past would now have to be reversed and rapid
structural changes encouraged if Greek industry
was to survive the rigours of EEC competition.
The disadvantages of Greek industries in terms of
size, concentration and available markets would
have to be countered by greater development of
intra and inter-branch specialisation. The idea
popularised at the time of the accession of '270
million customers for Greek products' has to be
seen more in terms of internal adjustments,
rather than just exports. In terms of specific
sectors, the abolition of tariffs was expected to
be felt more on edible oils and margarine, flour,
drinks, garments, shoes, paper products, rubber,
plastics, glass, metal pipes, tin products,
electrical motors and appliances. The effects of

the unified tariff towards third countries
appeared to threaten domestic markets rather than
offer direct competition to Greece's export to the
EEC. In this area the most vulnerable sectors were
canned foods, edible oils, flour, textiles and
garments.

    In appraising the overall effects of Greece's
accession to the EEC in general, and those on
industry in particular, one must account for
static and dynamic factors contributing to these
effects. The static elements include the impact
of reduced tariffs, although by 1981 a great deal
of tariff protection had already gone. The
dynamic aspects are more complex because they will
involve the effects of competition on markets
characterised by high concentration and operating
under long term structural imbalances. It is not
therefore surprising that when it came to putting
some monetary values on the costs and benefits
of Greece's membership, the CAP would figure
prominently in the calculations precisely because
it involved direct money flows that could be
aggregated. Similar considerations applied to
sums received or paid to various EEC funds. Thus
on the simplest possible basis one could examine
the financial flows between the EEC and Greece,
and particularly those with the Agricultural Fund
(FEOGA), in order to estimate the benefits of
membership. The costs of the membership could
then be measured in terms of the higher prices
that consumers had to pay for agricultural goods
once Greece became a full member. During the
years 1981-83 Greece received from the agricultural price support fund of FEOGA some 131.2
billion drks or about 44 billion drks per annum.
These figures exclude any sums payable by FEOGA
for restructuring or redirecting farming
activities etc. The annual inflows were equal to
about 11% of the gross agriculture production or
about 13% of value added in agriculture. The
major part of these payments were received by the
tobacco sector (27.4%), vegetables and fruit
(25.5%) and cotton and rice with 15.1% and 12.4%
respectively [13]. The particular projects and
activities under which these payments were
disbursed also makes interesting reading. As can
be seen from Table 6.1, production subsidies were
paid directly to farmers in the cases of wheat and
edible oils. Exports, processing, and tobacco
subsidies were paid, not to the actual farmers,
but to exporters and middlemen and in particular,

producers of juices, tinned foods etc. The subsidies enabled them to pay farmers the minimum guaranteed prices as established by the EEC. In other words, only 15% of the funds went directly and exclusively to the actual producers of the goods. It requires elementary economic analysis to show that the extent to which buyers of farm products can exercise monopsonistic pressures on isolated groups of farmers will determine the proportion of the subsidy that they will receive. This particular aspect of the FEOGA payments policy has drawn a sustained barrage of criticism in Greece as it obscures the consequences of farm price policies on individual as opposed to sectoral income distribution. It has long been a complaint of Greek farmers that the weakness of their own cooperative movement and the oligo- polistic nature of wholesaling and marketing of farm products deprived them of a fair share of retail prices. The subsidy systems did nothing to change the distribtuion of food products, but increased the spoils available to wholesalers rather than to producers.

TABLE 6.1 Percentage allocation of FEOGA
         (guarantees) payments to Greece 1981-83.

Export subsidies	11.8
Production subsidies	15.2
Tobacco and other subsidies	41.2
Processing subsidies	18.0
Storage costs	7.1
Other activities	6.7

Source : <u>Oikonomikos Tahydromos</u>, 14/6/84, p.20.

The inflows from the price support schemes for agriculture represented the positive side of the picture. Upon assuming full membership, Greek consumers had to pay higher prices for food as access to the international markets was now limited because of the high price policies of CAP. Greek farmers, however, enjoyed the higher prices guaranteed by the EEC. So there was a transfer of income from Greek consumers of agricultural products to the EEC farmers and another transfer from EEC funds to Greek farmers. The net sum of these flows yielded the 'trade' cost or benefit of the application of CAP to

The EEC

Greece [14]. As Table 6.2 shows these flows were
negative throughout the period under examination.

TABLE 6.2   Net benefits to Greece of the
             application of CAP, 1981-83 (first ten
             months of 1983) billion drks.

	1981	1982	1983	1981-83
Trade costs	-10.3	-11.4	-10.4	-32.1
Other inflows	10.1	39.9	65.5	115.1
Net effect	-0.2	28.5	55.1	83.0

Source : Oikonomikos Tahydromos 7/6/84   p.25

    At the same time, however, Greece received a
net inflow from other EEC funds, including from
FEOGA (other than price support), Regional Development, Social funds etc. Adding these flows to
the trade cost yields an overall positive result.
So the initial application of CAP plus the
budgetary receipts from EEC yielded a net inflow
for Greece. It is important , however, to keep in
mind three points. Firstly, these calculations do
not make any allowances for any changes in
personal income distribution, especially with
regards to sums received by farmers. Secondly,
there is a deadweight loss caused by both subsidies and tariffs that has to be accounted for as
well and which is not included in the costs.
Finally, and most important, these figures do not
allow for any positive or negative effects on
industry and on the consumers of industrial goods.
    Joining a common tariff area will cause trade
diversion as well as creation. In the case of
Greece, the most striking aspect of trade
diversion took place in agricultural imports.
Greece's geographical distribution of trade is
shown in Table 6.3 starting with the period just
prior to full membership in 1981 and the years
after it. Allowing for the fact that the total
value of trade declined during the 1980s because
of the international recession, there was no
rapid redirection following full membership in
1981, although the EEC's share of both imports and
exports rose.
    The picture however changes significantly
when imports are divided into their industrial and
agricultural components. This is done in Table 6.4.

210

Agricultural imports from EEC increased by a spectacular 91% between 1980 and 1981 but at the same time agricultural imports from the rest of the world declined by 50%. If this diverted trade

TABLE 6.3   Geographical distribution of Greece's external trade, 1979-1983, $ml, current prices.

	Exports to :		
Year	EEC	Rest of World	ECC as % of total exports
1979	1612.6	2319	41
1980	1640.6	2452.8	40
1981	1666.1	3104.9	34.9
1982	1541.5	2599.5	37.2
1983	1610.2	2494.8	39.2
	Imports from :		
Year	EEC	Rest of World	EEC as % of total import
1979	4364.6	5744.9	43
1980	4234.7	6668.3	38.8
1981	4795.0	6708.7	41.4
1982	4695.4	5372.6	46.6
1983	4419.0	5072.1	46.5

Source: Bank of Greece, Monthly Statistical Bulletin, April 1984.

is subtracted from the increase in imports from EEC, the overall increase comes to less than 22%. This is a crude estimate which does not allow for any effects of changing foreign exchange rates or differences in inflation rates, but it still shows that the trade diversion effect, although sub-stantial, was hardly drastic. Industrial imports from EEC declined after 1981 as did imports from the rest of the world [15]. The trade diversion of agricultural goods, however, requires further analysis as it does pinpoint one area that the impact of full accession is unlikely to have a

'once-and-for-all' effect. As Table 6.5 shows,
most of the increase in the imports of agricultural goods is accounted for by meat and dairy
products. There is nothing unusual in this since

TABLE 6.4   Import of industrial and agricultural
             products, current prices, 1979-1983
             (first ten months of 1983), $ml

| Year | Agricultural Imports from: | |
	EEC	Rest of the world
1979	311.1	593.7
1980	362.2	529.2
1981	704.3	266.2
1982	907.8	316.2
1983	772.0	218.5

| Year | Industrial Imports from: | |
	EEC	Rest of the world
1979	3,247.4	1,384.4
1980	3,168.9	1,626.6
1981	3,313.7	1,450.8
1982	3,253.1	1,479.6
1983	2,583.8	1,040.9

Source: Oikonomikos Tahydromos, 2/2/84, p.9. The
         figures in this table exclude imports of
         fuel and vehicles and hence are not
         comparable to those of Table 6.3.

Greece has always been a net importer of these
products. The overall deficit in the agricultural
trade of Greece with the EEC, however, increased
after accession but was not counterbalanced by an
improvement in the surplus of Greece's
agricultural trade with the rest of the world. In
relative terms this is still a small percentage of
the total deficit in Greece's external trade [16].
Taken, however, in conjuction with the relative
underdevelopment of Greece's meat and dairy
industry and the prospect that CAP policies will
become less rather than more liberal, this

TABLE 6.5   Agricultural trade balance, current prices, million drks, 1979-82.

Year	E E C			Rest of the World		Trade Balance with:	
	Imports from	Exports to	Imports of animal/dairy products (% of total imports)	Imports from	Exports to	E E C	Rest of the world
1979	12,089.5	19,416.8	6,479.1 (53.5)	24,024.2	24,051.9	+7,327.3	-27.7
1980	16,494.7	23,556.3	9,476.3 (57.4)	24,420.1	33,951.5	+7,061.6	+9,531.4
1981	37,932.1	29,625.6	22,238.8 (58.6)	19,005.0	34,067.8	-8,306.5	+15,062.8
1982	61,744.5	42,234.6	40,881.1 (66.2)	24,236.5	42,548.4	-19,509.9	+18,311.9

Source : P. Kolyris in Oikonomikos Tahydromos, 7/6/84 ,   pp. 25 and 26.

particular deficit is likely to persist or even grow.

Three years (1981-83) is too short a time to start to approximate the long term impact and effect of the full membership on Greece's economy. The external trade data presented are likely to be dominated by trade diversion effects and once-and-for-all adjustments. It is not yet possible even to begin to estimate the effects on industry. Greece's Memorandum in 1982 and the subsequent acceptance by EEC of at least some of its points, indicate that Greece's original conditions of membership will not remain unchanged. The reimposition in 1982 of special duties on furniture, clothing, drinks and electrical goods effective till 1989, the postponement of the introduction of VAT and the exemption granted to Greece over the rules that forbid preferential treatment of domestic producers for state supplies, are all further indications that Greece's membership is not truly "full" as yet. But it is also important to remember that by 1981 import duties were 40% down on their 1961 levels and they represented an effective 8.1% duty on industrial goods. By 1983 they were reduced to 5.5%, even taking into account the subsequent reimposition of special duties [17].

The Greek industrial sector still enjoys some protection although there is no comparison with the situation in 1961 levels. The dynamic effects, however, of future competition and long term capacity of the Greek industry to adjust, especially in the sector of high technology, remain doubtful. Some evidence has already been presented in relation to the poor record of productivity, the high energy consumption, especially in the export oriented sectors, and the relatively low value-added of important exports such as textiles.

EEC turned out to be neither the panacea nor the instrument of destruction of the Greek economy. Trade diversion did take place but during a period of declining international trading activities. The accession, however, will put a number of sectors to the test of competition and rapid change. There is at present no concrete evidence to judge the overall effects or to make predictions about the future. Greece has put great store in the development push it expects to get from the Integrated Mediterranean Schemes (IMS).

The fact that in terms of financial flows the first three years of membership yielded a surplus and the likelihood that more funds will be forthcoming from the IMS indicate that the EEC in the near future will still be offering Greece a range of opportunities. It will be up to Greek producers, farmers and administrators to use and exploit them.

6.3   RETROSPECTS AND PROSPECTS

Hindsight, it has been said, is an exact science. In the case of Greece's economic history there are periods that allow a degree of precision in drawing conclusions, others which are more open to speculation. This volume has concentrated on the years between 1920 and 1980. In some respects in the case of Greece it is difficult to separate or classify stages of economic development and events. This is because in the prewar period there was a relative degree of continuity in Greece's economic history despite the violent shocks of the Asia Minor disaster and depression of the 1930s. Greece entered the decade of 1920s with effectively the same structure of industry, and to a lesser extent, of agriculture, as it entered the 1950s. Once the 'tsiflik' estates were broken up, smallholdings became almost universal. Currants declined in importance whilst tobacco had taken their place as the key export good. Wheat production had been encouraged and it expanded rapidly, partially for strategic reasons of self sufficiency. Industry had turned inwards under the protective environment of bilateral clearing arrangements, restricted capital movements and overall decline in international trade. Had the war not taken place or had Greece remained neutral, then the economy would have grown happily along the same lines with the exception that the trade restrictions would have eased the balance of payments deficits.
   The repeated economic crises of 1893, 1922-26 and 1932 were all connected with finance and external borrowing in particular. Greece's political ambitions and just aspirations from its emergence as an independent state in 1833 till the finalisation of the frontiers after 1922 meant that it had to fight a number of costly wars and participate as an unequal partner in the power politics of the UK, France, Germany and Russia. Greek economic historians have tended to

overstress the dependence of Greece on external finances without at the same time emphasising that the majority of the loans were used by the government, and the lion's share of public expenditures went on defence. As the developments after 1930 showed, Greece could minimise its dependence on foreign trade and could plot and follow an autarchic course in its economic policies. However, the burden of servicing loans meant that exports had to be supported and encouraged. Therein developed an interesting contradiction in that successive Greek administrations considered imports as a source of tax revenues rather than as a drain of foreign exchange. This helped to develop a peculiarly perverse dependence. As foreign trade declined, the revenue from import duties fell, which made recourse to foreign borrowing all the more likely thus generating further need for foreign exchange earnings to service these loans. The final outcome of these repeated loans was, of course, political domination by the creditor countries. The imposition of an international economic control on Greece in 1897, the abrupt withdrawal of promised credits and loans in 1922 which led to the financial crisis and the 'bisection' of the currency, are just two of the several incidences when Greece was treated as a client state. Even the foundation of the Bank of Greece was the outcome of conditions imposed for further access to the international financial market. This incident in itself turned out to be highly beneficial as the events after the 1929 crisis showed. The existence of a central bank and the stabilisation of the currency ensured that Greece faced the oncoming depression better prepared and with a more coherent set of policies.

Perhaps the most painful and frustrating episode in Greece's economic history was the unwillingness or inability of the post-civil war right-wing governments to push forward with a concrete industrialisation programme. Admittedly, as Chapter Four has shown, there was pressure from the United States to steer Greece away from plans that emphasised rapid industrialisation and the building of the necessary infrastructure because the US would have had to foot the bill. The civil war coming so soon after the occupation had resulted, once again, in the complete dependence of the Greek state on external financial sources, in this case US aid. This dependence, ensured

that even if there was political will to act
otherwise, it had to submit to the realities of
financial plans that were drawn by the Greeks but
approved by and paid for by the Americans. This
perhaps casts the USA as the villain of the
piece. The right-wing governments in Greece were
great believers in market forces and private
enterprise. There would have been no great
contradiction in their ideology, and that of the
United States, if they had put forward indicative
plans that were based on private investment
decisions with the role of the state in a
secondary position. But, as will be presently
shown not even this minimum planning model was
implemented.

Kintis has summarised aptly the circumstances that led Greece away from a path of a self
sustained industrial take off [18]:

'The most important choices with
reference to the policies of industrialisation that were followed in the
postwar period in Greece were made at
the beginning of the 1950 decade. It is
important to understand that the
decisions taken and the omissions in
these decisions were key determinants of
the shape and degree of the industrial
development of the country. The decade
of 1950s was the period during which it
was both possible and appropriate to lay
the foundations for an autonomous
economic and industrial development,
exactly as it happened with the rest of
the European countries. But the
combination of the political powers that
emerged at the end of the civil war, the
dreadful state of the economy, the
foreign intervention and the short-
sighted and pessimistic views that won
the day regarding the potential of
industrial development in the country,
did not allow the formation and the
application of a long term strategic
plan capable to lead to self-sustaining
economic development'.

It was a key characteristic of the approach
to economic policy in this period, that the Greek
state abandoned, early on, even the pretence of
indicative planning and relied totally on market

forces for the direction taken by the economy. In
view of the extensive state participation in
reconstruction and development in one way or
another in the UK, France, Italy and Germany,
Greece's policy stood out in its pathetic reliance
on free markets at a time when the economy lacked
both the infrastructure or even the bare basis of
leading sectors that would act as the dynamos for
further development. Given that a socialist
centralised planning was out of the question, both
because of the post-civil war situation and
because the United States would not have allowed
it by simply withdrawing its aid, the alternative
of indicative planning with the state playing a
limited but important role would have been an
acceptable and realistic alternative. The 1953
devaluation was a bold move precisely because it
laid the emphasis on the market mechanism, but
could not have succeeded in the context of an
economy still recovering from war and occupation.
The quotations from official statements in
Section 4 of Chapter Four are indicative of the
reliance of the policy makers on foreign capital.
As Chapter Five has shown, foreign investment in
Greece did not generate the conditions necessary
for the growth of inter-branch dependence or
export orientation. It was futile and completely
unrealistic to expect foreign investors to take
and make developmental decisions and policies.
The final proof of the failure of this approach
that relied on foreign investment, no state
intervention and free enterprise in a country
which was primarily deficient in the first and
third items, was the great emigration wave of the
1960s. The private sector in industry and
agriculture just could not generate the investment
that would have provided appropriate employment
opportunities.

Against this background, any appraisal of the
long term development of the Greek economy within
the institutional and economic framework of the
EEC cannot but be guardedly optimistic. Greece's
future is now linked to whatever chances it may be
able to exploit in the EEC and in an international
economy which is growing more competitive. Given
the extensive penetration of foreign enterprises
in Greece's industrial sector and the fact that
political and institutional factors would limit
state initiatives in investment, the routes open
to industrial policies narrow down considerably.
Nevertheless , within the EEC framework and the

218

continuous renegotiations of the conditions of the accession, Greece may still exploit some of its comparative advantages. Heavy industry and mechanical engineering are on the decline or under severe competitive pressures everywhere. The growing importance of high technology sectors and products could offer a challenge and lead to more export intensive developments. But all this would require consistent policy-making, the recognition of the international competitive process as an integral part of investment decisions and finally, a revamping of the educational system. The prospects for agriculture are much brighter but again the adjustment must come at the expense of the smaller farmers. Consolidation into bigger farming units will be inevitable in Greece. An active cooperative movement would have helped to soften the blow and ease the transition. At present Greece has put great store in the integrated Mediterranean Programmes which treat the relatively underdeveloped regions in the EEC as an overall EEC problem. Again this will be a matter of pushing and fighting for Greece's interests in a community not famous for taking altruistic decisions and which is rapidly changing its views on the way its financial resources are allocated and spent.

In the Introduction to this volume it was pointed out that Greece has endured massive economic shocks and sustained ill-management and maladministration for long periods in its history. Despite these setbacks it did manage to survive as an intact socio-economic unit. The EEC will not offer a second chance at making up for the lost chances of the 1950s, nor was Greece's accession to the community a shock in the way the Asia Minor disaster was. What the EEC will offer is a consistent, but considerably more restrictive framework, in which to exploit the possibilities still open to Greece for another attempt at a more integrated economic development but fully linked to the international economy.

Notes

[1] S.G. Triantis, Common Market and Economic Development, Centre of Planning and Economic Research, Athens, 1965, Ch.3, passim.
[2] Details drawn from various sections of the Reports of the Governor of the Bank of Greece for 1978, 1979, and 1980, Bank of Greece,

The EEC

Athens 1979, 1980 and 1981.
[3] See *Oikonomikos Tahydromos* for 7/4/83 pp.
19-24 and 14/4/83 pp. 20-21.
[4] For a comprehensive discussion of the problem
that face Greece's agriculture within the EEC
see the following three references. It is
important to note, however, that as all three
were published under the auspices of the
Greek communist party they are, naturally,
highly critical of Greece's accession to the
EEC.
(a) *Tria Hronia stin Eok* (proceedings of a
conference), Syhroni Epohi, Athens 1984,
passim.
(b) G. Panitsides, *I Symfonia gia tin Entaxi
stin Eok kai i Agrotiki Oikonomia mas*,
Syhroni Epohi, Athens 1980, passim.
(c) G. Panitsidis (Ed.), *Domikes Allages stin
Agrotiki Oikonomia mas*, Syhroni Epohi,
Athens 1980, passim.
[5] *Tria Hronia*, passim.
[6] See article by V. Patikis in *Oikonomikos
Tahydromos*, 30/8/84, pp.21-24.
[7] A. Kintis, *I Anaptyxi tis Ellinikis
Viomihanias*, Gutenberg, Athens 1982,
pp.135-153.
[8] K.P. Prodromidis, *Exoterikon Emporion tis
Ellados*, Kentro Programmatismou kai
Oikonomikon Ereunon, Athens 1976, pp.273-279.
[9] Dimokratiki Panepistimoniki Kinisi, *I Eok kai
ta Provlimata tis Ellinikis Viomihanias*
(proceedings of a conference) Gutenberg,
Athens 1984, p.76.
[10] *I Eok kai ta Provlimata*, pp. 85-88.
[11] T.Giannitsis, *I Elliniki Viomihania*,
Gutenberg, Athens 1983, p.238.
[12] The results were reported in three separate
publications:
(a) I. Hassid, *Ellas kai Eok*, Instituto
Oikonomikon kai Viomihanikon Ereunon,
Athens 1977, passim.
(b) I. Hassid, Elliniki Viomihania kai
Koinotita, in *Proetoimasia gia tin
Entaxi*, pp.41-51.
(c) I. Hassid, *Elliniki Viomihania Kai Eok*,
Volumes I and II, Insititouto Oikonomikon
kai Viomihanikon Ereunon, Athens 1980,
passim.
The summary points in the text draw heavily
from item (b).
[13] See report in *Oikonomikos Tahydromos*, 14/6/84,

pp.17-22.
[14] P. Kolyris, article in Oikonomikos
Tahydromos, 7/6/84, pp.23-26.
[15] N. Nicolaou, article in Oikonomikos
Tahydromos, 2/2/84, pp.10-11. See also
Oikonomikos Tahydromos for 25/5/84, pp.21-22.
[16] An official EEC publication reported in the
Oikonomikos Tahydromos, 24/5/84, p.22 put it
thus: (trade figures measured ECUs)
'.... the additional burden to Greece's
external trade in agricultural products with
other EEC members (after netting out the
improvement of the trade balance with the
rest of the world) does not exceed in any
case 3% of the total deficit in Greece's
external trade or 6% of her deficit with
other EEC members.....'
[17] N.Nicolaou in Oikonomikos Tahydromos,
pp.10-11.
[18] Kintis, Anaptyxi, pp.154-155. See also
pp.155-157 for a discussion of the postwar
industrial policy.

SELECT BIBLIOGRAPHY

Books only in English are listed here

General introductions to Greece's political and economic history

1800s to 1970s

1) D. Dakin, The Unification of Greece 1770-1923, St. Martins Press, London, 1972.
2) E.S. Forster, A Short History of Modern Greece, Methuen, London, 1958.
3) J. A. Levantis, The Greek Foreign Debt and the Great Powers 1821-1878, Columbia University press, New York, 1944.
4) N.P. Mouzelis, Modern Greece: Facets of Underdevelopment, Macmillan. London, 1978.
5) C. Tsoukalas, The Greek Tragedy, Penguin, London, 1969.

Economic History, 1920-1940

1) M. Dorizas, The Foreign Trade of Greece: The Economic and Political Factors Controlling, Philadelphia, 1925.
2) E. Mears, Greece Today: The Aftermath of Refugee Impact, London, 1930.
3) D.E. Protecdicos, Greece, Economic and Financial, Eyre & Spottiswoord, London, 1930.
4) Surveys of International Affairs for 1936 and 1937, Oxford University Press, 1937 & 1938.
5) South Eastern Europe : A Political and Economic Survey, The Royal Institute of International Affairs, London, 1939.

Select Bibliography

Economic History, 1945-1980

1)   W.O. Candilis, The Economy of Greece
     1944-66 Praeger, New York,1968.
2)   B. Sweet-Escott: Greece, Political and
     Economic Survey 1939-53, Royal Institute of
     International Affairs, London,1954.
3)   X. Zolotas, Monetary Equilibrium and Economic
     Development, Princeton University Press, 1965.
4)   The Greek Economy Today, Centre of Planning
     and Economic Research, Athens 1981 (This
     contains mostly data).

The Centre of Planning and Economic Research publishes a large number of specialised monographs on a wide range of issues on the Greek economy. Most of the publications are in English and they provide an excellent source of information and empirical evidence on the postwar Greek economy, especially for the 1960-1970 period. Extensive reference has been made to these sources in the footnotes of individual chapters. The OECD publishes in English regular country surveys which include Greece. These reports provide useful background information and data.

Index

225

Index